Understanding Mass Violence

A Social Work Perspective

Shulamith Lala Ashenberg Straussner

Ehrenkranz School of Social Work, New York University

Norma Kolko Phillips

Lehman College, City University of New York

Boston • New York • San Francisco
Mexico City • Montreal • Toronto • London • Madrid • Munich • Paris
Hong Kong • Singapore • Tokyo • Cape Town • Sydney

We dedicate this book to the memory of our parents
who taught us about surviving trauma
Shmuel Aszenberg and Ruth Apelcweig Ashenberg —SLAS
and
David Kolko and Rose Suchenky Kolko —NKP
and to our fervent hope for world peace

Series Editor: *Patricia Quinlin*
Senior Editorial Assistant: *Annemarie Kennedy*
Marketing Manager: *Taryn Wahlquist*
Senior Editorial-Production Administrator: *Beth Houston*
Editorial-Production Service: *Walsh & Associates, Inc.*
Composition and Prepress Buyer: *Linda Cox*
Manufacturing Buyer: *JoAnne Sweeney*
Cover Administrator: *Joel Gendron*
Electronic Composition: *Omegatype Typography, Inc.*

For related titles and support materials, visit our online catalog at www.ablongman.com.

Library of Congress Cataloging-in-Publication Data

Understanding mass violence : a social work perspective / Shulamith Lala Ashenberg Straussner, Norma Kolko Phillips, editors.
p. cm.
Includes bibliographical references and index.
ISBN 0-205-37523-5
1. Social service. 2. Victims of crimes—Services for. 3. Victimes of terrorism—Services for. 4. Violence—Psychological aspects. 5. Mass murder—Psychological aspects. 6. Post-traumatic stress disorder. I. Straussner, Shulamith Lala Ashenberg. II. Phillips, Norma Kolko.

HV40.U56 2003
362.88—dc21

2003056333

Printed in the United States of America

10 9 8 7 6 5 4 3 2 1 07 06 05 04 03

Contents

Preface

We wish that this book did not have to be written and that there would not be a need in the future for social workers to deal with the consequences of mass violence. However, following the terrorist attacks of September 11, 2001, when social workers and social work agencies were suddenly put in the center of the response efforts and were expected to provide services to people affected in profound and diverse ways by the attacks, it became clear to us that there was a need for this kind of book.

While the social work profession in the United States has a long history of providing services to war veterans and victims of natural disasters, the vast majority of social workers and social service agencies today have had no experience helping people with the traumatizing effects of intentional, human-caused mass violence. It is now necessary to prepare a growing number of social workers who will be working in this area.

This book brings together existing knowledge with new knowledge being developed by social workers as they have responded and continue to respond to incidents of human-caused mass violence. It is organized into five sections that encompass the broad scope of social work practice. The first section includes a chapter providing an overview of social work practice in the context of mass violence. The section on direct practice includes chapters on interventions with individuals and families, with traumatized children, and with the elderly. The third section deals with the impact of mass violence on organizations and communities and includes chapters on mass violence in schools, the workplace, and in communities. A chapter on the impact of mass violence on law enforcement personnel illustrates the difficulties faced by first responders. Section Four deals with specific clinical issues that social workers need to be alert to, including retraumatization of people previously traumatized, the important role that spirituality and religion might play with people experiencing trauma, and the phenomenon of secondary traumatization, which is experienced by many people providing services to victims and survivors of mass violence. The book concludes with a section linking mass violence with social welfare policy and with social justice.

We are indebted to the authors for their courage in addressing the difficult and often painful issues that are discussed in this book and for their abilities in bringing a scholarly perspective to these highly charged topics. We thank Professor Madeline H. Moran for her ongoing encouragement and also her reading and comments on Chapter 12. We appreciate the help from Robin L. Donath with the literature review and the ceaseless assistance of Eugene Laper of the Lehman College Library. Norma Phillips is grateful to Herbert Lehman College, City University of New York, for granting her a sabbatical, without which the timely completion of this book would have been impossible. The support from the editorial staff of Allyn and Bacon has facilitated this effort; we are grateful to Patricia Quinlin for her immediate recognition of the urgency of this book and to Annemarie Kennedy for her ongoing support.

S. Lala Ashenberg Straussner

Norma Kolko Phillips

Contributors

Marygrace Berberian, MSW, MA, ATR-BC, is Director, World Trade Center Children's Mural Project, and is Adjunct Instructor at the Graduate Art Therapy Program, New York University.

Lisa Bialkin, MSW, JD, is in private practice and is presently in training at the New York University Psychoanalytic Institute and the Institute for the Psychoanalytic Study of Subjectivity in New York City.

Sondra Brandler, MSW, DSW, is Associate Professor and Social Work Program Coordinator at College of Staten Island/City University of New York.

Linda Lausell Bryant, MSW, is Associate Commissioner for the Office of Youth Development, New York City Administration for Children's Services. She is a doctoral candidate at Ehrenkranz School of Social Work, New York University.

Graciela Castex, MSW, EdD, is Associate Professor at Department of Sociology and Social Work, Lehman College/City University of New York.

Jane E. Cranston, MSW, is in private practice and is an executive coach and President of "Coaching Your Potential."

Barbara Dane, MSW, DSW, is Professor and Director, Advanced Certificate Programs in Clinical Social Work and in Palliative and End-of-Life Care at Ehrenkranz School of Social Work, New York University.

Arlene Gellman, MSW, PhD, is in private practice and Adjunct Assistant Professor at Ehrenkranz School of Social Work, New York University.

Richard Holody, MSSW, DSW, is Assistant Professor at Department of Sociology and Social Work, Lehman College/City University of New York.

Jessie Klein, MEd, MSW, PhD, is Assistant Professor at Department of Sociology and Social Work, Lehman College/City University of New York.

Gerald Landsberg, MSW, PhD, is Professor and Director of Institute Against Violence at Ehrenkranz School of Social Work, New York University.

Madelyn Miller, MSW, is Adjunct Associate Professor and a doctoral candidate at Ehrenkranz School of Social Work, New York University. She chairs the Disaster Trauma Working Group of the New York City Chapter of NASW and the Public Education Committee of the International Society for Traumatic Stress Studies. She has a private practice in New York City.

George T. Patterson, MS, PhD, is Assistant Professor at Ehrenkranz School of Social Work, New York University.

Norma Kolko Phillips, MSW, DSW, is Associate Professor and Social Work Program Director at Department of Sociology and Social Work, Lehman College/City University of New York.

William Steele, MSW, PsyD, is Director of The National Institute for Trauma and Loss in Children (TLC), a program of the Children's Home of Detroit, Michigan.

Shulamith Lala Ashenberg Straussner, MSW, DSW, is Professor and Director of Post-Master's Program in the Treatment of Alcohol and Drug Abusing Clients at Ehrenkranz School of Social Work, New York University.

Grace A. Telesco, MSW, PhD, is Assistant Professor at East Stroudsburg University and Adjunct Assistant Professor at John Jay College of Criminal Justice/CUNY and the Graduate School of Social Service, Fordham University. She is a retired Lieutenant from the New York City Police Department.

Carol Tosone, MS, PhD, is Associate Professor at Ehrenkranz School of Social Work, New York University.

Section I

Overview

1

Social Work Interventions in the Context of Mass Violence

Shulamith Lala Ashenberg Straussner and Norma Kolko Phillips

> *The Oklahoma City National Memorial is only eight blocks from Cathy Coulter's downtown office, yet she detours to avoid passing the huge bronze gates and the 168 chairs symbolizing each person killed in the 1995 bombing here. Her friends died there, and she nearly died, too. The memories are too painful...*
>
> *Employees like Ms. Coulter, who survived the bombing by crouching in a darkened bathroom, are terrified to return daily to the Murrah area.... [Even thinking about it makes her feel that her] "stomach is shaking so bad right now that it's just like I'm going to throw up.... It's hard to breathe."*
>
> *Ms. Coulter is still haunted by the darkness of that bathroom where she crouched during the blast. Every night, she switches on a night-light before bed, as if she were a child. "Seven years later, we still have nightmares.... And I'm still afraid of the dark. I read somewhere that the people in New York are healing. Well," she said, "they're not. It's going to take a long time." (Yardle, 2002, p. 1)*

The impact of mass violence is profound, widespread, and often long lasting. While social workers have a long history of dealing with people in crisis situations (Golan, 1978; Parad & Parad, 1990), few of the current generation of social workers in the United States have been prepared to deal with the tragic consequences of terrorism and other deliberate human-caused mass violence. Incidents such as school shootings, the terrorist attacks on the World Trade Center in 1993 and on the Alfred P. Murrah Federal Building in Oklahoma City in

1995, the attacks on New York City and Washington, DC, of September 11, 2001, and the sniper attacks in the Washington, DC, area in 2002 have demonstrated the dramatic need for social workers and social work agencies to be prepared to intervene during and following incidents of mass violence. As pointed out by Waters (2002) following September 11, 2001: "Never before in American history has the mental health community been asked to play, or has volunteered to play, such a prominent role in dealing with a national crisis" (p. 52).

The purpose of this chapter is to present an overview of social work interventions in the context of deliberate human-caused mass violence. It will discuss the impact of mass violence on individuals, families, communities, and organizations; the nature of trauma and posttraumatic stress disorder, and special aspects of social work practice with people affected by mass violence.

The Impact of Mass Violence

The term *mass violence* is defined as "intentional violent criminal acts...that result in physical, emotional or psychological injury to a sufficiently large number of people" (U.S. Department of Justice, Office for Victims of Crime, 2000, p. 1). The resulting act can affect every aspect of individual and communal life. The most common psychological reaction to mass violence is *trauma.* According to Arroyo and Eth (1996), "Psychic trauma refers to a sense of profound helplessness in the face of overwhelming danger, anxiety, and arousal when confronted with an external situation in which there is a high risk of death or injury to oneself or to another" (p. 54). The stress resulting from trauma due to mass violence affects individuals on emotional, cognitive, and behavioral levels (National Center for Post-Traumatic Stress Disorder [NCPTSD], 2001).

While trauma can result from various types of incidents, *deliberate human acts,* such as war or terrorism, tend to have the greatest psychic impact. As noted by the NCPTSD (2001), "deliberate violence creates longer lasting mental health effects than natural disasters or accidents" (p. 1), or even technological disasters. Norris (2001), in her comprehensive review of the literature, points out that 67 percent of individuals who experienced intentional mass violence were severely impaired, in contrast to 34 percent of the those who experienced technological disasters, such as the 1979 nuclear accident at Three Mile Island, and 42 percent of those who experienced natural disasters, such as earthquakes or hurricanes. Among acts of intentional mass violence, terrorist acts, which by definition are "deliberate and purposeful acts against a group of people or places symbolizing societal values with the purpose of inciting fear and sabotaging a way of life" (NCPTSD, 2001), have a particularly damaging impact.

Exposure to Mass Violence

An individual's experience of trauma can result from exposure to one or more catastrophic incidents. There are a number of ways people can become exposed to mass violence:

1. *As a "surviving victim" or a "survivor" of an incident of mass violence.* Cathy Coulter (described at the opening of this chapter), who was in the Murrah Federal

Building in Oklahoma at the time the bomb went off, is an example of a "surviving victim." Whether an individual views him- or herself as a "victim" who survived a traumatic incident or as a "survivor" of the incident is more than a simple matter of linguistics—it represents one's sense of "agency," or sense of self, and reflects one's feelings of either helplessness or of empowerment (Norman, 2000; Reiker & Carmen, 1986).

2. *As a witness to mass destruction.* For example, a U.S. college student spending her junior year studying in Jerusalem witnessed the bombing of a city bus immediately after she got off; some of her schoolmates were still on this bus.
3. *As family member, friend, or a peer of a victim.* For example, a flight attendant who lost several friends during the plane crashes of September 11th was unable to return to work. After using up her sick days she decided to quit her job.
4. *By seeing or hearing the details of the incident.* Due to mass media and the use of the Internet, it is not unusual today for people to be traumatized by seeing images of mass violence that may be taking place in other parts of the world. For example, an immigrant from Sierra Leone who has lived abroad for many years became traumatized as he watched scenes of his devastated community on a live telecast from his hometown.

   Social workers and other helping professionals who work with people traumatized by mass violence can also experience the symptoms of trauma—a phenomenon known as *secondary trauma*—through hearing the details of the event as these are reported by their clients and by ongoing exposure to their clients' intense emotional reactions to traumatizing events. For example, a social work student from Tennessee attending school in New York City volunteered to help family members of victims of the September 11th attacks to fill out missing person's reports. After three days of volunteering, she became overwhelmed and felt unable to continue; she made plans to drop out of school and return home.
5. *By experiencing ongoing fear of mass violence in reaction to previous exposure to danger.* This phenomenon, which can be termed *anticipatory trauma,* was seen in the United States following the deaths of several people due to anthrax shortly after September 11th. It was also seen in Israel during the Gulf War, when more deaths occurred as a result of heart attacks related to fear reactions and accidents during air raids than were caused by actual missile attacks (Solomon, Laor, & McFarlane, 1996).

Trauma and Posttraumatic Stress Disorder

Exposure to incidents of mass violence is always traumatizing. Not every person, however, becomes so traumatized that he or she becomes dysfunctional; many individuals have a high degree of resilience or develop greater resilience as a consequence of surviving and coping with mass violence (Norman, 2000). Nonetheless, for some people the traumatic exposure to incidents of mass violence leads to the development of the psychiatric condition of posttraumatic stress disorder (PTSD). This dysfunctional reaction to the experience of trauma has been recognized for centuries, particularly as it related to the profound impact of mass violence on men in combat.

Historical Views of PTSD

Historically, the symptoms that we associate today with PTSD have been closely connected to combat and mass violence. During the Civil War the set of symptoms exhibited by traumatized soldiers was referred to as "irritable heart," while World War I made the terms "shell shock," "combat fatigue," and "effort syndrome" part of the psychiatric vocabulary (Kaplan & Sadock, 1998, p. 620). World War II saw soldiers suffering from "war neurosis," "battle fatigue," and "combat stress reactions" (Goode, 2001). The psychological impact of mass violence on the millions of civilians in war-torn Europe and Asia, however, was basically ignored, although some researchers, such as John Bowlby and Anna Freud, studied the psychological impact of the separation of children from their parents in Great Britain during World War II.

It was only in the 1960s, when writings of various novels and memoirs about the war by European authors such as Gunter Grass, Jerzy Koszinski, Primo Levi, Bruno Bettelheim, Elie Wiesel, and many others became popular that the profound impact of mass violence on individuals, families, and communities became more widely recognized. Studies of survivors of the Holocaust (Krystal & Niederland, 1968) and Hiroshima (Lifton, 1967) identified the long-lasting impact of mass trauma and introduced concepts such as "survivors' guilt" into our vocabulary.

However, the full impact of the trauma of war became evident only after the return of U.S. soldiers from Vietnam. The destructive psychological impact of the Vietnam War on the very young men who fought it so far from home resulted in the emergence of the diagnostic category of Posttraumatic Stress Disorder, which, for the first time, was included as a formal diagnosis in the third edition of the *Diagnostic and Statistical Manual* (DSM), published by the American Psychiatric Association in 1980.

With regard to the impact of trauma on women, however, it took the women's movement in the 1980s and 1990s to recognize the critical role of violence in the traumatization of many women. Even today, while there is extensive literature related to the impact of domestic violence, sexual abuse, and rape on women, studies focusing on the impact of mass violence on women are rare; this is so despite the fact that women are known to have twice the risk of developing PTSD as men (van der Kolk, 2000).

Diagnosing PTSD

Posttraumatic Stress Disorder is currently classified as an *anxiety disorder* brought on by either a single traumatic event, or several such events, and resulting in a set of psychological and physiological symptoms. In order for an individual to be diagnosed with PTSD today, he or she must meet the set of criteria described in the latest *Diagnostic and Statistical Manual for Mental Disorders,* Fourth Edition, Text Revision (DSM-IV-TR) (American Psychiatric Association, 2000):

1. *Exposure to a traumatic event.* Such event must include the witnessing of death or serious injury of others or the experience of a threat of serious injury or death to oneself or others, and result in feelings of intense fear, helplessness, and horror.

2. *Re-experiencing of the event,* via one or more of the following:
   a. Recurrent and intrusive re-experiencing of images and thoughts of the trauma.
   b. Recurring nightmares about the trauma.
   c. Acting or feeling that the event is reoccurring, which may include flashbacks, illusions, or hallucinations.
   d. Intense psychological distress when confronted with actual or symbolic cues of the event.
   e. Physiological reactions when confronted with actual or symbolic cues of the event.
3. *Avoidance and emotional numbing* regarding the event, via at least three of the following:
   a. Avoiding talking or thinking about the incident.
   b. Avoiding activities, places, or people related to the event.
   c. Inability to recall important aspects of the event.
   d. Feeling of detachment from people.
   e. Restricted affect.
   f. Sense of doom about the future.
4. *Persistent symptoms of increased arousal,* reflected by at least two of the following:
   a. Difficulty falling or staying asleep.
   b. Anger or irritability.
   c. Difficulty concentrating.
   d. Hypervigilance.
   e. Heightened startle reactions.
5. *Clinically significant distress or decreased level of functioning* in work, self-care, or interpersonal relationships.
6. *Long duration of symptoms.* The timing and duration of symptoms following the traumatic event is an important factor when diagnosing PTSD. Symptoms must last *at least 30 days;* only then can the diagnosis of Posttraumatic Stress Disorder be used. Symptoms lasting less than one month but more than two days result in the diagnosis of *Acute Stress Disorder.* The specifier of *Acute PTSD* is used when the duration of symptoms is more than one month but less than three months, while the term *Chronic PTSD,* which occurs when there is a failure to resolve or diminish the impact of the traumatizing experience over time (van der Kolk, 1987), is used when the duration of symptoms lasts three months or longer. Finally, since symptoms of PTSD may not show themselves until months or even years after the trauma, the specifier of *PTSD With Delayed Onset* is used if at least six months have passed before the onset of symptoms. Symptoms have been known to show more than thirty years following the trauma (Kaplan & Sadock, 1998), and it is not unusual for elderly individuals exposed to mass violence to have led a productive life for many years and only begin to show symptoms of PTSD as they become physically or psychologically disabled in old age.

According to Herman (1992a), while the typical symptoms of PTSD are relevant to survivors of one-time traumatic events, they may not represent the range of symptoms that can develop in response to trauma that has occurred over a prolonged period of time. She, therefore, introduced the concept of *Complex PTSD,* which applies to those who have experienced ongoing trauma; this can be seen in victims of political torture, ongoing terrorism, prisoners of war, or victims of concentration camps.

Prevalence of PTSD

Prior to 2001, the prevalence, or the lifetime rate of PTSD among civilians in the United States, ranged between 1 and 3 percent, with an additional 5 to 15 percent experiencing a subclinical, or milder version, of this disorder. The prevalence among those exposed to war was much higher, with about 30 percent of Vietnam veterans experiencing lifetime PTSD and an additional 25 percent experiencing a subclinical form of the disorder (Kaplan & Sadock, 1998).

Studies show no significant associations of PTSD with race, education, or place of residence, although there appears to be greater prevalence of PTSD among unmarried people and people of low socioeconomic status (Kaplan & Sadock, 1998). Women are more likely than men to have been diagnosed with PTSD mostly triggered by physical assault or rape. Responses to traumatic events also tend to vary with age, with the very young and the very old having more severe reactions to such events than those in middle age (Kaplan & Sadock, 1998).

Another group with high rates of PTSD are immigrants who have experienced trauma prior to or during the process of migration. Such individuals are at great risk for developing delayed PTSD or of being retraumatized should they experience additional traumatic incidents following their migration (Castex, 1997; Perez Foster, 2001)

Following the September 11th attacks in New York City, studies of residents of Manhattan found that the rates for PTSD tripled. Among those surveyed, 7.5 percent met the criteria for PTSD. Proximity to the World Trade Center increased the reaction, with 20 percent of those living near the towers exhibiting symptoms of PTSD (Susser, Herman, & Aron, 2002). These findings corresponded with the data following the bombing of the Murrah Federal Building in Oklahoma City, where 7.8 percent of city residents and 34 percent of survivors who were in or near the building developed symptoms of PTSD (Susser et al., 2002). Studies of children in New York City following the 2001 attacks found that 10.5 percent of the city's public school children suffered from PTSD (Susser et al., 2002).

Comorbidity of PTSD and Other Disorders

A growing number of studies are finding a high rate of the coexistence, or comorbidity, of other disorders among those experiencing stress reactions and PTSD (Breslau, Davis, Andreski, & Peterson, 1991). Among the most common comorbid disorders are substance abuse; affective disorders, particularly depression; personality disorders; somatoform disorders (physical symptoms that are not based on any medical condition); and other anxiety disorders, such as phobias (Kessler, Sonnega, Bromet, Hughs, & Nelson, 1995). Breslau and colleagues (1991) found that when any one of these disorders exists prior to the traumatic event, individuals are at greater risk of developing PTSD after exposure to a stressor.

Studies show particularly high rates of comorbidity between PTSD and substance use disorders (Kessler et al., 1995). Among males diagnosed with PTSD, 52 percent had alcohol and 35 percent had drug use disorders, while among females with PTSD, 30 percent had alcohol and 27 percent had drug use disorders. Vietnam veterans in treatment for PTSD have a particularly high rate of comorbidity—between 60–80 percent of those veterans diagnosed with PTSD have a current alcohol and/or drug problem (Kessler et al., 1995).

Impact of Mass Violence on Individuals

There is no uniform response to mass violence. How an individual responds to a potentially traumatic experience is influenced by biological, psychological, social, familial, and experiential factors (Foa, Keane, & Friedman, 2000). While some people become highly traumatized and may experience profound short-term or long-lasting effects, including PTSD, others show greater resilience and cope much better under the same circumstances. People may also develop a range of symptoms other than PTSD. For example, studies of survivors and witnesses of the September 11th attacks in New York City found that 9.7 percent reported symptoms of major depression, a rate much higher than in the population at large (Galea et al., 2002). Other studies found that cigarette smoking and alcohol use increased in the weeks following the attacks (Susser et al., 2002).

Foa and colleagues (2000), Herman (1992b), and van Der Kolk (1987) have identified the following variables that impact how one experiences trauma: physiological reactions, age at the time of the trauma, chronicity of trauma, history of previous traumatic events, preexisting mental disorders and substance abuse problems, family history of mental disorders or trauma, and social and community supports. In addition to these factors, Frankl (1959/1992), in his vivid description of his survival in a Nazi concentration camp, identified the crucial role of one's attitude toward adversity and suffering, including spiritual beliefs, in a person's ability to cope with severe trauma.

Physiological Reactions to Traumatic Events

The experience of trauma leads to changes in the brain and body chemistry. According to van der Kolk (2000), a traumatic experience can change a person's biological capacity to cope and alter how she or he perceives a threat. Moreover, recent studies utilizing positron emission tomography (PET) scans of the brains of individuals in the process of remembering traumatic events have found changes in the area of the brain (known as the Broca's area) that is used to identify and verbalize internal emotional experiences. These changes may account for the fact that people in the midst of actual traumatic experience, or those who are reliving traumatic memories, may have difficulty verbalizing their feelings. This phenomenon is especially common among traumatized children and adolescents, who are then likely to act out their feelings (van Dalen, 2001).

Another important brain chemical that is affected by traumatic stress is *cortisol,* a steroid hormone produced in the adrenal glands. Cortisol leads to the release of so-called fatty acids, an energy source from fat cells used by the muscles and brain. The secretion of cortisol increases in response to stress in the body, regardless of whether the stress is due to a physical situation, such as an injury or chronic illness, or is of psychological origin, such as stress due to trauma. Such increase in cortisol ensures that the brain receives adequate sources of energy, thereby enabling the individual to deal with stressors. However, excessive levels of stress deplete the supply of cortisol. Studies have found that individuals with PTSD tend to have significantly lower levels of cortisol than those who have not been diagnosed with PTSD (Yehuda, Kahana, Binder-Brynes, Southwick, & Mason, 1995). This makes it more difficult for them to deal with existing stress, much less cope with any additional trauma(s). It is also believed that high levels of cortisol may inhibit the formation of long-term memories. Consequently, it is not uncommon for survivors of mass violence not to remember parts of their traumatizing event (van der Kolk, McFarlane, & Weisaeth, 1996).

Age and Reactions to Mass Violence

It is important to consider the common reactions to mass violence during different ages and life stages as these are major determinants to the nature of the individual's reactions.

Reactions of Children and Adolescents. A child's reaction to mass violence will depend on several factors, most important of which is whether the child lost a parent or relative because of the violence. Another factor contributing to the reaction of a child is how much of the disaster the child witnessed directly. It has been seen, however, that children can also be profoundly impacted even when not directly exposed to mass violence. For example, two years after the Oklahoma City bombing, 16 percent of children who lived approximately 100 miles from the blast and who were not related to victims who were killed or injured reported significant PTSD symptoms related to the event (Pfefferbaum et al., 2000). Another important factor is the extent to which the child has experienced trauma in the past.

A crucial dynamic related to children's reaction to mass violence is the age of the child. Typical reactions to mass violence in children 5 years of age and younger include fear of being separated from a parent, fear of the dark, increased crying, clinging to the parent, and regressing to younger behavior, such as thumb-sucking and bedwetting (Pynoos & Nader, 1988). Children aged 6 to 11 may show withdrawal and disruptive behavior, have difficulty with concentration and school work, develop sleep problems, show irritability and outbursts of anger, and complain of stomachaches or other psychosomatic symptoms (Straussner & Straussner, 1997).

Common responses seen in children and adolescents exposed to traumatic events include loss of trust in adults and fear of the event occurring again (Pynoos & Nader, 1988; Straussner & Straussner, 1997). In general, older children tend to understand the potential danger of their situation, whereas younger children believe and take comfort in the reassurance of their parents and teachers. The key factor accounting for resilience among children is the support of adults, in particular their parents. Studies of children who survived the Holocaust have found that those who stayed with their parents did better, even if they lived in much worse conditions and suffered more deprivations, than children who were cared for by other adults (Danieli, 1985).

Symptoms exhibited by older adolescents resemble those of adults, including flashbacks, nightmares, emotional numbing, depression, substance abuse, and antisocial behavior. Responses of college students to mass violence may be complicated by geographical separation from family and support systems, increasing their levels of anxiety and feelings of isolation. Many college students find it difficult to concentrate on schoolwork and are at high risk of dropping out if not provided with appropriate support (Arroyo & Eth, 1996).

Reactions of Adults. While adults may feel and express their reactions to mass violence in a variety of ways, most of those impacted by violence experience some or all of the following:

- **Emotional reactions,** such as sorrow, shock, a sense of hopelessness, anhedonia, disinterest, powerlessness, and emptiness.
- **Cognitive reactions,** such as difficulty concentrating, confusion, worry, short-term memory loss, feelings of unreality, and unwanted memories.
- **Physical reactions,** including fatigue, changes in appetite, heart palpitation, rapid breathing, gastrointestinal problems, severe headache or sweating when thinking about the event, being easily startled, sexual dysfunction, worsening of chronic physical conditions, and sleeping difficulties.
- **Interpersonal reactions,** such as conflict with others, withdrawal from relationships, high need for control, and feelings of rejection. (NCPTSD, 2001)

Reactions of Older Adults. Older adults, particularly those who are emotionally or physically frail, are highly vulnerable to being traumatized by mass violence (Kaplan & Sadock, 1998). Those with a previous history of trauma may experience retraumatization, while those who were experiencing diminishing physical and mental abilities prior to the event of mass violence might feel an increased sense of helplessness and hopelessness following the event. In addition, the concrete and psychosocial needs of the elderly may be severely affected by mass violence. There may be temporary or permanent loss of supports and services, such as home care and medical and pharmaceutical services. Isolation from family and community support systems and the destruction of orienting landmarks may further increase their level of depression as well as anxiety, resulting in panic reactions.

Impact of Mass Violence on Families and Communities

> *A middle-aged widow rarely gets out of bed when the sun is up. Another staves off the pain with mounds of paperwork and nonstop errands. One young mother, inconsolable and financially overwhelmed, has scared friends with dark suggestions that she and her children might join her husband in heaven. For a mother coping with a lost son, spirituality has become a comfort and a crusade.... Six months after the destruction of the World Trade Center, there is little normalcy for the 34 households here [in a small New Jersey community] that lost a family member. If anything, the surviving family members*

> *say the daily struggles with sadness and anger have become more debilitating. The shock and numbness, the whirl of condolence visits, and the bewildering distractions of...(holidays) have given way to unrelieved bleakness. (Jacobs, 2002, p. 1)*

The sudden and unexpected loss of a family member due to mass violence is difficult to bear. During and following traumatic events most individuals seek "natural supports" of family, friends, neighbors, and co-workers. However when community support systems have also been affected by mass violence, it is even more difficult to find the necessary help.

As discussed below, trauma resulting from ongoing mass violence may have long-lasting and wide impact not only on the individuals and families involved, but also on communities and future generations.

Intergenerational Transmission of Trauma

The impact of parental traumatic experience on offspring originated with studies of children of Holocaust survivors (Danieli, 1985). Later studies found the association of paternal PTSD observed in Vietnam War veterans with PTSD symptoms in their children. Rosenheck and Nathan (1985) coined the term *secondary traumatization* to describe this phenomenon, which today is more commonly referred to as *intergenerational transmission, transgenerational transmission,* or *multigenerational transmission* of trauma. Recent studies also indicate that the impact of massive trauma appears to continue throughout the generations. According to Auerhahn and Laub (1998), "massive trauma has anamorphous presence not defined by place or time and lacking a beginning, middle, or end.... it shapes the internal representation of reality of several generations, becoming an unconscious organizing principle passed on by parents and internalized by their children. Traumatic memory thus entails a process of evolution that requires several generations to play itself out" (p. 22).

The intergenerational transmission of trauma has been further examined in a 1998 book edited by Yael Danieli, which explored the generational impact of survivors of the atomic bombs in Japan as well as survivors of trauma from the former Yugoslavia, Cambodia, Nigeria, and Chile, among others. The authors identified common psychological symptoms in *second and even third generation* offspring, including symptoms such as anxiety, depression, narcissistic vulnerability, excessive guilt, problems in regulation of aggression, restlessness, difficulty concentrating, unresolved mourning, chronic nightmares, and psychosomatic disorders. In addition, dysfunctional dynamics in the families of traumatized individuals, including enmeshment, intrusiveness, overprotection, and problems with separation-individuation, appear to be fairly common across different cultures (Danieli, 1998).

More recent studies have focused on biological or hereditary vulnerability to PTSD and intergenerational hormonal impact related to massive trauma. According to the *DSM-IV* (American Psychiatric Association, 2002), relatives of people with a history of depression may have greater vulnerability to developing PTSD if faced with severely traumatic events, while studies of children and even grandchildren of Holocaust survivors with PTSD found that they tended to have lower cortisol levels and therefore diminished ability to handle stress and trauma; this was so even if they themselves had not experienced trauma (Yehuda et al., 1995).

Impact of Mass Violence on Communities

Reactions to mass violence are not limited to individual and families; they also have a profound impact on communities (Zinner & Williams, 1998). The term *communal bereavement* has been used to refer to the sadness, distress, and diminished sense of well-being and safety within their communities that individuals tend to feel after a major catastrophe (Talbot, 2001).

Anger is another common communal response, which usually develops as a reaction to people's feelings of helplessness. Within a community setting, such anger is often contagious and can easily become directed toward other individuals or groups who are seen as responsible for the event. One potential consequence of such anger is the scapegoating of innocent individuals or groups. For example, following the famous Coconut Grove nightclub fire in Boston in the 1940s, "the Jews were blamed, while after the *Andrea Doria* and *Titanic* disasters, the Italians were the scapegoats. During wartime anger is usually canalized against the enemy" (Edwards, 1976, p. 944). It was clear that following the September 11th attacks, anger was focused against Muslims, and consequently individuals, as well as Muslim groups, were scapegoated in many communities throughout the United States.

Interventions with Individuals and Families

As discussed previously, an individual's response to the processing of trauma is influenced by biological, psychological, social, familial, and experiential factors (Foa et al., 2000). Consequently, all of these factors need to be taken into account during the helping process.

Unlike grief and bereavement states, severe stress reactions due to profound trauma do not necessarily resolve themselves over time (Lindy & Titchener, 1983). According to Kaplan and Sadock (1998), "about 30 percent of patients [with PTSD symptoms] recover completely, 40 percent continue to have mild symptoms, 20 percent continue to have moderate symptoms, and 10 percent remain unchanged or become worse" (p. 622). Thus it is important that appropriate professional help be provided. Moreover, it is essential to offer help as soon as possible, since the shorter the duration of symptoms, the better the prognosis for recovery (Kaplan & Sadock, 1998).

Goals and Strategies of Intervention

Since people process and respond differently to mass violence, social workers need to be prepared with a range of goals and intervention strategies. Typically, clinicians need to help traumatized individuals to accomplish the following goals:

- Re-establish feelings of safety
- Manage their anxiety and anger
- Address issues related to comorbidity

Re-establishing Feelings of Safety. After incidents of mass violence, many individuals no longer experience the world as a safe place. They may have greater feelings of helplessness and vulnerability and feel a decreased sense of control over their lives and their future. Professional help needs to be multimodal and supportive, as well as provide active listening with acknowledgment that most reactions reflect normal feelings and behaviors to an abnormal situation.

Managing Anxiety and Anger. Following incidents of mass violence, people tend to have high levels of anxiety that often interfere with their daily life. Consequently, it is important that clients be taught a variety of skills that can help them cope with their feelings, such as relaxation techniques and breath control, in order to diminish their levels of anxiety. Another important technique is exposure therapy, in which the individual gradually and repeatedly relives the frightening experience under controlled conditions to help him or her work through the trauma (Ehlers & Clark, 2000). A newer treatment technique that has been proven effective with traumatized individuals is Eye Movement Desensitization and Reprocessing (EMDR) (see Shapiro, 2001 and Wilson, Becker, & Tinker, 1995 for more information). In addition, research studies have demonstrated the effectiveness of cognitive behavioral therapy, group therapies, and narrative therapy (Ehlers & Clark, 2000; Foa et al., 2000; Norman, 2000).

Research studies also have shown that various psychotropic medications can help ease symptoms of depression and anxiety that often are associated with mass violence and help promote sleep, thereby increasing an individual's ability to deal with daily activities. Currently, researchers are attempting to determine which treatments work best for which type of trauma (National Institute of Mental Health, 2001a, 2001b).

As indicated previously, in addition to feelings of anxiety and depression, common reactions of people who experience mass violence include feelings of rage against the perpetrators. Unfortunately, those who act upon their feelings of anger and their desire for revenge usually increase their rage and levels of stress, rather than obtaining relief as they expected. The challenge for helping professionals is to aid traumatized clients to reframe their experiences in a way that allows for feelings of empowerment rather than victimization (Norman, 2000).

Addressing Issues Related to Comorbidity. An important aspect of intervention with people affected by mass violence is the need to address comorbidity. Assessment and treatment or appropriate referral for problems such as depression, anxiety, substance abuse, and sleep disorders need to be included in every encounter with a survivor of mass violence. Finally, given the special issues related to preexisting traumas among many immigrant groups, it is essential that help be available in the language of the client and that appropriate outreach services to such at-risk groups be undertaken.

Use of Critical Incident Stress Debriefing

One of the most frequently used approaches when providing help immediately following a major disaster is Critical Incident Stress Debriefing (CISD). Developed by Mitchell (1983) in order to help first responders such as emergency medical personnel, this approach has become used with a broad population of individuals who have experienced trauma due to unforeseen disaster.

CISD is a structured approach aimed at helping people talk about their experiences and reactions to the traumatic event, thereby normalizing their reactions and decreasing their risks of future anxiety and stress-related disorders (see Mitchell, 1983, for a detailed description of CISD). While research findings regarding the value of this approach are contradictory, it is important to keep in mind that "debriefing" is not a treatment modality that is designed to stand alone, but should be a component of a comprehensive critical incident stress management program that includes disaster preparation and post-incident follow-up care, as well as ready access to trained professionals with specialized debriefing skills.

Intervention with Children

According to Terr (1991), children who do not receive treatment for their psychic trauma are much more likely to later develop a number of serious disorders. She found that children suffering long-term trauma exhibit massive denial and psychic numbing; they may forget whole segments of childhood and demonstrate indifference to pain, lack of empathy, failure to acknowledge feelings, and avoidance of intimacy. Such children may be misdiagnosed as having conduct disorders, attention deficit disorders, or depression, while the source of their trauma may be ignored or its impact minimized. Moreover, the child's adaptations to ongoing trauma may lead to character changes and possibly result in the development of narcissistic, antisocial, borderline, or avoidant personality disorder, as well as dissociative disorders (Terr, 1991).

Age-appropriate intervention by clinicians experienced with working with traumatized children is not only critical in helping relieve the suffering of such children, it can also prevent long-term dysfunction and minimize the costs to society at large (van Dalen, 2001). It is also important to empower parents and other adults so that they can help children cope with mass violence. Parents and teachers need to be helped to recognize that it is important for them to listen to children without passing judgment, to allow them to express their feelings, and to let them know that it is normal to cry, to be afraid, and to be sad following such traumatic experiences.

Working toward Empowerment

As noted previously, people who have experienced mass violence tend to see themselves as either victims or survivors, while many professionals prefer to view such clients as survivors. Janoff-Bulman and Frieze (1983) advocate for the use of the term "victim" for survivors of any individual or mass trauma, based on their belief that this term "relieves… [people] of responsibility for their victimization" (p. 13). Although victims of mass violence are not responsible for what happened, they still need to assume responsibility for their own recovery.

Ultimately, part of the process of recovery is to enable the individual to see him- or herself less as a victim and more as a survivor. Part of empowerment is helping people to realize that there are still positive things they can do to address their feelings, and that there are activities, such as reading a book, seeing a movie, or going to a ball game, that can still give them pleasure. It is also important to help people to find meaning in their survival

(Frankl, 1959/1992) and to help them see their importance to their loved ones and their community. Nonetheless, we need to be careful that in our efforts to encourage empowerment of clients, we do not neglect to accept the clients' real feelings of vulnerability and disempowerment by events outside their control.

Interventions with Communities

Interventions cannot be limited to individuals and families; help must also be offered to communities. Providing community-wide activities, such as memorial services, drop-in discussion groups, and focus groups on unmet needs and services tend to destigmatize individual reactions and enhance long-term social support. Of particular importance is the provision of help during anniversaries of the original trauma (Gabriel, 1992) and whenever there are incidents that may resemble the original trauma, regardless where they occur. For example, schools in which students have experienced mass violence need to pay special attention and acknowledge student and staff reactions whenever mass violence occurs in another school.

Mass media also plays a crucial role during and following incidents of mass violence; it is important to advocate for informative and helpful—as opposed to sensationalized and destructive—media coverage. For example, the repeated television images of the World Trade Center buildings falling down in New York City on September 11th led some children to think that many other buildings were falling down and that those who lived in tall buildings were in ongoing danger of being destroyed.

Impact of Mass Violence on Helping Professionals and Social Agencies

The treatment of people affected by trauma raises particular countertransferential concerns, which have been referred to as *secondary trauma, vicarious victimization, vicarious traumatization,* or *compassion fatigue.* All these terms generally refer to trauma that is transmitted from client to the helping professional within the counseling experience (Figley, 1999). While social workers need to provide a holding environment that can tolerate the feelings and the testing of their traumatized clients, bearing witness to others' traumatic experiences heightens their own sense of vulnerability. This is particularly difficult when the patient and helping professional have been exposed to the same trauma. Studies of helping professionals have found problems in blurring of boundaries, inappropriate disclosure of feelings of anger and guilt, and a compulsion to rescue (Danieli, 1985).

Social agencies need to help staff to become culturally and historically attuned to the events of mass violence experienced by their client population. The provision of appropriate supports to staff dealing with clients who have experienced mass violence is crucial. Agencies also need to pay attention to their own staff members who have been traumatized. Good clinical supervision, agency-wide acknowledgment of the difficulty of the tasks, ongoing in-service training and other educational opportunities, and opportunities for staff members to network with each other around their common experiences are essential aspects of good agency practice when providing services to individuals and communities impacted by mass violence.

Conclusion

As mass violence has become an inescapable part of our lives, the social work profession needs to be better prepared to respond: We must be prepared to provide direct services to clients and communities; to design agency and community programs aimed at providing help to people affected by mass violence; to have emergency response procedures and appropriate personnel in place; to work as policy practitioners and ensure support for affected individuals, communities, and agencies; and to promote social work research that addresses difficult questions surrounding best practices, appropriate provision of services, and evaluations of outcomes. In addition, the social work profession needs to advocate for a nationally supported mechanism to ensure the preparation of a cadre of skilled social workers who are able to do this work.

All of these activities are geared toward providing the best intervention approaches and to fostering resilience of individuals, families, and communities during and following times of mass violence. Ultimately, of course, reducing the risk of traumatic stress reactions due to mass violence is best accomplished by preventing war, terrorism, and other traumatic stressors. As pointed out by Ofri, Solomon, and Dashberg (1995) "the impact of man-made disasters...that include intentionality and murderous cruelty that absolutely subvert the basic sense of security and meaning by which we all live, affect[s] not only the victims, but all of humanity" (p. 240).

References

American Psychiatric Association. (2002). *Diagnostic and statistical manual of mental disorders (DSM-IV)* (4th ed.). Washington, DC: Author.

Arroyo, W., & Eth, S. (1996). Post-traumatic stress disorder and other stress reactions. In R. J. Apfel & B. Simon (Eds.), *Minefields in their hearts: The mental health of children in war and communal violence* (pp. 52–74). New Haven, CT: Yale University Press.

Auerhahn, N., & Laub, D. (1998). Intergenerational memory of the Holocaust. In Y. Danieli (Ed.), *International handbook of multigenerational legacies of trauma* (pp. 21–41). New York: Plenum.

Breslau, N., Davis, G. C., Andreski, P., & Peterson, E. (1991). Traumatic events and posttraumatic stress disorder in an urban population of young adults. *Archives of General Psychiatry, 48,* 216–222.

Castex, G. (1997). Immigrant children in the United States. In N. K. Phillips & S. L. A. Straussner (Eds.), *Children in the urban environment: Linking social policy and clinical practice* (pp. 43–60). Springfield, IL: Charles C. Thomas.

Danieli, Y. (1985). The treatment and prevention of long-term effects and intergenerational transmission of victimization: A lesson from Holocaust survivors and their children. In C. R. Figley (Ed.), *Trauma and its wake: Vol. 1. The study and treatment of post-traumatic stress disorder* (pp. 248–313). New York: Bruner/Mazel.

Danieli, Y. (Ed.). (1998). *International handbook of multigenerational legacies of trauma.* New York: Plenum.

Edwards, J. G. (1976, April 17). Psychiatric aspects of civilian disasters. *British Medical Journal,* 944–947.

Ehlers, A., & Clark, D. (2000). A cognitive model of posttraumatic stress disorder. *Behavior Research and Therapy, 38,* 319–345.

Figley, C. R. (1999). Compassion fatigue: Toward a new understanding of the costs of caring. In B. H. Stamm (Ed.), *Secondary traumatic stress: Self-care issues for clinicians, researchers, and educators* (pp. 3–28). Baltimore, MD: Sidran Press.

Foa, E. B, Keane, T. M, & Friedman, M.J. (2000). *Effective treatments for PTSD: Practice guidelines from the International Society for Traumatic Stress Studies.* New York: Guilford.

Frankl, V. (1959/1992). *Man's search for meaning.* Boston: Beacon Press.

Gabriel, M. (1992). Anniversary reactions: Trauma revisited. *Clinical Social Work Journal, 20*(2), 179–192.

Galea, S., Ahern, J., Resnick, H., Kilpatrick, D., Bucuvalas, M., Gold, J., & Vlahov, D. (2002). Psychological sequelae of the September 11 terrorist attacks in New York City. *New England Journal of Medicine, 346,* 982–987.

Golan, N., (1978). *Treatment in crisis situations.* New York: Free Press

Goode, E. (2001, November 20). Treatment can ease lingering trauma of Sept. 11. *New York Times,* p. F1.

Herman, J. (1992a). Complex PTSD: A syndrome in survivors of prolonged and repeated trauma. *Journal of Traumatic Stress, 5,* 377–391.

Herman, J. (1992b). *Trauma and recovery.* New York: Basic Books.

Jacobs, A. (2002, March 9). Six months later, reality sets in for a New Jersey town. *New York Times,* p. A1.

Janoff-Bulman, R., & Frieze, I. H. (1983). A theoretical perspective for understanding reactions to victimization. *Journal of Social Issues, 39,* 1–18.

Kaplan, H. I., & Sadock, B. J. (1998). *Synopsis of psychiatry* (8th ed). Philadelphia: Lippincott, Williams & Wilkins.

Kessler, R. C., Sonnega, A., Bromet, E., Hughs, M., & Nelson, C. B. (1995). Posttraumatic stress disorder in the National Comorbidity Survey. *Archives of General Psychiatry, 52*(12), 1048–1060.

Krystal, H., & Niederland, J. (1968). (Ed.). *Massive psychic trauma.* New York: International University Press.

Lifton, R. J. (1967). *Death in life: Survivors of Hiroshima.* New York: Random House.

Lindy, J. D., & Titchener, J. (1983). Acts of God and man: Long-term character change in survivors of disasters and the law. *Behavioral Sciences and the Law, 1,* 85–96.

Mitchell, J. T. (1983). When disaster strikes: The critical incident stress debriefing process. *Journal of Emergency Medical Services, 8,* 36–39.

National Center for Post-Traumatic Stress Disorder [NCPTSD], Department of Veteran Affairs. (2001). What are the traumatic stress effects of terrorism? Retrieved October 2002 from www.ncptsd.org.

National Institute of Mental Health (NIMH). (2001a, October). Workshop to reach consensus on best practices. Retrieved December 17, 2002, from www.nimh.nih.gov/events/prmassviolence.cfm.

National Institute of Mental Health. (2001b, October 1, updated). Relieving trauma. Retrieved December 20, 2002, from www.nimh.nih.gov/publicat/reliving.cfm.

Norman, J. (2000). Constructive narrative in arresting the impact of post-traumatic stress disorder. *Clinical Social Work Journal,* 28(3), 303–319.

Norris, F. (2001). *The range, magnitude, and duration of effects of natural and human-caused disasters: A review of the empirical literature.* National Center for PTSD Fact Sheet. Washington, DC: National Center for PTSD.

Ofri, I., Solomon, Z., & Dashberg, H. (1995). Attitudes of therapists towards Holocaust survivors. *Journal of Traumatic Stress, 8* (2), 229–243.

Parad, H. J., & Parad, L. (Ed.). (1990). *Crisis intervention, Book 2.* Milwaukee, WI: Family Service of America.

Perez Foster, R. M. (2001). When immigration is trauma: Guidelines for the individual and family clinician. *American Journal of Orthopsychiatry, 71,* 153–170.

Pfefferbaum, B., Nixon, S., Tucker, P., Tivis, R., Moore, V., Gurwitch, R., Pynoos, R., & Geis, H. (1999). Posttraumatic stress responses in bereaved children after the Oklahoma City bombing. *Journal of the American Academy of Child and Adolescent Psychiatry, 38,* 1372–1379.

Pynoos, R., & Nader, K. (1988). Psychological first aid and treatment approach to children exposed to community violence: Research implications. *Journal of Traumatic Stress, 1,* 445–473.

Reiker, P. P., & Carmen, E. H. (1986). The victim to patient process: The disconfirmation and transformation of abuse. *American Journal of Psychiatry, 56,* 360–370.

Rosenheck, R., & Nathan, P. (1985). Secondary traumatization in children of Vietnam Veterans. *Hospital and Community Psychiatry, 5,* 538–539.

Shapiro, F. (2001). *Eye movement desensitization and reprocessing, basic principles, protocols and procedures* (2nd ed.). New York: Guilford.

Solomon, Z., Laor, N., & McFarlane A. C. (1996). Acute posttraumatic reactions in soldiers and civilians. In B. A. van der Kolk, A. C. McFarlane, & L. Weisaeth. *Traumatic stress: The effects of overwhelming experience on mind, body, and society* (pp. 102–113). New York: Guilford.

Straussner, J. H., & Straussner, S. L. A. (1997). Impact of community and school violence on children. In N. K. Phillips & S. L. A. Straussner (Eds.), *Children in the urban environment: Linking social policy and clinical practice* (pp. 61–77). Springfield, IL: Charles C. Thomas.

Susser, E. S., Herman, D. B., & Aaron, B. (2002). Combating the terror of terrorism. *Scientific American, 287,* 70–78.

Talbot, M. (2001, December 9). Communal bereavement. *New York Times Magazine,* 62.

Terr, L. (1991). Childhood traumas: An outline and overview. *American Journal of Psychiatry, 148,* 10–20.

U.S. Department of Justice, Office for Victims of Crime. (2000). *Responding to terrorism victims: Oklahoma City and beyond* (NCJ 183949). Washington, DC: Author.

van Dalen, A. (2001). Juvenile violence and addiction: Tangled roots in childhood trauma. *Journal of Social Work Practice in the Addictions, 1,* 25–40.

van der Kolk, B. A. (1987). *Psychological trauma.* Washington, DC: American Psychiatric Press.

van der Kolk, B. A. (2000). Posttraumatic stress disorder and the nature of trauma. *Dialogues in Clinical Neuroscience,* 7–22.

van der Kolk. B. A., McFarlane, A. C., Weisaeth, L. (Eds.). (1996). *Traumatic stress: The effects of overwhelming experience on mind, body and society.* New York: Guilford.

Waters, R. (2002). Our greatest challenge. *Psychotherapy Networker, 26,* 52–62.

Wilson, S. A., Becker, L. A., & Tinker, R. H. (1995). Eye movement desensitization and reprocessing (EMDR) treatment for psychologically traumatized individuals. *Journal of Consulting and Clinical Psychology, 63,* 928–937.

Yardle, J. (2002, April 11). Survivors in Oklahoma City fear new office at bomb site. *New York Times,* pp. A1, A31.

Yehuda, R., Kahana, B., Binder-Brynes, K., Southwick, S., & Mason, J. (1995). Low urinary cortisol excretion in Holocaust survivors with PTSD. *American Journal of Psychiatry, 112,* 982–986.

Zinner, E., & Williams, M. B. (Eds.). (1998). *When a community weeps: Case studies in group survivorship.* Philadelphia, PA: Bruner/Mazel.

Section II

Impact of Mass Violence on Individuals and Families

2

Interventions with Individuals and Families Affected by Mass Violence

Madelyn Miller

The global scope of human-caused mass violence, with its enormity of trauma and violent loss of life, encompasses a wide range of historical reference points. Included are the unfathomable devastation to Hiroshima and Nagasaki, Japan, and the violation of Nanking, China; the still-unimaginable horror of the Holocaust across Europe and genocides in Cambodia, Rwanda, and Armenia; as well as the sorrowful troubles of Northern Ireland, the despair of the Israeli-Palestinian violence, the horror within the former Yugoslavia, and the terror across Latin America. The impact of mass violence has also been felt as a result of the Tokyo metro sarin attack, the Pan Am 103 flight over Lockerbie, Scotland, the U.S. Embassy bombings in Kenya and Tanzania, and the Oklahoma City bombing. We have all experienced the catastrophic tragedy of September 11, 2001—terror unparalleled in the history of the United States.

Each of these cataclysmic disasters helps us understand more about survival and coping strategies after trauma and traumatic loss (Brooks & McKinlay, 1992; Scott, Brooks, & McKinlay, 1995; Shalev & Ursano, in press; Sitterle & Gurwitch, 1999; Tucker, Dickson, Pfefferbaum, McDonald, & Allen, 1997; Ursano & Fullerton, 1997) and the intersection of individual and collective experience after mass violence, with implications for restorative experiences in both domains (Bolton, 1999; Kleber, Figley, & Gersons, 1995; Nader, Dubrow, & Stamm, 1999; Zinner & Williams, 1998). The pervasive impact of mass violence touches individuals, families, and communities across cultures (DeSpelder, 1998; deVries, 1996; Green, 1996; Kleber et al., 1995; Zinner & Williams, 1999), long beyond immediate acts of devastation. The profound effects of mass violence therefore need to be seen within an extended time frame. Social work intervention may occur at any point along a continuum, which may begin immediately following a catastrophic tragedy, later as individuals or families are in need of information and care or identify concrete needs, and during the weeks, months, and years that follow, as their experiences evolve. Intervention may also occur at times of anniversaries, when one experiences new trauma or loss, or re-experiences trauma or loss from the past. Further, literature regarding the intergenerational transmission of trauma and responses to traumatic loss, regarding the impact of trauma passing from generation to generation, dramatically extends the time frame for intervention (Danieli, 1998).

This chapter explores the range of immediate and long-term social work interventions with individuals and families affected by mass violence. It provides a context within which we can examine the dynamics of people's responses to massive disaster, become familiar with the range of characteristic responses that follow, and determine appropriate interventions.

Impact of Trauma

Traumatic experiences are defined broadly as catastrophic life events that overwhelm human capacities to cope, exerting a complex biopsychosocial impact (Bloom, 1997; Herman, 1992; van der Kolk, McFarlane, & Weisaeth, 1996). Formally defined in the *DSM-IV* (APA, 1994) within a diagnostic context, traumatic experiences are identified as incidents of actual or threatened death or serious injury or threat to the physical integrity of others. Safety, security, and predictability in the world are threatened after trauma, and the world is experienced as changed. Following the trauma of mass violence, however, many individuals experience deep uncertainty, incongruity of unfathomable experience, exhaustion, profound losses, relocation, exposure to horror, dehumanization, and isolation (Shalev & Ursano, in press).

Terrorism typically involves a strike that comes with no warning and brings with it the threat of recurrence and unknown health effects (Flynn, 1996; Myers, 2001). Terrorism that results in mass violence is both an individual and a collective trauma. It affects individuals and families, as well as their communities, and includes those who were exposed either directly or indirectly. The intentionality of human-caused catastrophe to terrorize whole communities, the invisibility of the means of terrorism, the possible introduction of weapons of mass destruction, the magnitude of loss of life, and proximity to this loss are all overwhelming issues with long-term impact. Significant time is required for people to process these realities in a variety of ways. The often sustained terror and anxiety of terrorism may be coupled with lingering sensory aftermath.

Loss and Bereavement Following Mass Violence

Traumatic loss is often a central feature of the experience of mass violence. Sudden, traumatic death occurs with no preparation, no process, and no goodbye for surviving loved ones, co-workers, or friends. There is no chance to repair a relationship, deal with ambivalences, or return a long-overdue call. Such death is not only unexpected; it occurs within the context of trauma, horrifying imagery, and fear, thereby intensifying the experience of survivors. Multiple losses may be common after mass violence.

Accompanying the loss of a loved one, friend, or acquaintance, there are numerous other losses. These may include the loss of one's home, workplace, or school, a beloved pet, emotional and physical safety, comfort in living, and trust in the future. There may also be loss of financial stability through loss of income and additional expenses. And there may be loss of a sense of fairness, control, identity, meaning, and hope. Traumatic loss affects individuals, families, communities, and the collective experience of all survivors.

Dealing with traumatic loss within the context of mass violence involves unique issues: the nature of deaths; the numerous systems to negotiate; the painful public intrusion into highly private experience by agencies, law enforcement, the media, and the medical examiner; determining when a loved one is no longer missing, but has died; determining whether DNA is needed for identification and the identification process itself; and determinations regarding a memorial or religious service. The long, uneven, unpredictable, and uniquely felt and expressed process of grieving requires living through holidays and seasons, often without a timetable. It can take the form of a long-delayed process, not experienced until years have passed, or as an acute, intense grief reaction, lasting close to a year or more before slowly receding and becoming less intrusive.

Individual Responses

It is important for the social worker to appreciate the severity of exposure to profound violence and destruction after mass catastrophe and to frame an understanding of human response accordingly (Shalev, in press; Shalev & Ursano, in press). Three characteristic areas are experienced intermittently after trauma: (1) *intrusive reexperiencing,* such as persistent imagery, sensations of the experience, flashbacks, or nightmares; (2) *numbing,* or detached, dissociated experiences, including traumatic amnesia; and (3) *hyperarousal,* for instance, heightened startle reactions when hearing a loud noise or siren, difficulty sleeping, and poor concentration. These responses, which are normal reactions to abnormal and overwhelming experiences, need to be normalized with clients in each intervention format and defined as expected responses that can persist for a significant length of time.

It is only if individuals are unable to minimally function in their normal life or if posttrauma reactions worsen or remain intractable many months after traumatic exposure has subsided that they are considered to have posttraumatic stress disorder (PTSD). Otherwise, these posttrauma reactions are a complex, yet normal, repertoire of reactions to the devastation of violence on massive proportions. Factors contributing to the severity of these responses, and the possibility of future vulnerability, include: proximity to the site of destruction; exposure to loss of life, injury, or threat to safety; multiple losses; history of previous mental health problems; history of previous trauma, loss, or disruption; individual coping capacities; and the availability of social supports. Additionally, the powerful dynamic of intergenerational transmission of trauma and traumatic loss must be considered (Rousseau & Drapeau, 1998).

Each person's response to traumatic loss is unique and, like trauma itself, one can expect a wide range of time frames, behaviors, and evolving reactions (Doka, 1996). How a person responds to traumatic loss cannot be compared to how the person has responded to other deaths, as the factors of trauma and the scope of loss place this in a different realm of experience. For example, denial is a common protective mechanism for people experiencing traumatic loss. Out of the necessity to first integrate some aspect of the loss and re-establish identity, or in order to become familiar with a newly created daily existence without a loved one before facing the finality of loss, some individuals maintain hope that a loved one will be found at a site of devastation, even long after extensive searching. Others may need to continue to search, unable to consider the possibility of death, perhaps out of a desire not to abandon a loved one or a sense of loyalty.

A range of biopsychosocial and behavioral reactions may be seen as part of the post-trauma experience for individuals, including worsening of physical problems and somatization, staying awake to avoid nightmares, using alcohol and other drugs, increased interpersonal violence, becoming isolated, or overengaging in physical or work activity to avoid intrusive feelings and imagery. Physical manifestations of anxiety following mass violence are pervasive. The almost universal expression of a variety of sleeping problems includes difficulty falling asleep, interrupted sleep, or awakening early in a state of anxiety. These reactions also may be accompanied by visual or auditory associations to the trauma. For example, hearing thunder may be interpreted as an exploding bomb or lightning as the bright light of an explosion. In Oklahoma City, significant sleeping problems were experienced by the general population at least through the first year following the bombing incident (North et al., 1999). In Tokyo, the single use of chemical terrorism in the metro resulted in significant somatic problems across the population well past the fifth year (Asukai, 2001). Additionally, in New York City, reactions of hyperarousal continued to be expressed over many months after September 11th by people jumping at the sound of a police or fire alarm or ducking at the sound of a low-flying plane. Other commonly shared reactions include difficulty concentrating and focusing, poor memory, changes in eating, and pervasive agitation. Studies looking only at PTSD and depression found significant impact (Galea et al., 2002; Schuster et al., 2002). More intense reactions are common for those individuals with prior trauma and loss, especially if these parallel the dynamics of a recent mass disaster. These reactions include not only memories, but a revisiting of the emotional state of vulnerability and compromised resourcefulness experienced during the previous trauma.

The wide impact of mass violence must also be considered, and it is important to work not only with those disaster survivors who can be clearly identified, but to include those who are marginalized and disenfranchised by the event. These may be individuals experiencing discrimination, those who are racially profiled, or who are experiencing human rights violations as a result of a particular tragedy.

Responses of Families

The trauma of mass violence may profoundly disrupt families in a variety of ways. All aspects of a family's routine, and expected roles, schedules, and activities may be lost or disrupted. They may experience loss of significant people—relatives, friends, neighbors, healthcare providers, or they may lose places that symbolize community ties, such as a workplace, a house of worship, a school, a favorite store, restaurant, community center, or the community itself. Some families may lose their dwellings and be left homeless and without any essential or uniquely meaningful possessions. For those in rural areas, land and animals may also be lost; accompanying their loss of livelihood are the losses of those connections. Families may spend months trying to return to their earlier residences or communities, despite determinations of their uninhabitability.

Family cohesion is often challenged, as there is increased strain on sometimes already stressed relationships among partners and among various family members. Children and adolescents may revisit earlier losses, disruptions, and traumas, including changing homes, families, or countries. Parents who are overwhelmed or experiencing severe post-trauma reactions themselves need support in order to balance their own needs against urgent demands of their children and other family members. Particular stress is placed on single parents, especially those with minimal financial resources and few support systems, who must also cope with severe trauma and the traumatic loss reactions of their children. Those recently divorced or separated, those with legally unrecognized relationship status or with undocumented immigration status, or those suffering other losses, chronic illness, physical disability, or mental health problems are particularly emotionally vulnerable. For families with a history of sexual or physical abuse or other family trauma, such as domestic violence or substance abuse, mass violence may lead to further vulnerability and an increased risk that those behaviors may worsen or experiences may reoccur once again.

Studies of children's reactions to mass violence indicate that regardless of the ages of children, the most important factor in the outcome is parental coping. The literature underscores the dramatic impact of parents' capacities to instill confidence in their children that they will get through their experience (Norris, 2001; Perez Foster, 2001; Pynoos, Steinberg, & Goenjian, 1996). After mass violence, children tend to reflect the affect and deepest expressions of stress and loss within the family and are highly sensitive to the conflict and distress, as well as coping abilities and dysfunctions of their parents. Children with parents who are able to be supportive and capable, even in the midst of profound devastation and chaos, are tied to the resourcefulness of their parents and are thus less vulnerable to the negative impact of trauma (Pynoos et al., 1996). Unfortunately, in a family where a parent has been killed, the surviving parent or caretaker may be experiencing deep bereavement, making him or her emotionally unavailable to their children. Moreover, as in any situation in which a child, young or mature, has been killed, the surviving family will experience a spectrum of traumatic loss responses challenging their own stability.

Considerations of family history and the level of functioning of individual family members are significant factors in addressing the complexity of previous trauma and loss and current accompanying stressors, traumas, and losses.

Older adults within the family may be particularly vulnerable if they are in poor health, immobilized, isolated, and without other social supports. Compounding the developmental context of issues of mortality and loss, aging itself may bring back experiences of earlier trauma and loss, sometimes many decades later (Aarts & Op den Velde, 1996; Tucker et al., 1997). The exposure to overwhelming experiences of mass violence results in a revisiting of earlier traumas, losses, and disruptions, often without the context to safely process them. For example, an increased likelihood of depression and PTSD was cited in a study of older Bosnian refugees (Mollica et al., 2001). At the same time, some studies have identified the resilience of older adults, underscoring their life experiences and their becoming natural resources for others at the time of catastrophe (Norris, 2001).

Cultural Considerations

Cultural factors often have a fundamental impact on how an individual or family responds to traumatic death (Doka & Davidson, 1998). The nature of death as a result of mass violence may violate strongly held cultural patterns related to death and mourning rituals (Doka & Davidson, 1998), thus introducing prolonged uncertainty. For example, in some ethnic cultures, family members cannot begin to mourn without their loved one's body for burial or cremation. Yet, after an aviation tragedy or a building explosion, a body or identifiable remains may never be found; thus a funeral cannot be held and the resulting completeness may not be experienced. While a memorial service may take place instead of a funeral, its meaning is not the same. For some there is a lack of a physical place, such as a gravesite, to serve as a link to the deceased and provide a place to mourn. These experiences, referred to by some as "ambiguous loss," have been shared by survivors of those lost to mass violence across the world (Turner, Wieling, & Boss, 2002).

Individual and family inclusion in community healing through cultural and familiar rituals after the collective bereavement of mass violence supports a process of reconnection, restoration, and a recommitment to life (Linenthal, 2001; Zinner & Williams, 1998). Participating in the shared experiences of mourning provides essential links to others and a sense of belonging, which are particularly important after the disruption to everyday life and important relationships that follows mass violence. This may include participation with others in spontaneous memorials, anniversary services, or local commemorative activities. The many individuals who do not use social services find their only social connection and mourning process through such engagements with others. An understanding of the collective, community context of individuals and families after mass violence, and its influence on individual and family experience, is important for social workers so that they can actively support participation in a full range of community experiences as an essential resource.

Issues in Intervention

Recognizing and supporting the continuing bonds felt by individuals and family members with those who are missing or who died and appreciating the need to relearn how to live in the world after such profound loss become important aspects of clinical practice (Attig, 1996; Klass, Silverman, & Nickman, 1996). Such perspectives can enhance work with bereaved individuals who have lost not only important relationships, but also their future dreams and life expectations. A central challenge to social workers and other helping professionals is helping clients to find meaning and hope after surviving mass catastrophe (Frankl, 1959/1992; Laub & Auerhahn, 1993; Lifton, 1979). It is meaning and hope that permeate the experience of survival, and it is the focus on these features that become the central aspects of social work interventions with those impacted by mass violence.

Stage-Specific Interventions

No one method of intervention is appropriate for all survivors of mass violence. Instead, a chosen intervention must respond to the particular stage along the life cycle of mass violence in which a survivor is situated. Informal engagement, support, and an active presence may be most appropriate techniques at one point following devastation, while helping the client process the overwhelming experience of trauma and loss may be a better approach at another time.

It is important to consider two essential dimensions following mass violence: at what point in the aftermath of a catastrophe are interventions offered and with whom. Needs occur along a continuum as the realities of mass violence unfold, and the spectrum of survivors requiring intervention changes over time. Whether intervention occurs during a disaster, in the immediate aftermath, within a day, week, or month, on an anniversary, or years later is highly significant, just as the social context, culture, and meaning become significant factors in intervention.

Shalev and Ursano (in press) identify several overlapping, nonlinear stages occurring after mass violence. They include the impact phase, immediate post-impact or rescue phase, early recovery phase, and return to life. As clients progress from the immediacy of devastation and danger to the aftermath of mass violence and then to a process of reintegration, both the role of the social worker and provision of services change. The process moves from direct engagement at the site of devastation and protection, to provision of concrete needs, to a responsive presence, and then to the ongoing clinical work. This latter stage continues to include support for community engagement and social interaction.

The helping professional complements and respects the naturally unfolding process of survival. People need time to integrate reality, reappraise the experience, reconnect to others, and become ready to express their experience, all before formal intervention takes place. It is essential to support individuals and families in reengaging with their natural social and community supports. Certainly, if an individual is experiencing extreme anxiety, physical pain, dissociation, substance abuse, or severe insomnia, further specialized treatment is necessary.

Interventions with Individuals and Families

Basic principles for all intervention in the aftermath of mass violence transcend distinctions among the various intervention models and styles. These principles include:

- Respecting and normalizing the complexity of trauma and traumatic loss responses, including the fact that individual and family reactions are unique and most often occur over a long, often delayed, process.
- Providing additional information when appropriate about expected responses, the importance of support networks, coping strategies, and strategies for taking care of oneself in the future.

It is essential that any immediate response is understood as a first point along a continuum of care, rather than as a final intervention. As we have learned from the catastrophes of

Northern Ireland, Oklahoma City, Tokyo, and various aviation disasters, including the Lockerbie disaster (Brooks & McKinlay, 1992; North et al., 2001; Scott et al., 1995; Sitterle & Gurwitch, 1999; Zinner & Williams, 1998), there are delayed and extended expressions of trauma and loss following such tragedies. Therefore, there is a crucial need for the provision of diverse services as time evolves, both for those most immediately affected and for the community at large.

Immediate Interventions

The immediate aftermath of mass violence encompasses chaos, confusion, disorganization, poor communication of information regarding the devastation, and the overwhelming experience of being in danger. Emergency personnel may have difficulty gaining access to victims and survivors, and those immediately involved may be searching for loved ones, friends, and co-workers. Once out of danger, food, shelter, medical, and mental health needs become central issues. Family and friends of those missing will immediately be in search of information, approaching providers, hospitals, disaster-specific organizations, and the media in their search.

Intervention is at first informal. It may include helping to bring someone to safety, staying engaged, and providing human contact. It is important to provide as accurate information as is available on the unfolding situation. The social worker under these conditions is her- or himself exposed to trauma and may be even in a life-threatening situation. Conscientious attention to the essential need for support and self-care is required (Charney & Pearlman, 1998; McCann & Pearlman, 1990; Pearlman, 1995; Pearlman & Saakvitne, 1995a, 1995b; Saakvitne, 1996, 2002; Tauber, 2002). The prolonged waiting and living with uncertainty weigh heavily on both survivors and service providers. Many will be looking for ways of communicating with loved ones to register their safety. If a community has the human and financial resources after mass violence to establish a survivor or family center, this can provide a centralized location for attention and care. The location offers a sense of grounding and becomes a protected space, providing a context for community and a sense of belonging.

A variety of perspectives exist regarding the most effective intervention models in the immediate aftermath of traumatic events. Shalev (2002) and Shalev and Ursano (in press) suggest that studies on these models are inconclusive. They state that before deciding on any intervention model, providers need to first understand the uniqueness of individual experience as a key to creating a therapeutic rapport. It is then possible to respond to survivors' basic needs. At this early stage, intervention goals are categorized as: (1) reducing psychobiological distress, often through the reduction of secondary stressors, such as helping someone to safety, providing a phone, linking with family members, or an information source; (2) treating specific reactions that interfere with natural healing—for instance, providing specialized referrals in response to extreme levels of anxiety, sleep disruption, physical pain, or self-harm behaviors, as well as allowing discussion and assimilation of the traumatic experience; and (3) supporting normal healing by providing encouragement and facilitating enhancement of support systems—for instance, providing support to overwhelmed parents who can then better support their children.

For many but not all individuals, group interventions can provide beneficial opportunities for interpersonal engagement, the safe experience of being with others who have shared mass violence, the expression of grief and trauma, and the normalizing of a broad range of characteristic reactions. Such shared experience allows for the development of a sense of community to counter the disruptive and isolating impact of terrorism or other mass violence and offers the support of strengths and coping strategies. Additionally, the group provides a context for expression of aloneness, fear, anxiety, and despair. It is one of several formats for the development of interpersonal connections and for providing meaning and hope. Specialized group models of intervention after mass violence should not be used unless the mental health professional comprehensively understands the complexities and dimensions of trauma and traumatic loss. Social work practitioners must also assess their own capacities to listen to clients' trauma and traumatic loss in the midst of their own feelings of helplessness so as to avoid their own retraumatization. The importance of ongoing support among colleagues is an essential aspect of all trauma intervention (Charney & Pearlman, 1998; McCann & Pearlman, 1990; Pearlman, 1995; Pearlman & Saakvitne, 1995a, 1995b; Saakvitne, 1996, 2002; Tauber, 2002).

Regardless of the type of group model used, there is wide support for using groups after trauma (Foy, Eriksson, & Trice, 2001). In this context, all such groups are based on the model of providing for safe expression and social support, with a goal of helping to establish a sense of safety and control. Several models include supportive, psychodynamic, cognitive-behavioral, and psychological debriefing groups. Others used in the immediate aftermath of mass violence include small and large group crisis intervention, acute trauma debriefing, critical incident stress debriefing (Mitchell, 1983), critical incident stress management, and family interventions. After September 11th, among these other models, a variety of debriefing groups have been frequently used.

Debriefing group formats, originally developed to deal with police and fire personnel critical incidents, generally begin with introduction of self and group, group discussion of events and reactions, psychoeducation about normal responses to traumatic events, discussion of social supports, basic coping skills, future expectations, self-care, and suggestions for additional help.

Some debriefing groups are offered for several sessions. Many debriefing groups, however, are offered only on a one-time basis, leading trauma and disaster specialists to express concerns regarding the ability to respond to complex and long-term dimensions of posttrauma experience through such single intervention (Foy et al., 2001; Gist & Devilly, 2002; Shalev, 2002; Shalev & Ursano, in press). Briere (2001) maintains that a single psychological debriefing is not helpful; rather, group interventions should be provided over multiple sessions. He suggests that because responses to trauma are normal and many recede with time, professional assistance should be indicated only if an individual requests it, if symptoms interfere significantly with functioning and persist for more than a few months, and if suicide ideation, aggression, or psychotic symptoms occur.

All crisis or short-term debriefing groups used in the context of terrorism, mass disaster, and violence need to be understood within a framework of continuity of care, carefully determined to be the best intervention for the given situation, and offered at an appropriate time in the process. Participants in these groups are encouraged to express their experiences in a manageable way with an emphasis on immediate coping, while the range of their responses is normalized. Participants are also helped to prepare for future reactions by anticipating traumatic triggering of memories and emotions, such as at anniversary dates, new life events, media coverage and news, trials, and holidays. The focus is on beginning to help individuals to develop basic skills for coping and self-care and establishing support networks.

With Individuals. Helping individuals anticipate traumatic triggers (Pynoos et al., 1996)—that is, the reminders that may viscerally bring an individual back to the experience of trauma—is an important aspect of any intervention after trauma. This may include helping an individual to consider the profound and often unexpected impact of attending a memorial service or returning to the site of devastation. Preparing individuals for the range of reactions possible may help them to understand or even minimize the impact of such traumatic triggers, which can result in a return of previous emotional experience and the resurfacing of characteristic posttrauma reactions. It may also help them to make informed choices about exposure.

Traumatic expectations (Pynoos et al., 1996)—that is, the beliefs transferred from trauma to relationships with people and to how one sees one's relationship to the world—also require attention. For instance, an older woman who has lost a niece in an aviation disaster en route to the Dominican Republic within months after the September 11, 2001, tragedy now expects all travel to be dangerous and constantly worries that all her relatives are in danger. In time, intervention will need to help her to contextualize these experiences as she becomes more comfortable.

In any intervention the complexity and broad range of characteristic individual responses to traumatic loss need to be normalized and understood as occurring over an uneven, evolving, long-term, and complex grief process. Helping a client deal with loss without confirmation or information about a missing loved one requires that the clinician also develop the ability to live with ambiguity. Allowing individuals their hopefulness while acknowledging the unknown gives clients permission to progress at their own pace in this profoundly difficult process of traumatic bereavement.

Preparing individuals for anniversary reactions and holidays and helping them to revisit loss at personally meaningful times engages survivors in an active process. Clinicians must anticipate increased vulnerability, diminished resourcefulness, and intensified posttrauma reactions at these times. Bearing witness, listening deeply, and bringing an active presence to any interaction with a suddenly bereaved individual allows for a respectful engagement process. The clinician offers an authentic presence and allows for the uniqueness of clients' expressions, including their silence. Ultimately, this helps in grieving, rather than in forgetting. For example:

> Two months after the death of several co-workers, the relocation of his workplace, and a minor injury, Mr. C., a recently divorced Latino man, 38, who narrowly escaped the World Trade Center collapse, is experiencing anxiety, interrupted sleep, and intrusive imagery about his co-workers' experiences. Despite remaining engaged at work and involved with supportive siblings, his posttrauma reactions continue. He never before worried about his

health and how long he would live, but now he cannot stop thinking about this. Referred to a social worker in a community mental health clinic, he states that he has not cried about his experience and wonders if his recent realization of depression is an improvement over being so cut off from his feelings previously. His social worker is providing a context for safe engagement and the development of trust within the relationship and is balancing his exploration of current experience with a careful pacing to ensure safety. She normalizes his still early responses to mass violence and the constant exposure to anthrax threat, high-alert designation, and subway delays, offering her understanding of his range of physical, emotional, and interpersonal reactions as fully expected responses. She continues to assess his gradual and consistent progress, such as Mr. C's slow resumption of reading books, one of his favorite activities in the past. She acknowledges how his keeping weekly appointments is an expression of his social engagement and taking care of himself. She carefully examines her own shared experience after sessions, understanding her own parallel reactions. She is staying active in her peer support group at her workplace where discussion focuses on the impact of working in the midst of ongoing terrorism.

Another client, Mr. R., a 29-year old African American man, was having a difficult time a month after the trauma of September 11th. While he did not lose any close friends or family, he was close enough to watch horrifying aspects of the devastation from his office window. Also, his twin sister had been missing for five hours that day until she was able to safely call family. Currently, he is unable to concentrate at work, worries about his job security, and is still somewhat uncomfortable traveling to work. He has occasional nightmares about what he has seen and has become more isolated from family and friends. His social worker is helping him understand his current functioning in the context of trauma after mass violence, normalizing his reactions in this early stage of postdisaster experience. She is supporting his reengagement with his social network and providing a consistent and safe setting for his expressions of terror and fear of loss. She is affirming his resourcefulness from earlier experiences and assessing her own experience of bearing witness.

With Families. Parents need help to understand not only their own experiences but also their children's responses in a developmental context. They need to expect intensified behaviors and may need help to address, talk to, and help their children and adolescents cope with grief, death, trauma, loss, disruption, and the inevitable emotional overload. Help given to parents on how to discuss terrorism, mass violence, and their own feelings, as well as how to best address their children's teachers, can benefit the whole family. Enabling parents' expression of their feelings of helplessness and also safety ultimately becomes a model for them as they talk to other family members.

Earlier family trauma and loss are often revisited after mass violence, and an intensification of vulnerable relationships may become overwhelming. Revisiting their own and their children's previous vulnerabilities and previous capacities to deal with disruption may help frame their present experience. Family dynamics may be stressed in unexpected ways in times of crisis. The following illustration points to the subtle, often unexpressed, yet profound experiences of family members in the midst of mass violence.

Mrs. B., a 57-year-old widow, worked in a church across from the Twin Towers. She recently arrived in the United States from rural South Asia to stay with her son, 28, after the loss of her husband. She had minimal command of English and several chronic health problems.

She found herself on the street the morning of September 11th, running through thick smoke and debris in an unfamiliar neighborhood until she could find a phone to call her son. He found her several hours later, stunned and terrified, with an excruciating migraine headache.

Her son took her to a doctor in their community with whom she could communicate and introduced her to other women from their country at a local house of worship. She began to feel somewhat calmer and less alone. After several weeks, her migraines continue to come and go, and she is only now beginning to eat better and is more animated at home with her son.

While Mrs. B. has only seen a counselor to speak about benefits at a busy local center and has not spoken about her experiences, her son sought support after realizing how much this disaster has touched him. As he has become aware of his complex family roles and responsibilities within his cultural context, he has been left with a sense of pervasive helplessness. The weekly sessions with a social worker are providing a format for his exploration of family expectations, and he is becoming more able to share his fear of losing his mother. Within an increasingly uncertain social climate, he has also expressed concerns for his own safety on the street, fearing becoming the target of a hate crime. The social worker continues to support his identification of these realities and encourages him to meet and speak more openly with other friends sharing these fears. The social worker gives much thought to his emotional responses to this client's experiences of vulnerability and his family dynamics. He is assessing his countertransference reactions and vicarious trauma after each session.

Long-Term Interventions

Long-term interventions after mass violence include both ongoing work with previous clients and long-term work with new clients experiencing delayed reactions to trauma. Interventions with ongoing clients, using both individual and group modalities, utilize the same principles discussed previously. The clinician needs to continue to bear witness, listen intently, and normalize the broadest expressions of the characteristic spectrum of posttrauma and traumatic loss reactions. Preparation for long-term, delayed, uneven experience that may threaten principal foundations of trust in oneself, others, the world, and the future becomes a necessity for unfolding work. Clinical interventions require ongoing creativity and flexibility in order to help clients deal with changing realities. The clinician may also experience the compounded reality of working within an intense atmosphere exposed to trauma, sharing this experience with clients, and experiencing vicarious trauma resulting from the cumulative empathic engagement with traumatized clients. Adopting a strengthened perspective on the significance of the treatment relationship to healing, within the broader context of connection and belonging, provides a sense of continuity and connection dramatically missing from the world in the aftermath of mass violence, and allows for the development of a renewed sense of safety.

What should we expect in the long term? Literature abounds regarding the long-term effects of those surviving mass violence (Jensen & Agger, 1996; Lindy, 1985; Ursano, Fullerton, & McCaughey, 1994; Zinner & Williams, 1998), those closely affected, and the mental health workers immediately engaged with them (Linenthal, 2001; Saakvitne, 2002). Each study found the existence of delayed expressions of posttrauma experience, with some people experiencing severe consequences such as PTSD, substance abuse, family violence, self-harm, and a range of other difficult behaviors (Norris, 2001). Literature from the Oklahoma City bombing suggests it may take many months for individuals to pass through the shock and denial stages before beginning to cope with the reality of their losses (e.g., Long-term effect of terrorist attacks, 2001).

With Individuals. What may be most challenging in long-term work with survivors of catastrophic tragedy is the interplay between previous trauma and loss and more recent experiences. The unexpected but common occurrence of memory transporting an individual back to previous traumatic experiences may occur with or without conscious awareness. The profound difficulty in facing both the past and the present dimensions of experience taxes the individual and challenges the clinician. For example,

> Ms. P., a 50-year-old single woman, was in long-term treatment after a history of severe sexual abuse in childhood. She was deeply aware of years of pain, isolation, shame, and social discomfort and was greatly affected by the recent experience of mass devastation in her city even though she was living and working far from the site of the disaster, neither losing someone she knew nor being affected on a concrete level. She began re-experiencing intrusive imagery and flashbacks from childhood that she had not felt for years. The "impending doom" that she was experiencing from her history of threatening abuse was more intensely experienced as she faced the current devastation following mass violence. Her earlier posttrauma reactions were no longer distinguished from her current reactions of being overwhelmed from recent experience. Her familiar fear could not be differentiated from current trauma. She was unable to use public transportation, wouldn't sleep to avoid the possibility of horrifying nightmares, and was unable to answer her phone at night, fearing the dangerous intrusion of others into her carefully constructed safety.
>
> Intervention required the social worker to help contextualize the experiences of impending doom in the past as separate from the profound fear and shock of her current trauma, with its closely related questions about human cruelty, helplessness, and near-annihilatory fear. The social worker's empathic engagement and responsive presence, coupled with a normalizing and gentle contextualizing of her experience, eventually allowed Ms. P. to recall the resources that she was able to engage during past years to protect herself. She bought several new books so she could read, decided to organize her apartment to enhance the comfort of her home, and conscientiously met several colleagues after work for coffee in order to begin socializing again. Her ongoing participation in a long-term group with other women survivors of abuse provided additional support and validation, as her experience was understood in its complexity.

As time evolves after mass violence, more grief may arise, more difficult imagery heretofore protected by hypervigilance may be available, and questions about meaning may become more central. Existential questions may include how to consider living one's life after profound loss, and how to create meaning in an unsafe and uncertain world.

With Families. The collective exposure of families to mass violence results in complex shared experience and subtle responses to one another's coping. Family history, current stress, and the unique impact of catastrophe in relation to past experience become central aspects of consideration. For those experiencing strain and difficulty communicating, the tragedy of mass violence may unsettle any measures of progress, or it may allow a family to transcend devastation and risk connection, as illustrated below:

> Mr. L. was a Vietnam veteran in his mid 50s with a history of alcoholism. He was the father of two sons who had been estranged from him for most of their adult years. Eight months after the World Trade Center disaster, Mr. L. was called by his younger son, who had been in therapy at the Veterans' Administration since his return from the Gulf War. His son had been re-experiencing frequent flashbacks after September 11th, which he had not experienced for years. He became too frightened to leave his apartment and decided to seek out his father for support. The father realized that his own war experience in Vietnam meant something to his son at this time of crisis. Along with his two sons, the father saw a social worker in a community agency for ongoing family work. The relationship of neglect and abuse by Mr. L., and the shame, impotence, and trauma resulting from it across the years, became the dual centerpiece of treatment. The grief of lost bonds and the unique traumas of each family member were apparent during the sessions. The social worker established a safe setting for engagement and communication and provided a context for articulating their hopes and disappointments, expectations and hurt, rage and shame. He helped Mr. L. and his sons balance their hope for unconditional closeness with their unfolding discovery of pain, loss, and echoes of despair, within the context of their active search for connection.

Conclusion

This chapter has introduced a context and a perspective within which to begin addressing the immediate and long-term social work interventions with individuals and families following mass violence. In working with survivors of mass violence, it is important to appreciate the breadth of reactions inevitably experienced by many, ranging from initially acute reactions that can last for a significant course of time to often delayed, uneven, and intermittent, as well as long-endured consequences that may cross the generations. And it is important to include the collective context of mass violence as both an influence and a resource for individuals and families.

Depathologizing and destigmatizing the spectrum of responses after overwhelming life experience requires a critical assessment of treatment models and a continual appreciation of survival-driven evolution of human reactions. We need to humanize our interventions and respect the varied timing and pacing of individual and family responses after overwhelming experience and unfathomable sorrow. Clients who begin new treatment after mass violence, as after other traumas, must begin to develop a sense of safety and trust in the treatment relationship before any uncovering of trauma can take place. Given a context of fear, anxiety, and danger, it is essential that the pace of intervention moves slowly and that clients are provided with the time needed to allow the intimacy of the therapeutic context to become comfortable.

In addition, it is of central importance that we assess our own experience with clients, acknowledge the relative sense of helplessness accompanying our experience, the demands of providing services in the aftermath of mass violence, and the complications resulting from sharing painful realities with our clients. We need to recognize the inevitability of vicarious trauma in our work with trauma survivors as a result of empathic engagement and our sense of responsibility, and commit ourselves to self-care, including engaging in supportive and informed supervision, consultation, peer groups, and other support with colleagues. This will allow us to more easily listen to our clients and provide a balance for them as they express fears, helplessness, and anxiety. Our attention to collegial support and collective engagement provides the foundation for finding meaning in our own experience. Learning about resilience from colleagues and communities across the world can contextualize our own situation, providing not only a perspective for our own experience, but a sense of hope for the future.

The complexity of clinical work, with its particular demands and challenges reflective of the intensity following mass violence raises many issues: How do we responsively acknowledge, and integrate the profound realities after trauma and traumatic loss into our work? What is our role in the treatment dyad regarding our shared experience of exposure to overwhelming circumstances? How do the current issues of mass violence intersect with clinical work with earlier traumas and losses? What adaptations to a catastrophic tragedy are considered to be out of the norm? How do we engage in the development of meaning, hope, and enhanced interpersonal connections if our own perspective is challenged?

These questions are some of the challenges we bring into our work as we balance attunement to clients and to ourselves, keeping our work informed by our shared experience and often parallel reactions. It is our striving to enhance interrelatedness, connection, and active social engagement that ultimately offers the foundation for creating meaning and hope in survival. With appreciation of the human capacity to survive in the midst of often life-threatening experience and recognition of the exquisite sensitivity and equal resiliency in the face of tragedy of individuals, families, and our community, we can approach our work in this uncertain world with a sense of possibility and continuity.

References

Aarts, P. H., & Op den Velde, W. (1996). Prior traumatization and the process of aging: Theory and clinical implications. In B. van der Kolk, A. McFarlane, & L. Weisaeth (Eds.), *Traumatic stress: The effects of overwhelming experience on mind, body, and society* (pp. 359–377). New York: Guilford.

American Psychiatric Association (APA). (1994). *Diagnostic and statistical manual of mental disorders* (4th ed.) Washington, DC: Author.

Asukai, N. (2001, May). *Somatic complaints among survivors of the 1995 Tokyo metro sarin attack.* Presented at the annual European Conference on Traumatic Stress (ECOTS) of the European Society of Traumatic Stress Studies, Edinburgh, Scotland.

Attig, T. (1996). *How we grieve: Relearning the world.* New York: Oxford University Press.

Bloom, S. (1997). *Creating sanctuary: Toward the evolution of sane societies.* New York: Routledge.

Bolton, D. (1999). The threat to belonging in Enniskillen: Reflections on the Remembrance Day bombing. In E. Zinner & M. B. Williams (Eds.), *When a community weeps: Case studies in group survivorship* (pp. 191–212) Philadelphia: Brunner/Mazel.

Briere, J. (2001). *Facts sheet for mental health professionals working with acute traumatic stress.* International Society for Traumatic Stress Studies. Retrieved August 1, 2002, from www.istss.org.

Brooks, N., & McKinlay, W. (1992). Mental health consequences of the Lockerbie disaster. *Journal of Traumatic Stress,* 5, 527–543.

Charney, A., & Pearlman, L. (1998). The ecstasy and the agony: The impact of disaster and trauma work on the self of the psychologist. In P. Kleespies (Ed.), *Emergency psychological services: The evaluation and management of life threatening behavior* (pp. 418–435). New York: Guilford.

Danieli, Y. (Ed.). (1998). *International handbook of multigenerational legacies of trauma.* New York: Plenum.

DeSpelder, L. (1998). Developing cultural competency. In K. Doka & J. Davidson (Eds.), *Living with grief: Who are we, how do we grieve?* (pp. 97–106). Philadelphia: Taylor & Francis.

deVries, M. (1996). Trauma in cultural perspective. In B. van der Kolk, A. McFarlane, & L. Weisaeth (Eds.), *Traumatic stress: The effects of overwhelming experience on mind, body, and society* (pp. 398–413). New York: Guilford.

Doka, K. (Ed.). (1996). *Living with grief after sudden loss.* Bristol, PA: Taylor & Francis.

Doka, K., & Davidson, J. (Eds.). (1998). *Living with grief: Who we are, how we grieve.* Philadelphia: Taylor & Francis.

Flynn, B. W. (1996, April). *Psychological aspects of terrorism.* Presented at the First Harvard Symposium on the Medical Consequences of Terrorism.

Foy, D., Eriksson, C., & Trice, G. (2001). Introduction to group interventions for trauma survivors. *Group Dynamics, 5,246–251.*

Frankl, V. (1959/1992). *Man's search for meaning.* Boston: Beacon Press.

Galea, S., Ahern, J., Resnick, H., Kilpatrick, D., Bucuvalas, M., Gold, J., & Vlahov, D. (2002). Psychological sequelae of the September 11 terrorist attacks in New York City. *New England Journal of Medicine, 346,* 982–987.

Gist, R., & Devilly, G. (2002). Post-trauma debriefing: The road too frequently traveled. *The Lancet, 360,* 741.

Green, B. (1996). Cross-national and ethnocultural issues in disaster research. In A. Marsella, M. Friedman, E. Gerrity, & R. Scurfield (Eds.), *Ethnocultural aspects of post-traumatic stress disorder* (pp. 341–361). Washington, DC: American Psychological Association.

Herman, J. (1992). *Trauma and recovery.* New York: Basic Books.

Jensen, S., & Agger, I. (1996). *Trauma and healing under state terrorism.* New Jersey: Zed Books.

Klass, D., Silverman, P., & Nickman, S. (Eds.). (1996). *Continuing bonds: New understandings of grief.* Washington, DC: Taylor & Francis.

Kleber, R., Figley, C., & Gersons, B. (1995). *Beyond trauma: Cultural and societal dynamics.* New York: Plenum.

Laub, D., & Auerhahn, N. (1993). Knowing and not knowing massive psychic trauma: Forms of traumatic memory. *International Journal of Psychoanalytic Analysis, 74,* 287–302.

Lifton, R. J. (1979). *The broken connection: On death and the continuity of life.* Washington, DC: American Psychiatric Press.

Lindy, J. (1985). The trauma membrane and other clinical concepts derived from psychotherapeutic work with survivors of natural disasters. *Psychiatric Annals, 15,*153–160.

Linenthal, E. (2001). *The unfinished bombing: Oklahoma City in American memory.* New York: Oxford University Press.

Long-term effects of terrorist attacks. (2001). *Mental Health Weekly, 11* (37), 1–4.

McCann, I. L., & Pearlman, L. A. (1990). Vicarious traumatization: A framework for understanding the psychological effects of working with victims. *Journal of Traumatic Stress, 3,* 131–149.

Mitchell, J. (1983). When disaster strikes. *Journal of Emergency Services, 8,* 36–39.

Mollica, R., Sarajlic, N., Chernoff, M., Lavelle, J., Sarajlic-Vukovic, I., & Massajli, M. (2001). Longitudinal study of psychiatric symptoms, disability, mortality, and emigration among Bosnian refugees. *Journal of American Medical Association, 286,* 546–554.

Myers, D. (2001). *Weapons of mass destruction and terrorism: Mental health consequences and implications for planning and services.* Presented at a conference *The Ripple Effects from Ground Zero: Coping with Mental Health Needs in Times of Tragedy and Terror.* American Red Cross of Greater New York. New York City.

Nader, K., Dubrow, N., & Stamm, B. H. (Eds.). (1999). *Honoring differences: Cultural issues in the treatment of trauma and loss.* Philadelphia: Brunner/Mazel.

National Center for Post-Traumatic Stress Disorder, Department of Veteran Affairs. (2001a). *How terrorist acts may affect veterans.* Retrieved August 22, 2002, from www.ncptsd.org.

National Center for Post-Traumatic Stress Disorder, Department of Veteran Affairs. (2001b). *What are the traumatic stress effects of terrorism?* Retrieved July 19, 2002, from www.ncptsd.org.

Norris, F. (2001, September). *50,000 disaster victims speak: An empirical review of the empirical literature, 1981–2001.* Prepared for National Center for PTSD and the Center for Mental Health Services (SAMHSA). Retrieved June 22, 2002, from www.istss.org/ISTSSDisaster/victimSpeak.htm.

North, C., Nixon, S., Shariat, S., Mallonnee, S., McMillen, J., Spitznagel, E., & Smith, E. (1999). Psychiatric disorders among survivors of the Oklahoma City bombing. *Journal of American Medical Association, 282,* 755–762.

Pearlman, L. A. (1995). Self-care for trauma therapists: Ameliorating vicarious traumatization. In B. H. Stamm (Ed.), *Secondary traumatic stress: Self-care issues for clinicians, researchers, and educators* (pp. 65–79). Lutherville, MD: Sidran Press.

Pearlman, L. A., & Saakvitne, K. W. (1995a). *Trauma and the therapist: Countertransference and vicarious traumatization in psychotherapy with incest survivors.* New York: W.W. Norton.

Pearlman, L. A., & Saakvitne, K. W. (1995b). Treating therapists with vicarious traumatization and secondary traumatic stress disorders. In C. R. Figley (Ed.), *Compassion fatigue: Coping with secondary traumatic stress disorder in those who treat the traumatized* (pp. 150–177). Philadelphia: Brunner/Mazel.

Perez Foster, R. M. (2001). When immigration is trauma: Guidelines for the individual and family clinician. *American Journal of Orthopsychiatry, 71,* 2.

Pynoos, R., Steinberg, A., & Goenjian, A. (1996). Traumatic stress in childhood and adolescence: Recent developments and current controversies. In B. van der Kolk, A. McFarlane, & L. Weisaeth (Eds.), *Traumatic stress: The effects of overwhelming experience on mind, body, and society* (pp. 331–358). New York: Guilford.

Rousseau, C., & Drapeau, A. (1998). The impact of culture on the transmission of trauma: Refugees' stories and silence embodied in their children's lives. In Y. Danieli (Ed.), *International handbook of multigenerational legacies of trauma* (pp. 465–486). New York: Plenum.

Saakvitne, K. W. (1996). *Countertransference and vicarious traumatization: The therapist in the eye of the storm.* Paper presented at the APA Division 39 Spring Conference, New York City.

Saakvitne, K. W. (2002). Shared trauma: The therapist's increased vulnerability. *Psycho Dialogues, 12,* 443–449.

Schuster, M., Stein, B., Jaycox, L., Collins, R., Marshall, G., Elliott, M., Zhou, A., Kanouse, D., Morrison, J., & Berry, S. (2001). A national survey of stress reactions after the September 11, 2001 terrorist attacks. *New England Journal of Medicine, 345,* 1507–1512.

Scott, R., Brooks, N., & McKinlay, W. (1995). Post-traumatic morbidity in a civilian community of litigants: A follow-up at 3 years. *Journal of Traumatic Stress, 8,* 3, 403–417.

Shalev, A. (2002). Treating survivors in the immediate aftermath of traumatic events. In R. Yehuda (Ed.), *Treating trauma survivors with PTSD.* Arlington, VA: American Psychiatric Press.

Shalev, A., & Ursano, R. (In press). *Mapping the multidimensional picture of acute responses to traumatic stress.* New York: Oxford University Press.

Sitterle, K. A., & Gurwitch, R. H. (1999). The terrorist bombing in Oklahoma City. In E. Zinner & M. B. Williams (Eds.), *When a community weeps: Case studies in group survivorship.* Philadelphia: Brunner/Mazel.

Tauber, Y. (2002). High holidays 2000 and aftermath: Doing psychotherapy with Holocaust survivors and the second generation in Israel during the sudden eruption of violence. *American Journal of Psychotherapy, 56,* 391–410.

Tucker, P., Dickson, W., Pfefferbaum, B., McDonald, N., & Allen, G. (1997). Traumatic reactions as predictors of posttraumatic stress six months after the Oklahoma City bombing. *Psychiatric Services, 48,* 1191–1194.

Turner, W., Wieling, E., & Boss, P. (2002, January/February). Ambiguous loss: Frozen grief in the wake of terrorism. *Family Therapy Magazine: The American Association for Marriage and Family Therapy.*

Ursano, R., & Fullerton, C. (1997). Trauma, time, and recovery. In C. Fullerton & R. Ursano (Eds.), *Posttraumatic stress disorder: Acute and long-term responses to trauma and disaster* (pp. 271–273). Washington, DC: American Psychological Association.

Ursano, R., Fullerton, C., & McCaughey, B. (1994). Trauma and disaster. In R. Ursano, B. McCaughey, & C. Fullerton (Eds.), *Individual and community response to trauma and disaster* (pp. 3–12). Great Britain: Cambridge Press.

van der Kolk, B. A., McFarlane, A. C., & Weisaeth, L. (Eds.). (1996). *Traumatic stress: The effects of overwhelming experience on mind, body, and society.* New York: Guilford.

Zinner, E., & Williams, M. B. (Eds.) (1998). *When a community weeps: Case studies in group survivorship.* Philadelphia: Brunner/Mazel.

3

Helping Traumatized Children

William Steele

When children and adolescents experience an overwhelming sense of terror that destroys their sense of safety and/or invokes intense feelings of powerlessness, they can suffer post-traumatic stress disorder (PTSD) reactions similar to those seen in adults (Udwin, 1993). Such reactions are commonly seen in children who are exposed to war, community violence, school violence, and religious cults that employ violence, as well as to family violence and other forms of assaultive victimization (Morse & Wiley, 1997; Pynoos & Nader, 1988; Saigh & Bremner, 1999; Schwarz & Kowalski, 1991b; Steele & Raider, 2001; Straussner & Straussner, 1997). It is important to state, however, that not every child who is exposed to violence becomes vulnerable to PTSD—it is the meaning that the child gives to the experience that helps to determine his or her vulnerability (Freud, 1965; Green, Wilson, & Lindy, 1985). For example, Webb (1994) reported on children trapped for five hours in an elevator at the New York World Trade Center following the bomb blast there in 1993, noting that the older children were more upset than the kindergarten children. This was probably due to the fact that "the older children understood the potential danger of their situation, whereas the younger ones were able to believe and take comfort in the reassurance of their teacher... 'that they would be down in no time' " (p. 52).

The dramatic increase in the forms of mass violence requires that clinicians gain the tools necessary to assist traumatized children. The abundance of research documenting the manifestation of trauma-specific reactions of children and adolescents exposed to violence will be helpful for clinicians, who must be able to identify reactions that are indicative of trauma and be prepared to provide children with interventions that are trauma-specific, developmentally appropriate, and designed to address both their short-term and long-term needs (Garbarino, 1993; Koop & Lundberg, 1992; Straussner & Straussner, 1997). The purpose of this chapter is to identify trauma-specific reactions of children and adolescents who have been exposed to mass violence. The chapter will discuss variables related to the severity of reactions, individual dynamics, and intervention strategies that are appropriate immediately following the trauma, in later weeks, and, when necessary, in the months or years that follow.

Exposure to Trauma

There are four ways a child can be exposed to trauma: (1) as a surviving victim, such as a survivor of the bombing of the Alfred P. Murrah Federal Building in Oklahoma City in 1995; (2) as a witness to mass destruction, such as the Columbine High School massacre on April 20, 1999, or the bombing of the World Trade Center on September 11, 2001; (3) as a person who is related to a victim, either as a family member or friend, or who is a peer living in the neighborhood, going to the same school, or similar to the victim in age, circumstances, and conditions related to the victimization (Milgram, Toubiana, Klingman, Raviv, & Goldstein, 1988); and (4) as a nonwitness exposed to hearing the details of the incident (Saigh, 1991; Steele & Raider, 2001).

The severity of reactions has been found to relate to one's physical proximity to the incident—the closer a child is to the actual incident, the more intense the reactions. Pynoos and colleagues (1987), in detailing research following a sniper attack in a California school, found that "the children in the area the shooting took place had a higher prevalence of PTSD (94.3 percent) than youth in the school building (88.9 percent), at home (44.2 percent), or on vacation (45.1 percent)." Children who were not at the school on the day of the shooting were also found to have a higher prevalence of guilt then those who were at school.

Related to physical proximity is direct victimization. Schwarzwald, Weisenber, Waysman, and Solomon (1994) reported that following SCUD missile attacks on Israel, youth who lived in the areas that were hit had a higher level of PTSD (62.0 percent) than youth living in communities that escaped the attacks (24.9 percent). He also found that children whose homes were hit by the missiles had a higher prevalence of PTSD (23.8 percent) as compared to those in the same neighborhood whose homes had not been hit (9.1 percent).

However, as noted previously in the Webb (1994) study, close proximity has not always been found to be directly related to trauma-specific reactions, particularly to the prevalence of PTSD. For example, following the 1993 New York World Trade Center bombing, Koplewicz and colleagues (1994) found that youth who experienced both high and low level of exposure—for example, children who were trapped in the elevators versus their classmates—had comparable prevalence of PTSD (69 vs. 66 percent). On September 11, 2001, children across the United States, not only in New York or Washington, also experienced high prevalence of trauma-specific reactions, especially those in cities in which their schools are surrounded by tall buildings (Steele, 2002).

The Milgram and colleagues (1988) study of 268 seventh graders following a tragic school bus accident suggested that personal involvement with the victims, in addition to the situation itself, could increase levels of PTSD. Saigh (1991) also found that nonwitnesses who hear of the details of an incident could, in fact, experience trauma-specific reactions. Saigh (1991) later reported that overall deliberate acts of violence, such as war, community violence, or school violence, appear to lead to a higher prevalence of PTSD than natural disasters or accidents, regardless of the type of exposure.

Children's Reactions to Trauma

Research over the past ten years has provided us with a clearer distinction between grief and trauma. It has also provided behaviorally descriptive definitions of trauma and posttraumatic stress disorder (PTSD) and categorization of behaviors by developmental levels of children and adolescents.

Trauma and Grief

If asked what one word best describes the experience of grief, the word "sadness" will be the common response; in trauma, that one word is "terror." While practitioners certainly appreciate the terror that children can experience when they are witnesses or are victims of violence, they do not necessarily view that terror as an element of trauma (Morse & Wiley, 1997; Steele & Raider, 2001). When in trauma, one is experiencing a continued threat to life, an absence of safety, and a sense of powerlessness. These are also the experiences that define terror. It is this ongoing state of terror that can leave children vulnerable to posttraumatic stress reactions. In addition to these reactions, trauma includes grief reactions (Jacobs, 1999).

While trauma reactions include grief, grief reactions can stand alone (Jacobs, 1999). In grief, anger is generally nonassaultive and oppositional; in trauma, anger is often nondiscriminatory, aggressive, and assaultive. In grief, guilt says, "I wish I would have/would *not* have. . . ." In trauma, guilt says, "It was my fault and it should have been me instead." Grief generally does not distort or disfigure our identity; trauma does distort and sometimes annihilates our identity. In grief, dreams are about the deceased; in trauma, dreams are about the dreamer him- or herself being in danger.

Types of Trauma

Lenore Terr (1991b) identified two types of trauma—Type I Trauma, which refers to reactions to single, sudden, isolated events that are limited in duration, and Type II Trauma, which refers to reactions to chronic, multiple, long-standing, repeated events, often of intentional human design, such as ongoing sexual assault or long-term combat. Unlike Type I Trauma, Type II Trauma often leads to significant character changes and personality problems in children. Children exposed to ongoing violence become vulnerable to Type II reactions and have symptoms such as numbing, denial, detachment, dissociation, and/or identification with the aggressor (Terr, 1991b).

Age-Related Symptoms

Since the early 1980s, Pynoos and his colleagues (Pynoos & Eth, 1986; Pynoos & Nader, 1988; Pynoos et al., 1987) have been studying school children exposed to a variety of violent situations, including a sniper attack at an elementary school. Utilizing three different assessment tools—the PTSD Reaction Index, Diagnostic Inventory for Children and Adolescents (DICA), and the Parent DICA—these researchers found different levels of symptomatic responses of children to violence, based on the children's developmental stages. Pynoos and Nader's (1988) classifications are categorized by school grade levels: preschool through second grade, third through fifth grade, and sixth grade and up.

Preschool symptomatology includes generalized fear, cognitive confusion, lack of verbalization, attributing magical qualities to traumatic reminders, sleep disturbances, anxious attachment, regressive symptoms, and anxieties. Children in the third through fifth grades experienced the following: preoccupation with their own actions during the event; specific fears; retelling and replaying of the event; impaired concentration and learning;

sleep disturbances; concerns about their own and others' safety; inconsistent behavior; somatic complaints; feeling confused, disturbed, and frightened by their grief responses; fear of ghosts; concerns for other victims and their families; and close monitoring of parents' responses. Adolescents' symptomatology includes detachment, shame, guilt, self-consciousness about their fears, vulnerability and other emotional responses, acting-out behavior, life-threatening reenactment, abrupt shifts in relationships, desires to take revenge, radical changes in life attitudes, and premature entrance into adulthood.

The various reactions specific to posttraumatic stress in children that have been identified in studies by Terr (1991a), Pynoos and Nader (1988), and Yule and Williams (1990) were summarized by Udwin (1993). These include sleep disturbance, loss of newly acquired skills, concentration difficulties, memory impairment, persistent intrusive thoughts and images, raised levels of both generalized and specific anxiety, heightened alertness (hypervigilance), and survivor guilt. Johnson (1993) also classified reactions by age and put them in four categories: cognitive, physical, emotional, and behavioral. For example, in the preschool child, he found that *cognitively,* the children experienced shorter attention span and confusion regarding events, locations, sequencing, death; *physically,* they experienced loss of appetite, overeating, bowel/bladder problems, and sleeping disturbances; *emotionally,* they experienced generalized fears, nervousness, anxiety, irritability, and fear of reminders; and *behaviorally,* they exhibited bedwetting, thumb-sucking, nightmares, repetitive play, anxious attachment, clinging, aggression, and disobedience. Petersen and Straub (1992) introduce additional reactions of adolescents not described by others—increased aggressive conduct, dullness, decreased ability to focus and concentrate, decreased trust in adults' ability to protect, sensitivity to feelings of shame and being stigmatized, and unforgiveness of their own behavior.

However, trauma is not always defined by age; children can experience adult-like reactions and vice versa. For example, a 27-year-old sister who ran to her younger brother after he had been shot said, "I was afraid to touch him. I thought if I touched him, he would die." This kind of magical thinking is typically seen in young children between 4 and 9 years of age.

Non-Age-Specific Reactions of Children

The following are descriptions of common reactions seen in children of all ages:

- ***Cognitive dysfunction:*** Refers to decreased abilities to concentrate on processing verbal information and impaired memory. "A" students become "C" students or fail altogether; children who once could complete two and three different tasks now have difficulty with a single task. Parents and educators often react negatively to this behavior because they simply do not understand its cause, resulting in the further negative impact on the child.
- ***Hypervigilance:*** Refers to the heightened state of fear or chronic readiness for danger. Victims are forever watching out for, and anticipating that they are about to be, or are, in danger; seeking safety spots in the environment, a certain place in the house, "holing up" in the bedroom; limiting activity to certain locations in school. Children

who sleep on the floor instead of their bed after a trauma do so because they fear the comfort of a bed will let them sleep so hard that they won't hear danger coming.

- ***Survivor guilt:*** Refers to the sense of accountability resulting in the feeling "I wish it would have been me instead." Students not in school at the time of a random shooting and subsequent death of a fellow student can feel accountable and experience survivor guilt. Some may respond to the overwhelming guilt by attempting or committing suicide.
- ***Intrusive images/thoughts:*** Refers to the unpredictable return of thoughts about what happened, visual memories of what happened, or images related to what was imagined to have happened. For example:

> Two years after the accidental murder of her mother during a gang shootout, teachers still noticed that Theresa, a 14-year-old girl, still engaged in a plucking motion with her hand. She did not know her mother was already dead when she ran to help her. When she rolled her mother over, her mother's mouth was filled with blood and broken teeth. The daughter began pulling the broken teeth from her mother's mouth so she wouldn't choke on them. She continued with these gestures for years when reliving her experience.

- ***Traumatic dreams:*** Refers to anxiety-inducing dreams of terror in which the dreamer is the victim, or potential victim, in his or her own dream. For example:

> Eleven-year-old Tommy was a survivor, not a witness, when we first met him one year after his sister was a victim of community violence. He was still having dreams of his own "guts" being "ripped out" by a man. His sister had been stabbed repeatedly in the chest and stomach area.

- ***Regressive behavior:*** Refers to engaging in behaviors that had actually ended prior to the trauma. For example:

> In addition to his nightmares following the murder of his sister, Tommy started to stutter, became eneuretic, and became more clinging to his mother.

- ***Startle response:*** Refers to those sounds, sights, and/or smells that were similar to those that existed at the time of the traumatic event and, when experienced again, startle the victim into a partial re-experiencing of the event. In mass violence, there are often numerous sensory elements that can later trigger the startle response. For example, a car backfiring may sound like an explosion.
- ***Emotional numbing:*** Refers to the deadening of one's emotions and feelings. Some victims act as if they are no longer afraid of anything or anyone, verbalizing that nothing ever scares them any more, and in the face of danger, respond inappropriately. For example:

> Fifteen-year-old Mary, whose sister was killed in the Oklahoma City bombing, had made new friends whom her mother described as "real trouble." She had received help, but the interventions were not trauma-specific. Fourteen months later, although still receiving treatment, she was emotionally detached from her feelings and had never cried for her sister. Still later, when she finally entered trauma-specific treatment, her tears were released. She reported that this was the first time she was able to cry for her sister.

- ***Aggressive/assaultive responses:*** Refers to the manifestation of an overwhelming sense of powerlessness experienced as a result of traumatic victimization. A child may become irritable, aggressive, act tough, and provoke fights. Identification with the aggressor is a well-known response of trauma victims, as it is a way to re-experience the power that was shattered by the terror of the experience. Victims may also verbalize a desire for revenge.
- ***Future orientation:*** Refers to the view one has about the future. In trauma, victims can become disconnected from any future orientation. A victim of trauma may develop a pessimistic view of the future, lose the resilience to overcome additional difficulties, lose hope and passion to plan for, survive, and enjoy life. This sometimes is manifested in suicidal ideation, becoming accident-prone, taking risks previously avoided, engaging in life-threatening situations, or reenacting the event as a victim or a hero.
- ***Repetitive play/behavior:*** Refers to the victim's attempts to gain mastery over some aspect of the traumatic experience or the terror created by that traumatic event. Children will sometimes engage in repetitive play scenarios as a way to try to regain a sense of control or make sense of what happened. Adolescents may also begin to engage in compulsive-like behaviors as a way to gain a sense of control.

The Impact of Trauma on Children's Abilities to Learn

Trauma can lead to changes in the processing of both verbal and nonverbal information, thereby altering the child's ability to learn. An intense state of fear or terror, also referred to in traumatology as a hyperarousal state, is a physiological alteration of the autonomic nervous system (van der Kolk, McFarlane, & Weisaeth, 1996). "Understanding the physiology of trauma is understanding the normal life-preserving survival responses of fight/flight/freeze in an individual and how they fulfill natures' species-preserving function. Investigating the disturbance of those responses forms the essential foundation for understanding the changes that result in Post-Traumatic Stress and Post-Traumatic Stress Disorder" (Grill, 1999, p. 3). It is important to understand that, while in an increased arousal state, there is a serious short-term memory deficit (Starknum et al., 1992). This memory deficit in ways resembles that found in Cushing's disease, in which there is a presence of high levels of cortisol in the blood. Verbal memory also decreases (Bremner et al., 1995). Physiological arousal also triggers trauma-related memories, and these memories then precipitate generalized arousal (van der Kolk et al., 1996). High levels of arousal also produce changes in neuronal excitability, often manifested in aggression or in an exaggerated withdrawal that serves as a safety response (LeDoux, Romanski, & Xagoraris, 1991). In essence, both memory and emotions are altered by trauma (Saigh & Bremner, 1999), which in turn leads to problems with learning, relationships, and performance—all distinct elements associated with childhood tasks.

In the hyperarousal state, the traumatized child may become unable to utilize the neo-cortex to process verbal information. Consequently, processing and storing verbal information become difficult. The traumatized child's dominant processes will be in the subcortical and limbic areas that deal with nonverbal information (Perry, 2000). Auditory, visual, tactile, and olfactory experiences are generally sent to the neocortex for analysis. In trauma (terror), the sensory experiences "bypass the neo-cortex and go directly to the amygdala, which mobilizes the organism for fight, flight, or freeze" (Morse & Wiley, 1997, p. 40). The body is poised to act, not because of what it thinks, but because of what it senses. In this way trauma is a sensory experience. While in the arousal state, hand gestures, facial expressions, and full body posturing all become far more important to survival than the cognitive processing of verbal information. These functions, therefore, make it difficult for the traumatized child, whose arousal level remains high, to effectively learn. Often this cognitive dysfunction, together with physiological effects of arousal, are mistakenly diagnosed as a learning disability or attention deficit hyperactivity disorder (ADHD) in children (Weinstein, 2000).

Understanding the sensory nature of trauma has led to varied treatments to deactivate the autonomic hyperarousal state by using the sensory elements of the body to resolve its symptoms (Rothchild, 2000). It is important to reduce or eliminate the arousal state so the survival reflex can complete its response and allow the victim to experience a "sensory relief" from the terror and regain a sense of safety. We have observed that by deactivating the arousal state we are able to restore a child's sense of safety, and the child can, in most cases, return to his or her previous state of calmness.

Interventions

Intervention with traumatized children needs to be structured, sensory-based, and designed to restore a sense of safety and feeling of empowerment. At the same time, it remains critical to understand that the level of fear and anxiety, as well as the duration of the sensations, will vary greatly among exposed children. Interventions, therefore, must begin with the least invasive or intrusive approaches, so as to protect children from further exposure or unnecessary treatment. Some children simply need reassurance and information; others will need additional structured, sensory-based intervention (Foa & Kozak, 1985; Malchiodi, 1998; Steele & Raider, 2001; van der Kolk et al., 1996).

Levels of Intervention

There are three levels of intervention that can help children find relief from their traumatic experiences. The first level is crisis intervention, the second is debriefing, and the third consists of structured, sensory trauma intervention.

1. *Crisis intervention* is most effective in the first two to five days following exposure. It includes information processing, proactive activities, and a restoration of a sense of safety through structured, consistent physical and verbal reassurance. During this period, children need adult presence in their life to feel safe. They need direction as well as information as to what has happened and what will be happening next. They need reassurance and someone to listen to them. In school settings, trauma protocol supports conducting classroom presentations to meet the above needs and crisis

teams to provide basic crisis intervention. Keeping children in school with friends and familiar surroundings and maintaining routines are important and comforting to most children.

Proactive activities also play a critical role in helping children regain a sense of safety following the trauma. Such activities can begin almost immediately following the traumatic event. Doing things together, such as collecting money, sending goods, sending letters, and participating in group demonstrations and discussions help children to reestablish a sense of control.

Adults play a critical role in restoring children's sense of safety. Maintaining order during chaos, providing direction, giving children the opportunity to talk and be heard, providing accurate information, giving reassurance, and providing children with the opportunity to be with those they are familiar with while engaging in daily routines and proactive activities are all components of crisis intervention with children following mass trauma.

2. *Debriefing,* the second level of intervention, is designed for children and adolescents who were most exposed to trauma—those who witnessed the incident first-hand and those who were related to the victims. Debriefing is designed to accelerate the healing process and is generally initiated on the third or fourth day following the incident. Critical incident stress debriefing (CISD), the formal debriefing process that is frequently used in community settings, needs to be modified to meet the unique needs and operating systems of schools. For example, while all staff need debriefing at the end of a critical incident, to ask 100 plus staff to remain after school for two hours simply is not practical. In situations such as this, the debriefing session must be abbreviated.

   The school environment itself is unique; interventions in schools must take into consideration not just the children, but all of the individuals working in the school—from the principal to the security and kitchen staff (Straussner & Straussner, 1997). Different models to accommodate developmental levels of students, needs of staff, needs of the crisis team members, and the needs of administrators have been developed (Steele, 1999). Debriefing can quickly restore the sense of safety and power that many victims initially experience, thereby minimizing the need for the more intense third level of trauma intervention. Most people participating in debriefing will find it very helpful and have no need for additional intervention.

3. *Short-term structured intervention* is an intense approach that may be needed when debriefing is not enough and acute stress reactions following exposure continue. The continuation of severe symptoms for a month following the trauma will lead to a change of the diagnosis from Acute Stress Disorder (ASD) to that of Posttraumatic Stress Disorder (PTSD). Even when all the criteria for PTSD are not met, trauma reactions may continue and interventions beyond debriefing may be needed. Prolonged traumatization and multiple traumas will generally necessitate the need for more intense intervention.

The National Institute for Trauma and Loss in Children (TLC) has developed and field-tested an effective intervention model called *Structured Sensory Interventions for Traumatized Children, Adolescents, and Parents (SITCAP)* (Steele & Raider, 2001).

The SITCAP Model of Intervention

The ability to learn to tolerate the intense fear and emotional reactions experienced as a result of a traumatic event is a critical part of recovery. The experience of trauma needs to be modified or reordered into a form that is acceptable and can be managed by the victim, resulting in a cognitive restructuring into a meaningful, integrative narrative (Steele & Raider, 2001). The SITCAP model of structured sensory intervention involves exposure, trauma narrative, and cognitive restructuring.

Exposure. Exposing or reexposing the child to the traumatic experience is a core component of trauma intervention. Exposure techniques are designed to help the trauma victim realize that the situation is no longer dangerous and conditioned responses, such as avoidance, are no longer necessary. Malleson (1959) used "in-vitro" exposure with adults as a way to reduce severe anxiety. Stampfl (1961) combined Malleson's exposure techniques with Freud's (1965) approach to develop "implosive therapy." The objective of implosive therapy is to identify the exteroceptive and interoceptive fear-inducing stimuli related to the trauma and then expose victims to stimuli repeatedly until they no longer trigger, or cause the person to experience, the reactions associated with the trauma (Saigh, Yasik, Oberfield, & Inamdar, 1999).

The ability to decrease fear or anxiety is dependent upon the controlled reliving of the fearful experience in a safe environment so as to be able to diminish the fear response to it (Foa & Kozak, 1985; Thompson, Charlton, Kerry, Lee, & Turner, 1995). Saigh and Bremner (1999) conducted a variety of single case studies with children of war and other traumatized populations and found "consistent evidence for the efficacy of imaginal and 'in-vitro' exposure in the treatment of PTSD" (p. 379).

The Use of Drawing as a Form of Exposure. The exposure method most frequently recommended for use with children is that of drawing, guided by specific tasks and trauma-specific questions (Golub, 1985; Herl, 1992; Roje, 1995; Steele & Raider, 2001; Webb, 1991). Saigh (1999), in discussing exposure by "flooding," indicates that children may not be able to imagine trauma scenes or tolerate prolonged in-vitro experiences. Instead, he suggests that "an effective adjunct to the more orthodox form of flooding is for traumatized children to prepare sketches of their stressful experience and verbally repeat (narrate) the content of their experience" (p. 370). Drawing provides children with an impetus to tell their story and to translate their traumatic experience into a narrative (Malchiodi, 1998). Riley (1997) indicates that the act of drawing is a form of externalization, a visible projection of self, one's thoughts, and feelings. Drawing provides a link between dissociated memories and retrieval into consciousness whereby the experience can be translated into narrative form and then reordered by the child's effort to integrate the experience into his or her life experiences. Beyers (1996) described the use of drawing with children and families with PTSD resulting from exposure to military conflict in the West Bank and Gaza Strip. In this work, Beyers cited numerous studies that illustrated the use of nonverbal media (drawing) to assist children with PTSD to access their trauma memories and to integrate the split-off parts induced by the trauma, demonstrating the successful reintegration of these into the child's current understanding of his or her world. Magwaza, Killian, Peterson, and Pillay (1993) achieved similar results with South African children exposed to community violence.

Drawing activities used within the SITCAP intervention program (Steele & Raider, 2001) have been found to help children by:

- Initiating focused, psychomotor activities to assist in triggering traumatic memories stored at the sensory level.
- Moving victims from a passive to an active involvement in their own healing process.
- Providing a vehicle to safely communicate what cannot be adequately described by words.
- Providing for the externalization of the trauma into a "container" (8 × 11-inch sheet of paper) that has boundaries, is concrete and tangible, and assists in bringing about a renewed sense of power over that experience.
- Creating a visual focal point as a reference and to tell the story.
- Giving the clinician or intervenor a visual representation of the way the trauma was experienced so the intervenor, as a witness, can see what the victim sees as he or she now looks at himself or herself and the surrounding world following the trauma.
- Allowing trauma sensations to be replaced with positive sensations.
- Re-establishing a connectedness to the adult world, which leads to a greater sense of safety and hope.

Examples of actual drawings and the drawing process related to traumatized children and their symbolic representation of the different elements of the trauma experience can be found in Steele and Raider (2001). Yet drawing is only one part of the intervention process. Forming a narrative and cognitive reframing are two additional strategies that are necessary components of successful intervention.

Trauma Narrative. The importance of utilizing narrative therapy as a core process in helping trauma victims integrate their experiences into consciousness is widely noted in the literature (Marks, 1972; Rachman, 1966). Van der Kolk and colleagues (1996) stated:

> Traumatic memories need to become like memories of everyday experience, that is they need to be modified and transformed by being placed in their proper context and restructured into a meaningful narrative. The purpose of full exposure is to make the fragments of the traumatic event lose their power to act as conditioned stimuli that reactivate effects and behaviors relevant to the trauma, but irrelevant to current experience. Thus, in therapy, memory paradoxically becomes an act of creation rather than the static (fixation) recording of events that is characteristic of trauma-based memories. (p. 420)

The trauma victim must be able to give his or her experience a language by forming a new narrative that limits the traumatic memory to the place and time it occurred, as opposed to generalizing that experience to everyday life. Trauma-specific questions are helpful in the formation of the narrative, the telling of the story. Questions are directed to major trauma themes or trauma sensations and reactions, such as fear, terror, worry, hurt, anger, revenge, accountability, the absence of safety, powerlessness, and "victim thinking" (Steele & Raider, 2001). The following are some examples of trauma-related questions:

- *What do you remember seeing or hearing?* This relates to the overall sensory imploding of detailed components of the trauma.
- *What is your biggest worry?* This relates to issues of safety and/or powerlessness.
- *What would you like to see happen to the person (thing) that caused this to happen?* This deals with anger and revenge.
- *Do you sometimes think it should have been you instead?* This is an accountability (survivor guilt) question.
- *What was the worst part for you?* This helps the child focus on, and relate to, the intervenor, the part of the experience that was the most difficult, frightening, and/or overwhelming.

Throughout the process, questions are specific to the theme being addressed. Their concreteness keeps the child focused on the specific theme, encourages the narrative (story) to be told for each theme, and encourages attention to detail. Details are critical to helping establish a sense of control and provide the intervenor with information needed to help the child.

Multiple questions need to be asked because specific trauma references will be different for each child. One child's trauma reference may be about the "hurt" experienced at a sensory level. For others it may be accountability and their fear for others. The systematic presentation of all questions and attention to all trauma themes are essential in order to give children the opportunity to make us a witness to their specific trauma experience.

Case Illustration. The following example involves one of the victims of a riot that broke out at a large cinema complex on New Year's Eve. The victim was Justin, an 18-year-old high school senior who was ushering at the movie complex. Justin was slated to graduate in the spring and had been accepted into the police academy. A football player, he was physically quite strong and stood over six feet tall. When several kids in the theater began to cause trouble, he attempted to get control but was unable to do so. He sought out the manager for help, but the manager was busy with other potentially unruly customers and told him he would have to handle it on his own. Justin took his post across the common area outside the doors of the movie he was responsible to monitor; however, the teens he had trouble with previously came out of the movie, rushed at him, knocked him down and started beating him, breaking his nose and several ribs. About one month later his parish priest, concerned that Justin was skipping school and not attending youth activities at church, referred him to a crisis clinic.

When seen by a trauma specialist, Justin was asked, "What was the worst part for you?" This trauma-specific question helps to encourage the telling of the story and focusing on specific details. The types of detail are unique to trauma, in which events seem to happen almost in slow motion. What is important to note is that when this case was presented in staff training and participants were asked to anticipate what the "worst part" must have been, their numerous responses rarely identified what the "worst part" was for Justin. Responses of the participants included anger he felt at the manager for leaving him on his own, embarrassment at being beaten, shame that he couldn't help himself, or the pain he felt during the beating. However, what we, as observer, assume to be the worst part may not necessarily be experienced as such by the victim. Only by giving the victim the opportunity to make us a witness can we truly know that trauma experience as he knows it. The teen's response was as follows:

> I can see it as if it is happening all over again. I'm on the ground and they're kicking me. As they are kicking and stomping on me I can see between their legs. As I'm looking between their legs, I see all these people standing around, and no one is helping me.

At that moment in time Justin experienced complete abandonment and felt betrayed by the adults in his world. Being unable to trust the adult world was the worst part of his experience. Without appropriate intervention this could have easily triggered self-defeating, and even destructive, responses. Justin already had begun to isolate himself, was missing school, and was putting his future in jeopardy. If he had gone much longer without help, it would not have been unusual if he began to identify with his aggressors by carrying a weapon or actively seeking out the kids who beat him with the intent of getting revenge. By asking this one trauma-specific question, the trauma specialist gave him the opportunity to tell his story while focusing on the sensory nature of trauma. He was then able to help Justin work through the abandonment he experienced—a central aspect of his experience that likely would have otherwise gone untreated.

Cognitive Restructuring. The basic premise of cognitive theory is that thought drives emotion. Similar situations may lead to different emotional states based upon the way that situation is interpreted (e.g., thought about) by different individuals. Disturbing, anxiety ridden, pathological emotional states are driven by dysfunctional thoughts. Cognitive therapy suggests that by changing the thoughts, the emotional states also change (Beck, 1972; Ellis, 1958; Marks, 1972). Cognitive therapy helps the individual first identify the thoughts (traumatic memories), evaluate their validity, challenge those thoughts that are erroneous or self-defeating, and then replace them with thoughts supportive of health or manageable emotional states (Saigh & Bremner, 1999). This process is referred to as *cognitive restructuring.* Outcome studies of the value of cognitive restructuring with individuals suffering from PTSD are limited, but clinical observations support their efficacy, especially as an adjunct to exposure therapy. Cognitive therapy has become a component of Stress Inoculation Training (Meichenbaum, 1974), one of the anxiety management treatments for PTSD that has been shown to be effective in the treatment of PTSD.

Cognitive therapy is useful in the integration of trauma memories into conscious memories. They are reordered in a way that allows these memories to become manageable. An example might be, "I survived this experience. I will survive other experiences because it has made me stronger." This is referred to as "survivor thinking" versus "victim thinking." Cognitive restructuring is also referred to as *reframing.* Cognitive statements are scripted into TLC interventions to ensure that the victim is provided with a survivor's way of making sense of the trauma experience. The goal is to help move the child to survivor thinking, which leads to empowerment, active involvement in his or her own healing process, and a renewed sense of safety and hope.

Age-appropriate activities can assist in supporting the restructuring or reframing of the experience. For example, in the case of Justin, the high school senior discussed earlier, having him draw what his fears looked like and later giving them a name helped him realize that he was responding as a victim to his own fear and that if the people at police academy found out what happened, they would never allow him to start his training. This was irrational, but not from a "victim's" viewpoint. The drawing also helped to identify his sense of shame resulting from his view of self as not being able to take care of himself. When asked why it was standard operating procedure for police officers to always work with a partner, he was able at the cognitive level to refocus on the reality that, even if there are people watching, protection and help are not always offered to a person. The fact that police officers work in pairs, he realized, dealt with the reality that even they could find themselves suddenly overwhelmed. Justin was then able to reframe that what happened to him was not his fault and that as a police officer he would be helping others, something that others had not been able to do for him. By recognizing that he would make an excellent police partner because of this experience, he was also able to reorder his experience in a way that gave his future new meaning. Subsequently, he was able to return to school and once again enjoy being with his friends and to participate in age-appropriate activities.

As a trauma intervenor, it is essential to accept that we cannot know what that trauma experience is like for a child. It is not our experience; it is the child's experience, and each child will experience similar incidents differently. This is why it is also important for the intervenor to truly be a witness, rather than a clinician in the traditional sense. Being a witness is a method of sitting back and letting the child show us how that experience was perceived and tell his or her story in a way that allows us to learn, at a sensory level, how this incident was experienced by the child. Once the child has given the traumatic experience a language through the story telling, we can help reframe it cognitively in a way that the child can manage to cope with it.

Cognitive restructuring, however, is rarely helpful until an individual can find relief from fear at a sensory or physiological level, while at the same time regaining the sense of power. Only then does a view of self and life change from that of being a victim to that of a survivor. It is an approach that works for children of all ages.

Parental Involvement

When working with traumatized children, one must also be prepared to work with their parents. Research studies have found that parents are critical to their children's ability to recover from trauma (Pynoos & Nader, 1988; Vogel & Vernberg, 1993). Studies following World War II showed that the level of upsetness displayed by the adult in the child's life—not the war itself—was the single most important factor in predicting the emotional well-being and recovery of the child (Beyers, 1996). We see the same relationship today. When a child has been traumatized, the parents may also experience extreme distress and often are unable to adequately respond to their children without professional intervention. Traumatized adults find it difficult to help their traumatized children (Schwarz & Kowalski, 1991). As pointed out by van der Kolk and colleagues (1996), "most children are amazingly resilient as long as they have caregivers that are emotionally available" (p. 432).

Parents generally underestimate the impact that trauma has on their own children. This is partially due to not understanding how trauma is different than grief and how it manifests itself in children, and partly because of the parents' own need to deny the trauma. For some parents, education about trauma is all that is needed; others may need brief help through debriefing. And still other parents may need short-term, structured sensory trauma intervention. Such help should begin with the least intrusive intervention (crisis intervention) and then, if needed, move to the more structured sensory interventions (Steele, 2001).

It is not uncommon that parents may also need additional intervention when they themselves have been victimized in the past and their child's trauma is now triggering those memories. Such parents will need to be helped to become aware of how their own unresolved fears block their ability to allow their children to openly tell their stories. Parents with their own traumatic history often discover that their child's experience threatens to bring all the terror of their own experience back to life. Unknowingly, they reject their child's cry for help, or minimize the child's terror, in hopes of calming the child and consequently calming themselves.

Conclusion

Trauma dictates a very specific intervention that is structured, moves slowly, and supports a process that keeps the child safe. To move too quickly into more intense forms of intervention immediately following exposure to trauma can place child survivors at unnecessary risk of being retraumatized. The intervention stresses the importance of having a structured process so as to create a safe environment. It is only in such a safe environment that children can re-experience the details of their trauma, tell their stories in order to find relief from the terror of their experiences, and regain a sense of mastery and power over themselves and their environment.

References

Beck, A. T. (1972). *Depression: Causes and treatment.* Philadelphia: University of Philadelphia Press.

Beyers, J. (1996). Children of the stones: Art therapy interventions in the West Bank. *Art Therapy: Journal of the American Art Therapy Association, 13,* 238–243.

Bremner, J. D., Randall, P., Scott, T. M., Bronen, R. A., Seibyl, T. P., et al. (1995). MRI-based measures of hippocampal volume in patients with PTSD. *American Journal of Psychiatry, 152,* 973–981.

Ellis, A. (1958). Rational psychotherapy. *Journal of General Psychology, 59,* 35–49.

Foa, E. B., & Kozak, M. J. (1985). Treatment of anxiety disorders: Implications for psychopathology. In A. H. Tuma & J. D. Maser (Eds.), *Anxiety and disorders.* Hillsdale, NJ: Erlbaum.

Freud, A. (1965). *Normality and pathology in children.* New York: International University Press.

Garbarino, J. (1993). Children's response to community violence: What do we know? *Infant Mental Health Journal, 14,* 103–115.

Golub, D. (1985). Symbolic expression in posttraumatic stress disorder: Vietnam combat veterans in art therapy. *The Arts in Psychotherapy, 12,* 285–296.

Green, B. L., Wilson, J. P., & Lindy, J. D. (1985). Conceptualizing posttraumatic stress disorder: A psychosocial framework. In C. R. Figley (Ed.), *Trauma and its wake: The study and treatment of posttraumatic stress disorder* (pp. 53–69). Philadelphia: Brunner/Mazel.

Grill, D. (1999). *Deactivation.* (In publication). Brentwood, CA: Treatment Center for Traumatic Life Experiences.

Herl, T. (1992). Finding the light at the end of the tunnel: Working with child survivors of the Andover tornado. *Art Therapy: Journal of the American Art Therapy Association, 9,* 42–47.

Jacobs, S. (1999). *Traumatic grief: Diagnosis, treatment, and prevention.* Philadelphia: Brunner-Routledge.

Johnson, K. (1993). *School crisis management: A hands-on guide to training crisis response teams.* Alameda, CA: Hunter House.

Koop, C. E., & Lundberg, G. (1992) Violence in America: A public health emergency. *Journal of the American Medical Association, 22,* 3075–3076.

Koplewics, H. S., Vogel, J. M., Solanto, M. V. Morrissey, R. G., Alonzo, C. M., Gallagher, R., Abekoff, H. B., & Novich, R. M. (1994, October). *Child and parent response to World Trade Center bombing.* Poster presented at the annual meeting of the American Academy of Child and Adolescent Psychiatry, New York.

LeDoux, I. E., Romanski, L., & Xagoraris, A., (1991). Indelibility of sub cortical emotional memories. *Journal of Cognitive Neuroscience, 1,* 238–243.

Magwaza, A., Killian, B. Peterson, I., & Pillay, Y. (1993). The effects of chronic stress on preschool children living in South African townships. *Child Abuse and Neglect, 17,* 795–803.

Malchiodi, C. (1998). *Understanding children's drawings.* New York: Guilford.

Malleson N. (1959). Panic and phobia: A possible method of treatment. *Lancet, 1,* 225–227.

Marks, I. A. (1972). Flooding (implosion) and allied treatments. In S. Argas (Ed.), *Behavior modification: Principles and clinical applications* (pp. 151–211). Boston: Little Brown.

Meichenbaum, D. (1974). *Self-instructional methods.* In F. H. Kanfer & A. P. Goldstein (Eds.), *Helping people change* (pp. 357–391). New York: Pergamon.

Milgram, N., Toubiana, Y., Klingman, A., Raviv, A., & Goldstein, I. (1988). Situational exposure and personal loss in children's acute and chronic stress reactions to a school bus disaster. *Journal of Traumatic Stress, 1,* 339–351.

Morse, R. K., & Wiley, M. (1997). *Tracing the roots of violence.* New York: Atlantic Monthly Press.

Peterson, S., & Straub, R. (1992). *School crisis survival guide.* New York: The Center for Applied Research in Education.

Perry, B. (2000). *Violence and childhood: How persisting fear can alter the developing child's brain.* The Child Trauma Academy. childtrauma@bcm.tmc.edu.

Pynoos, R., & Eth, S. (1986). Witness to violence: The child interview. *Journal of the American Academy of Child Psychiatry, 25,* 306–319.

Pynoos, R., & Nader, K. (1988). Psychological first aid and treatment approach to children exposed to community violence: Research implications. *Journal of Traumatic Stress, 1,* 445–473.

Pynoos, R., Nader, K., Arroyo, E., Steinberg, A., Eth, S., Nunez, F., & Fairbanks, L. (1987). Life threat and posttraumatic stress in school age children. *Archives of General Psychiatry, 44,* 1057–1063.

Rachman, S. J. (1966). Studies in desensitization–II: Flooding. *Behavior Research and Therapy, 4,* 1–6.

Riley, S. (1997). Children's art and narratives: An opportunity to enhance therapy and a supervisory challenge. *The Supervision Bulletin, 9,* 2–3.

Roje, J. (1995). LA '94 earthquake in the eyes of children: Art therapy with elementary school children who were victims of disaster. *Art Therapy: Journal of the American Art Therapy Association, 12,* 237–243.

Rothchild, B. (2000). *The body remembers.* New York: W. W. Norton.

Saigh, P. A. (1991). On the development of posttraumatic stress disorder pursuant to different modes of traumatization. *Behavior Research and Therapy, 29,* 213–216.

Saigh, P., & Bremner, J. (1999). *Posttraumatic stress disorder.* Boston: Allyn and Bacon.

Saigh, P., Yasik, A., Oberfield, R., & Inamdar, S. (1999). Behavioral treatment of child-adolescent posttraumatic stress disorder. In P. Saigh. & J. Bremner (Eds.), *Posttraumatic stress disorder* (pp. 354–374). Boston: Allyn and Bacon.

Schwarz, E. & Kowalski, J. (1991). Posttraumatic stress disorder after a school shooting: Effects of symptom threshold selection and diagnosis by DSM-III-R, or proposed DSM-IV. *American Journal of Psychiatry, 48,* 592–597.

Schwarzwald, J., Weisenber, M., Waysman, M., & Solomon, Z. (1994). Stress reaction of school age children to the bombardment by SCUD missiles: A one-year follow-up. *Journal of Traumatic Stress, 7,* 657–667.

Shaw, J. (1995). Psychological effects of Hurricane Andrew on elementary school population. *Journal of the Academy of Child and Adolescent Psychiatry, 34,* 1185–1192.

Stampfl, T. G. (1961). *Implosive therapy: A learning theory derived psychodynamic technique.* Unpublished manuscript, John Carroll, University of Cleveland. Cited In P. A. Starknum, M. N. Gebarksi, S. S. Berent, & D. E. Schterngart. (1992). Hippocampal formation volume, memory of dysfunction, and cortisol levels in patients with Cushing's syndrome. *Biology Psychiatry, 32,* 756–765.

Starknum, P. A., Gebarski, M. N., Berent, S. S., & Schterngart, D. E. (Eds.). (1992). Hippocampal formation volume, memory of dysfunction, and cortisol levels in patients with Cushing's syndrome. *Biology Psychiatry, 32,* 756–765.

Steele, W. (1999). *Debriefing handbook for schools and agencies.* Grosse Pointe Woods, MI: TLC Institute.

Steele, W. (2001). *Adults and parents in trauma: Learning to survive.* Grosse Pointe Woods, MI: TLC Institute.

Steele, W. (2002). *Student reactions to the attack on America* (unpublished manuscript). Grosse Pointe Woods, MI.

Steele, W., & Raider, M. (2001). *Structured sensory intervention for children, adolescents, and parents (SITCAP).* New York: Mellen Press.

Straussner, J. H., & Straussner, S. L. A. (1997). The impact of community and school violence on children. In N. K. Phillips & S. L. A. Straussner (Eds.), *Children in the urban environment: Linking social policy and clinical practice* (pp. 61–77). Springfield, IL: Charles C. Thomas.

Terr, L. (1991a). *Too scared to cry: Psychic trauma in childhood.* New York: Harper and Row.

Terr, L. (1991b). Childhood trauma: An outline and overview. *American Journal of Psychiatry, 148,* 10–20.

Thompson, J. A., Charlton, P. F. C., Kerry, R., Lee, D., & Turner, S. W. (1995). An open trial of exposure therapy based on de-conditioning for posttraumatic stress disorder. *British Journal of Clinical Psychology, 31,* 407–416.

Udwin, O. (1993). Annotation: Children's reactions to traumatic events. *Child Psychology and Psychiatry, 34,* 115–127.

van der Kolk, B., McFarlane, A., & Weisaeth, L. (1996). (Eds.). *Traumatic stress disorder: The effects of overwhelming experience on mind, body, and society.* New York: Guilford.

Vogel, J., & Vernberg, E. (1993). Children's psychological responses to disasters. *Journal of Child Psychiatry, 22,* 470–484.

Webb, N. (Ed.). (1991). *Play therapy with children in crisis.* New York: Guilford.

Webb, N. (1994). School based assessment and crisis intervention with kindergarten children following the New York World Trade Center bombing. *Crisis Interventions, 1,* 47–59.

Weinstein, D. (2000, Oct.). PTSD and ADHD. *ADHD Report,* 8 (5).

Yule, W., & Williams, R. (1990). Posttraumatic stress reactions in children. *Journal of Traumatic Stress, 3,* 279–295.

4

Mass Violence and the Elderly

Sondra Brandler

A biopsychosocial view of old age characterizes it as a period of life in which people generally experience a series of losses in their physical, psychological, and cognitive functioning, as well as diminution of their social networks (Butler & Lewis, 1983; Turner, 1992). The difficulties in coping with these developmental issues are compounded when the elderly are confronted with highly stressful events. The occurrence of mass violence, one of the most stressful experiences for people of all ages, may result in trauma so extreme that it threatens even the survival of the elderly.

The profound impact that mass violence can have on the elderly became evident following the September 11, 2001, attacks on the World Trade Center buildings in New York City. The 6,300 persons 65 years of age and older who lived within a few-block radius of these buildings were severely affected, and the event also had an impact on the additional 50,000 persons over age 60 who lived in the surrounding areas (Bermant, 2002). Some of these elderly lost family members and friends. Others witnessed the attacks from the street or from their apartment windows, and some had to be evacuated from the area, forced to leave their homes with nothing more than the clothing they were already wearing. About 700 older people are known to have insisted on remaining in their homes despite the urging of the authorities to evacuate, but it is likely that many more, afraid even to open their doors, stayed in their apartments during the evacuation of their buildings (O'Brien, 2002).

This chapter discusses the impact of mass violence on the elderly, the special needs of this population under such circumstances, and the implications for social workers, social service agencies, and policymakers.

Impact of Mass Violence on the Elderly

Mass violence and its aftermath have a unique impact on the elderly because many are dependent on the support of others for their day-to-day needs. The nature of this impact was clearly illustrated during, and in the aftermath of, the mass violence that occurred on

September 11, 2001. The struggles confronting the elderly were related to the disruption of daily living, the fact that many were severely affected by the loss of supportive relatives and friends, the psychological impact produced by mass violence, and the unmet special needs of elderly immigrants. These issues are elaborated in the following sections.

Disruptions of Daily Living

All individuals are affected by unexpected disruptions in the routines of their daily life. However, such changes can be particularly challenging for the elderly, many of whom have diminished coping capacities, few social supports, and difficulties adjusting to change. These dynamics presented unusual challenges for gerontological social workers attempting to help the elderly after the 2001 World Trade Center attacks, as they had no precedent for working with clients under such circumstances. Nonetheless, social workers and other helping professionals made efforts to minimize the disruption of their clients' customary daily routines, to restore them to their previous level of functioning, and to resume services that had been disrupted so suddenly.

Disruption in Communication, Transportation, and Access to Health Care. Following the attacks on the World Trade Center, some elderly people had difficulty shopping for food, obtaining needed medications, traveling to social activities, or accessing medical care (Lewis, 2002). While nearly all people living in the affected communities experienced cutoffs of telephone service, this was especially problematic for the elderly. Unable to be in contact with family members or health care providers, many were alone, frightened, and confused.

In addition to disruptions in communication, there were also extensive disruptions in transportation. Public transportation in the area around the World Trade Center was damaged, and fear of further acts of terrorism resulted in restrictions on private transportation, limiting access to private cars and special vehicles for the disabled elderly. Consequently, many older adults were unable to travel or experienced hardships when they ventured out. For example, a week after the attacks in New York City, a social worker who accompanied a frightened and anxious elderly woman recovering from a hip fracture to an appointment with her physician described how terribly difficult it was for her client to walk the several blocks from her apartment house to a place where she was finally permitted to meet a car service, thus adding physical pain to her existing psychological trauma (Zimmer, 2002).

Isolation of the Homebound Elderly. The attacks posed particular difficulties for the homebound elderly who were dependent on individuals providing in-home services, such as people delivering meals, home health aides, visiting nurses, physical therapists, and social workers (O'Brien, 2002). While volunteers provided some emergency meals in special vans donated for this purpose, in many instances the homebound elderly remained alone for days. The absence of their service providers brought about numerous deprivations for the homebound elderly. In addition to providing essential services, many service providers play a crucial role in the social functioning of the homebound elderly, particularly for those without caring family members living nearby. Relationships established with service providers become personally meaningful, and for many clients their service providers are their primary contact with the outside world.

Closing of Senior Centers. Senior centers, which offer daily meals as well as providing for the social and psychological needs of the elderly, were closed in the affected area for weeks after the attacks. Some of the elderly were able to be transported to other centers outside the area. However, due to closing of streets and security measures, even those centers had difficulty obtaining enough food for the increased number of older people.

Disruptions in Living Arrangements. While some people were isolated and unable to leave their apartments, others, including those living in congregate settings such as assisted living residences and senior housing, had to be evacuated. Alternative housing had to be found until their residences could be cleared of structural damage. Also affected were those who were not at home at the time of the attacks. They could not return until their apartments were deemed safe, and they too had to seek alternative housing outside the area. For example, a 90-year-old woman who left town early that morning with her nephew to visit her cousin in a hospital was unable to return home for days and had to stay in a hotel outside New York. While there she became disoriented and agitated and consequently had to be hospitalized herself.

Loss of Supportive Relatives and Friends

The anachronistic quality of being preceded in death by one's children or grandchildren may be the most difficult loss any person can sustain. In spite of this, however, little public attention is paid to the experience of the elderly when their children, grandchildren, or other relatives or friends are killed as a result of mass violence. In addition to the emotional experience of loss, many elderly people depend on family members and friends for financial support. For example, in addition to visits and providing emotional support, it is fairly common for adult children and other relatives and friends to contribute funds for the hiring of home care help, for the purchase of needed but expensive items, such as an air conditioner or television, or to send money regularly for meeting bills (Callahan, 1986; Shanas, 1982).

Nonetheless, when programs are developed to assist those impacted by mass violence, elderly relatives and friends of those who have been killed or injured are often ignored. Even if the elderly person had been receiving ongoing financial or emotional support from the deceased, he or she may not be considered for financial assistance or for other services, such as bereavement counseling, that are offered to immediate families of people who have been killed. For example, Mr. Thomas, an 82-year-old man who entered a nursing home in Virginia six years ago following a debilitating stroke, always looked forward to bimonthly Sunday visits with his granddaughter. She was his only living relative and was the one person who visited him, bought him clothes and treats, and provided those extras for him that his Medicaid personal allowance could not cover. When Mr. Thomas learned that his granddaughter was killed on September 11th while at work at the Pentagon in Washington, DC, he felt bereft of her devoted attention, as well as her concrete assistance.

He withdrew from all activities, rejected overtures of his friends to console him, and began to show signs of clinical depression and dementia. His personal loss also had a powerful impact on many other residents who were badly shaken, aware of the fragility of their connections and the possibility that their loved ones might also be in danger. Consequently, social work intervention had to address not only Mr. Thomas's loss, but also its impact on other residents, and even on the staff working with residents in the nursing home.

Psychological Impact

Although many older people demonstrate unusual resilience in managing under extremely difficult circumstances, others experience profound and long-lasting emotional trauma. In cases of terrorism, with its ongoing threats of harm, older people who are already emotionally fragile, especially those with histories of mental illness or previous traumas, are likely to be especially vulnerable psychologically (Aarts & Op den Velde, 1996). For example, mass violence might affect immigrants, such as those from Cambodia or Chile, who may have experienced tragic losses in the past and whose losses become compounded by the present trauma.

Constant media coverage of terrorist acts and threats of unknown future peril are exceptionally disturbing for frail, compromised elderly who are already experiencing a sense of loss of control over many aspects of their personal lives. Fears of what might happen in case of future terrorist attacks can reinforce their feelings of helplessness and powerlessness. After September 11th, many elderly people in New York City were afraid to leave their homes, even to obtain items necessary for day-to-day living. Symptoms of persistent anxiety and depression were common. In spite of this, very few of the elderly sought help at the free mental health counseling stations that were established near the attack site (Draper, 2002). Instead, they were much more likely to somatize their emotional reactions and seek medical treatment for stress-related physical problems (Chen, 2002).

After September 11th, it was discovered that lasting psychological trauma could be minimized if social workers reached out to clients immediately after the event (De Vivo, 2002). It appears that the adage that "an ounce of prevention is worth a pound of cure" was applied by many psychiatric facilities that provided assistance to already identified patients to help them weather the crisis. While there were still those who did not cope well, such immediate outreach generally appeared to reduce the incidence of more acute psychiatric episodes or rehospitalization.

It has been learned in providing social services to various traumatized populations that while emotional reactions to mass violence may be evident immediately, for some, reactions may appear months or even years later (Brodsky Cohen, 1991; Mui, 1998). Some of the elderly people who seemed to be doing well immediately following the Trade Center attacks were, in fact, not managing as well months after the event. For example, one elderly woman with no history of mental illness witnessed bodies falling from the Towers on September 11th. At the time of the attacks, her husband was ailing. Her closest friend had committed suicide a few months earlier. Months later she became depressed and withdrawn, and when she began talking to the visiting nurse about suicide, she was referred to a social worker who assessed her as needing in-patient treatment. After two weeks of hospitalization, she was released from the facility on a day pass. Once she got home, this woman committed suicide by jumping out of a window (Trische, 2002).

Impact on Elderly Immigrant Populations

Many immigrants now living in the United States have experienced tremendous suffering in their lives; some have fled from tyrannical regimes, ongoing civil wars, political oppression and torture, and other forms of mass violence. They have come to the United States seeking the American dream of freedom and liberty, viewing this country as a refuge, a safe haven from various kinds of persecution.

Yet, after they arrive, many are confronted with a society that is less than welcoming, that at times is discriminatory, and that does not provide the measure of security they expected. Even without the stresses created by mass violence, daily living can be difficult. Those who have family supports tend to rely on family members for assistance. Even when this is not available, either because there is no family to provide help or because family members do not have sufficient resources, many elderly immigrants are reluctant to seek help outside their immediate communities. While this may be in part because of language difficulties, it may also be a consequence of their unfamiliarity with available resources and policies and distrust of the government. Two immigrant groups, elderly Asian immigrants and survivors of the Holocaust, are discussed below to illustrate some of these issues.

The Elderly in New York's Chinatown

In very close proximity to the site of the World Trade Center is the Chinatown community, where more than 20 percent of the population is 65 years of age and older. Of these, 85 percent were born outside the United States (U.S. Bureau of Census, 1991). The elderly residents of Chinatown include not only those who come from China, but also from other Asian countries including Laos, Cambodia, and Vietnam—places that have experienced prolonged wars and genocide. Many of the Asians who came to the United States did so to escape dangerous political conditions in their countries of birth, and they carry with them the onerous burden of painful memories.

Many residents of Chinatown are reluctant to address those outside the Asian community. Difficulties with expressing themselves in English, status as undocumented persons, and a cultural stoicism may play a major role in the utilization of social services, even in the immediate community. Even venturing into the street on a normal day can be frightening for some older people. Some become targets of young muggers who are aware that crimes against immigrant elders, particularly those of Asian backgrounds, are not likely to be reported to the police, either because of the elderly person's fear of the authorities or because of fear of retaliation by their assailants (Chen, 2002).

Despite the fact that the stresses of immigration and acculturation increase their risk for depression (Gelfand & Yee, 1991), in general, Chinese immigrants are less likely to use mental health services, and Chinese elders are less likely to be identified or receive treatment from social workers than are their white counterparts (Beckett & Dungee-Anderson, 1992;

Mui, 1998). For many of these immigrants, the process of aging is expected to be difficult, and there seems to be no point in complaining about either the basic conditions of life or about substantive emotional struggles. There is evidence that elderly Asian immigrants have a higher rate of death due to suicide than do elderly white immigrants, and, in addition, the suicide rate for elderly Chinese immigrants is almost six times higher than for U.S.-born Chinese Americans (Yu, 1986). These factors placed elderly Asian immigrants at an even greater risk for being impacted by trauma, even prior to September 11th.

The attacks of September 11th had a profound impact on the Chinatown community in New York, and particularly on the elderly living in the community. People living in the Chinatown area were among those who lost telephone services for several weeks, and for months there were still pockets within the Chinatown community where the telephone service was spotty, resulting in isolation for many elderly people. While free cellular telephones were made available for the elders in the community, they proved to be of limited use since many elderly immigrants were unaccustomed to using such phones, especially those with voice mail and other technological features (Chen, 2002). In addition, although there were many volunteers and organizations attempting to be helpful in the Chinatown community, it was uncommon for older people to open their doors to people who they did not know and who were unable to communicate in their languages (Lee, 2002). Many homebound individuals were identified as in need of assistance only when a neighbor, family member, or another individual happened to become aware of the need and alerted the appropriate authorities (Lee, 2002).

In the aftermath of the attacks, the Chinatown neighborhood was reeling from the loss of businesses and employment. Tourism, a primary industry, was barely alive, particularly since transportation in and around the community continued to be limited. The Chinatown garment industry, a chief source of income for many newcomers who do not speak English, experienced a steady decline. There were many business closings with numerous layoffs of employees, and people could not easily acquire other work. Consequently, the older people in the community who were living with their families, or who were dependent upon the financial support of their relatives, were also struggling (Lee, 2002).

Social workers attempted to intervene in the interests of people affected by financial hardship. For example, in the days following the World Trade Center attacks in 2001, Mrs. Cho, 81 years old, could not reach the company that supplied her with adult diapers. Not only was her phone not working, but the company's phone was also down. Approved by Medicaid for diapers from one particular supplier only, she would be forced to purchase the costly diapers elsewhere, at her own expense. This presented a huge financial burden for her. A social worker in the community who knew Mrs. Cho sought her out to offer her services and was able to advocate with a Medicaid worker to make an alternative arrangement to serve this client.

There were many incidents where actions of the Chinese elderly reflected their stoicism. In keeping with cultural patterns, they did not request help for stress-related symptoms, and there was no significant increase in the use of mental health services by the Chinatown elderly after the attacks. On the other hand, the Chinatown Health Clinic did experience a 40 percent rise in the number of visits for medical services; most of the symptoms reported appeared to have been directly connected to stress-related issues (Lee, 2002). Stoicism prevailed for individuals and families, even in matters of the greatest significance. For example, a 76-year-old Chinese-born woman who worked in a senior center as a participant in an employment program for older persons, took three weeks before she shared her desperate situation with the staff. Her son, a banker with a history as a paramedic, had been killed in the Trade Center attacks when he stayed back to offer aid to others. In her grief, this elderly woman had to deal with the fact that she could not even obtain a death certificate for her son. He had been born in China and had no birth certificate. After finally sharing her dilemma, social workers acting on behalf of elderly clients in Chinatown were able to involve the Chinese authorities to establish his birth record (Chen, 2002).

Participation of aged persons in programs sponsored by ethnically sensitive senior centers is especially important for elderly immigrants, as such programs can help to establish and maintain a supportive community (Mui & Burnette, 1994). This connection played a major helping role during the crisis in Chinatown. Both during the September 11th crisis and thereafter, senior centers in Chinatown and its surrounding areas became the hub of activity for securing assistance for the aged residents of the neighborhood, as well as for elderly Chinese from other parts of New York City. Despite the difficulties in traveling from other boroughs to Chinatown, many elderly Chinese managed to find ways to get there, seeking the comfort of centers where their languages were spoken and cultural patterns were supported (Chen, 2002).

While the centers reinforced the common Chinese heritage of the participants, the collapse of the World Trade Center in their own backyard sharply emphasized the connection of these immigrants to their new country. The normally detached community of elders, who strive to connect to their Chinese ancestry first (Devore & Schlesinger, 1991), placed memorials to those lost in the attacks throughout the parks adjoining Chinatown, and elderly Chinese immigrants, for the most part quite poor, raised $20,000 to be donated to the charity fund for survivors and their families.

Elderly Holocaust Survivors

Among the elderly immigrants in New York City is a large group of Jewish Holocaust survivors. Many suffered physical disabilities as a result of their wartime experiences, and all, even as they capably conduct their normal daily activities, are scarred by unspeakable horrors of their pasts. For most elderly Holocaust survivors, incidents of mass violence trigger powerful memories of past catastrophic events, causing them to relive the very worst of their pain and grief, a renewal of the experience of losses of family, friends, homes, physical security and well-being, and, above all, of innocence (Brandler, 2000).

Many Holocaust survivors have a history of posttraumatic stress disorder (PTSD), and with new and terrifying occurrences, they are readily retraumatized. The degree of seriousness of PTSD, which can interfere with the most basic functioning—eating, sleeping, concentration on life tasks, and ability to relate to others—seems to depend upon specific factors, including the duration of the trauma, the specific nature of the trauma, whether there was a direct experience with the atrocities, including witnessing, and the extent of stressful events in the rest of their life experiences (Brandler, 2000; Kuch & Cox, 1992; Yehuda, Kahana, Schmeidler, Southwick, & Giller, 1995). Studies of Holocaust survivors in Israel have demonstrated that these individuals have more severe reactions to war and terrorist actions than those aged persons who did not experience the Holocaust (Solomon & Prager, 1992).

The peculiarity of circumstances leading to traumatization, such as in the case of the Holocaust, is that the requirements of survival left no time for mourning or opportunity for individuals to process the events immediately after they occurred. Circumstances demanded an automatic motion forward; losses were not addressed and certainly not resolved (Brodsky Cohen, 1991; Rosenbloom, 1995). Consequently, survivors remain especially vulnerable to retraumatization. The extent of this vulnerability can often be seen when Holocaust survivors retire. Along with the usual sense of loss of a work identity, they may experience the loss of a comforting distraction, leading to the intrusion of powerful long-buried memories (Brandler, 2000).

The events of September 11th contributed to the retraumatization of an already vulnerable population. Social workers dealing with Holocaust survivors report that after the events of September 11th, many clients who until then had been doing well were suffering extreme anxiety and depression (Brandler, 2002). For example, Mr. Rosenberg, 85 years old, thought he was "going crazy" because he started having nightmares. In his dream, he was back in Budapest sleeping in his room while the Nazis were breaking down the door to his house. The events of his dream had actually occurred in real life in Hungary during World War II. After September 11th, the nightmare terrorized him every time he tried to sleep. Eventually, he had to be medicated in order to get some rest. In addition to the fatigue, some of his anxieties spilled over into daytime activities, so that his medications had to be increased to calm him sufficiently to function in his daily activities. When seen months later, his symptoms, although eased by the drugs, persisted.

Impact of Mass Violence on Social Agencies Serving the Elderly

In an earlier time, when relatively few people lived into old age, the only assistance to the aged came through informal networks, such as family, friends, neighbors, and religious institutions. Today, with a large aged population, most of whom do not live with their adult children, formal networks of home health programs and various community care services are in place to attempt to address the concrete and psychological needs of older persons. These support services are designed to make it possible for people to remain in their homes, have productive and fulfilling activities, and manage fairly independently even into very late old age (Kropf, 1992).

Formal organizational structures that serve the aged, however, are less responsive and less flexible than the informal networks of friends and neighbors looking after each other during emergencies. For example, during the World Trade Center attacks, the Department for the Aging of New York City, with its main office located in lower Manhattan, had no operating telephones or computers, no access to records, and the building itself was temporarily evacuated during the emergency. Without this key resource, communities had to rely primarily on volunteer efforts to sustain their aged members.

Although many older people seem, perhaps by virtue of their long life experience, to be uniquely equipped to survive difficult times (Lewis, 2002), there are those physically and emotionally frail persons who must be better served by social services during times of crises. The capacity of the system to continuously identify those who are frail and at risk for harm, to assure that these individuals receive appropriate services and to ensure the continuity and flow of services is fundamental to maintaining older people in the community. Only with these assurances can premature, preventable, and inappropriate nursing home placements be avoided.

As social workers cope with the general impact of mass violence on various aged populations, it is important to differentiate particular aged populations for special consideration because of their special needs and vulnerabilities. For example, people in what has been termed the "old-old" age group, age 80 and older, generally are more frail and, if they are not living in communal settings, are likely to be more dependent on social and health services than are their "young-old" counterparts (Neugarten, 1968). With the disruptions inherent in situations of mass violence, the added stresses these situations present for the elderly, and the limitations that may be placed on usual and expected services, gerontological social workers and agencies providing services to the elderly must be particularly vigilant and provide for the safety and well-being of the most vulnerable elderly.

Searching for Solutions: The Role of Social Workers, Social Agencies, and Public Policies

What is most apparent from the experiences of the events of September 11th is that social workers and agencies serving the elderly need to put additional strategies in place in order to respond more effectively to situations growing out of mass violence. The primary issue is that currently there is no means to identify older individuals who may be impaired and in need of help during such an emergency. Assessment and intervention are impossible without identification of people in potential distress. Neither are there agency backup records held in other locations, should the local records of frail elderly persons become unavailable or be destroyed. In this "Information Age," when businesses and institutions maintain duplicate records at various sites, social agencies and organizations dealing with individuals who potentially are at the greatest risk during catastrophes also need to keep duplicate files at different locations.

Currently, some records of persons who are bedbound or who are dependent for survival on electrically powered machinery such as oxygen concentrators are kept by local fire stations and power companies. Should there be a fire in the home of a bedbound individual, the fire department is often aware of the special needs in this situation and able to act accordingly; similarly, with a failure in electricity, a backup generator is in place. There is, however, no central bank for information on these people should the local fire station or utility company be destroyed. It is essential that some organization of data about older individuals known to agencies be held in a central bank so they can be assisted in emergencies. Of course, those not affiliated with any formal network remain at highest risk.

Many communities prepare to address disasters by developing teams representing different city departments. Such teams include representatives of fire, police, and sanitation, as well as other departments, and are coordinated by an incident commander. They prepare for disaster response through pre-emergency planning and work closely together at the time of the crisis (Henry & Stapleton, 1992). In order to be prepared to step into immediate action and to provide necessary services to aged persons with special needs during such crises, social work representatives of public departments for the aging must be included in all stages of planning by such teams.

Some level of redundancy for every essential service must be built into plans for responding to crises of mass violence. As a necessary part of the plan, persons providing care to homebound or frail individuals must be given access to their clients, either to help by evacuating them or by remaining with them as necessary. Should the usual services be unavailable, a backup plan can be called into action. If care providers, for instance, cannot get to their clients by using normal public transportation during emergencies, an alternate arrangement must be in place to transport them. A disaster plan must also be in place so that those who have to be moved have appropriate alternative living arrangements already in place. For example, frail older people, unlike most other individuals, cannot "rough it" and stay overnight in a public school gymnasium until their usual housing is rendered safe. Spaces in more protective settings, such as hospitals or nursing facilities, must be designated as backup housing during disasters and additional services brought to the older persons at these sites. In communities with concentrations of non-English-speaking older residents, part of the backup disaster plan must include assignment of workers familiar with the language and culture of the residents (Ng, 2002).

Unlike the services offered by hospitals and the fire and police departments, social services are not typically available during nighttime hours, holidays, or weekends. Neither is there a hotline where emergency situations involving elderly persons can be reported and referred to appropriate agencies. Such situations might include notification that a care provider did not reach the client or that meals were not delivered as expected. A well-advertised hotline that responds to the needs of the elderly should be available ongoing during normal conditions; such a hotline is absolutely essential in circumstances in which there are major and even life-threatening disruptions in services. In communities with large groups of older adults, special training of community volunteers on how to be helpful to the elderly during times of disaster would be useful.

Programs providing for bereavement counseling to those who have lost family members or close friends must also take into account the impact of such losses on the elderly. As indicated previously, there is a tendency to overlook aged grieving parents, grandparents, other elderly family members, and even close friends who may not be on the scene at the time or at the place of the disaster. Yet, their extraordinary sorrow makes them vulnerable to illness and even to death.

Conclusion

During times of mass violence, social workers and other helping professionals providing direct client services must be particularly attuned to the impact of mass violence and its aftermath on those already having difficulty coping; to the losses of the elderly, as these may be hidden; and to the impact of the trauma on those who have been previously traumatized. Goals of interventions should be to maintain, restore, or replace the fundamental social and economic supports that help older adults remain as independent as possible and help preserve their physical and psychological health.

It has become apparent through the experiences of September 11, 2001, that it is essential to have professional and community networks in place that can be quickly mobilized to provide a consistent delivery of care and services to the aged population during incidents of mass violence and in the aftermath of the events. The focus must be on the problematic issues related to service delivery. These include the need for backup plans and safeguards to ensure that no elderly person is neglected; that gaps in services are identified, including both the underserved elderly and those not served at all; and that provisions are made for the special needs of the frail elderly.

References

Aarts, P. H., & Op den Velde, W. (1996). Prior traumatization and the process of aging: Theory and clinical implications. In B. van der Kolk, A. McFarlane, & L. Weisaeth (Eds.), *Traumatic stress: The effects of overwhelming experience on mind, body, and society* (pp. 359–377). New York: Guilford Press.

Beckett, J. O., & Dungee-Anderson, D. (1992). Older minorities: Asian, Black, Hispanic, and Native Americans. In R. L. Schneider & N. Kropf (Eds.), *Gerontological social work* (pp. 277–322). Chicago: Nelson-Hall.

Bermant, J. (2002). Interview with J. Bermant, Director of Research of the New York City Department for the Aging, June 14, 2002.

Brandler, S. (2000). Practice issues: understanding aged Holocaust survivors. *Families in Society, 81,* 66–75.

Brandler, S. (2002). Interviews with Holocaust survivors post September 11. Unpublished study.

Brodsky Cohen, H. (1991). Holocaust survivors and the crisis of aging. *Families in Society, 72,* 226–232.

Butler, R. N., & Lewis, M. I. (1983). *Aging and mental health.* New York: C. V. Mosby.

Callahan, D. (1986). Health care in the aging society: A moral dilemma. In A. Pifer & L. Bronte (Eds.), *Our aging society* (pp. 319–340). New York: W. W. Norton.

Chen, D. (2002, June 15). Interview with D. Chen, Social Work director, Chinese-American Planning Council, New York City.

De Vivo, J. (2002, June 30). Interview with J. De Vivo, Social Service Director, North Richmond Hospital.

Devore, W., & Schlesinger, E. G. (1991). *Ethnic-sensitive social work practice* (3rd ed). New York: Macmillan.

Draper, J. (2002, June 16). Interview with J. Draper, Mental Health Association of New York City.

Gelfand, D., & Yee, B. W. K. (1991). Influence of immigration, migration, and acculturation on the fabric of aging in America. *Generations, 15,* 7–10.

Henry, M., & Stapleton, E. (1992). *EMT pre-hospital care.* Philadelphia: W. B. Saunders.

Kropf, N. P. (1992). Home health and community services. In R. L. Schneider & N. P. Kropf (Eds.), *Gerontological social work* (pp. 173–201). Chicago: Nelson-Hall.

Kuch, K., & Cox, B. J. (1992). Symptoms of PTSD in 124 survivors of the Holocaust. *American Journal of Psychiatry, 149,* 337–340.

Lee, K. (2002, June 16). Interview with hospital administrator who works with the New York Coalition for Asian-American Mental Health.

Lewis, M. (2002, January). Thoughts on older people involved in the World Trade Center crisis. *NASW Newsletter,* Section on Aging, 3–4.

Mui, A. C. (1998). Living alone and depression among older Chinese immigrants. *Journal of Gerontological Social Work, 30,* 140–166.

Mui, A. C., & Burnette, D. (1994). A comparative profile of frail elderly persons living alone and those living with others. *Journal of Gerontological Social Work, 21,* 5–26.

Neugarten, B. L. (1968). *Middle age and aging. Chicago: University of Chicago Press.*

Ng, A. (2002, June 16). Telephone interview with A. Ng, Medical Director, Disaster Psychiatry Outreach.

O'Brien, N. (2002, June 16). Telephone interview with N. O'Brien, social worker/ researcher, International Longevity Center.

Rosenbloom, M. (1995). Implications of the Holocaust for social work. *Families in Society, 76,* 567–576.

Shanas, E. (1982, Fall). The family relations of old people. *National Forum, 62.*

Solomon, Z., & Prager, E. (1992). Elderly Israeli Holocaust survivors during the Persian Gulf War: A study of psychological distress. *American Journal of Psychiatry, 149,* 1707–1710.

Spalding, J. (1992). Post-traumatic stress disorder. In F. J. Turner (Ed.), *Mental health and the elderly* (pp. 396–424). New York: Free Press.

Trische, K. (2002, June 5 and June 16). Interviews with Dr. K. Trische, social worker with Village Care of New York, New York City.

Turner, F. J. (1992). The elderly: A biopsychosocial overview. In F. J. Turner (Ed.), *Mental health and the elderly* (pp. 1–9). New York: Free Press.

U.S. Bureau of the Census. (1991, September). *Census Bureau Press Release* (CB91-215). Washington, DC: U.S. Government Printing Office.

Yehuda, R., Kahana, B., Schmeidler, J., Southwick, S., & Giller, E. (1995). Impact of cumulative lifetime trauma and recent stress on current Post Traumatic Stress Disorder symptoms in Holocaust survivors. *American Journal of Psychiatry, 152,* 1815–1818.

Yu, E. S. H. (1986). Health of the Chinese elderly in America. *Research on Aging, 8,* 84–109.

Zimmer, A. (2002, November 15). Interview with Director, Institute on Mutual Aid/Self-Help Brookdale Center on Aging of Hunter College, New York City.

Section III

Impact of Mass Violence on Organizations and Communities

5

Mass Violence in Schools: The Role of Social Workers

Jessie Klein

School violence has always been a social problem, but the recent mass violence in and around schools has reached extraordinary proportions, calling for new prevention and intervention strategies. Between 1996 and 2001, fifteen boys, ages 11 to 18, killed a total of 32 children, 8 adults, and wounded 92 others in a spate of school shootings throughout the United States. This phenomenon has left a trail of youngsters mourning friends, parents burying their children, and schools devastated, tense, and lacking resources for support. Community networks and social service agencies have likewise been ill-prepared for the unexpected flood of people in need.

While most of the highly visible school shootings took place in the United States—consecutively in Washington, Alaska, Mississippi, Kentucky, Arkansas, Pennsylvania, Tennessee, Oregon, Colorado, Georgia, Michigan, California, and New York City—mass violence in schools has also occurred in other parts of the Western world, including Scotland, Canada, and Germany. In March 1996, Thomas Hamilton killed 16 children at a school in Dunblame, Scotland, before killing himself. In April 1999, a 14-year old boy in Canada, who had dropped out of school after he was severely ostracized by his classmates, came back and killed one student and wounded another at his high school; and in April 2002 in Erfurt, Germany, a recently expelled student, age 19, killed 13 teachers, 2 students, and 1 policeman (CBC News Online, 2002). In all these incidents, it is important to note the *one common denominator.* Males, and in particular teenage boys who felt powerless, ostracized, or otherwise rejected, picked up guns in order to demonstrate their power and ability to impact others and to extract revenge.

This chapter examines mass violence in schools, proposing that popular single-issue explanations, such as violence in the media, gun control laws, working parents, evil character, and pure chance, are at best incomplete. It explores the inclusion of gender role awareness in intervention programs and the need for trauma-related individual, group, and family counseling that is sensitive to gender issues and readily available to all students and community members. Social work intervention strategies with students, families, and school personnel are discussed.

Understanding Mass Violence in Schools

While a premeditated and calculated attack on a group of unarmed and unsuspecting people may be unfathomable, mass violence in community, workplace, and schools in the United States has increased in frequency during the 1990s. Incidents of massacres by adults in Florida, California, Georgia, and Alabama tended to relate to economic or employment loss and often involved the killing by men of their co-workers or supervisors (Flannigan, 1999; Sack, 1999a). The boys involved in school violence mostly killed their peers—the boys who attacked their masculinity or the girls who rejected them (Klein & Chancer, 2000). A consistent theme among most of the attacks is that men and boys who perceived themselves as powerless and unfairly dominated picked up weapons, and declared themselves, or their cause, victorious. The roots of mass school violence thus appear to be found in the social expectations of masculinity that pressure boys to use violence to demonstrate their manhood. This gender-based aspect of mass school violence, however, seems to be ignored in the literature. Public debates on the subject tend to be overwhelmingly devoted to single-issue symptoms, such as gun control, media violence, or lack of parental supervision.

Stricter gun-control laws have been acclaimed as the primary means to prevent massive school shootings (Dob, 1998; McCurry, 1999). While access to guns dramatically increases the capacity to kill and multiplies the death toll, it is important to note that school shootings also take place in countries with strict gun control laws, like Scotland and Germany.

Similarly, buttressed by evidence that several of the boys enjoyed violent video games, music, and movies, media violence has been blamed for the shootings (Leibovich, 1998). However, while media violence may be excessive, research findings are contradictory about whether violent imagery causes real violence (Schor, 2000; Wilson, 1974). Moreover, this perspective ignores the phenomenon that part of what is encouraged in the media is a hypermasculinity that is only realized when violence is enacted.

Child neglect is another explanation for mass violence in schools, with blame placed on working and single parents of the young perpetrators (Thomas, 1998). In reality, however, most of the boys who engaged in such killings came from a two-parent, white, middle-class, traditionally structured family (e.g., Harris and Klebold in Colorado, Carneal in Kentucky, Kinkel in Oregon). It is, therefore, important to understand the complex psychodynamic relationships within families, regardless of familial structure.

Boys who commit school shootings have also been described as "bad" or "evil" (Associated Press, 2001; Rodriguez, 1998). However, a closer examination of the boys' own comments following the crimes indicates that rather than acting badly, they believed they had demonstrated masculinity expectations of which others thought them incapable: "Murder is not weak and slow-witted, murder is gutsy and daring," announced 16-year-old

Woodham in Mississippi in 1997 (Holland, 1997, p. 1), after he killed the girl who had just broken up with him and aimed at boys who called him "gay." "One second I was some kind of heartbroken idiot," he explained, "and the next second I had the power over many things" (Popyk, 1998, p. 4). In Kentucky in 1997, 14-year-old Carneal also indicated increased self-regard after killing a girl who rejected him and targeting boys who had called him a "faggot." He told psychiatrists, "I was feeling proud, strong, good, and more respected" (Blank, 1998, p. 4). The pressure for boys to be aggressively violent to prove their masculinity may then be the underlying evil.

Still another effort to understand mass school violence views the child shooting sprees as random or unforeseen acts of violence (Schiraldi, 1998; Stolberg, 1999). Yet, when so many school shootings are committed by boys and directed predominantly at girls who rejected them and at boys who called the perpetrators "gay," further explanation is required (Klein & Chancer, 2000).

One aspect of this gender problem that did gain some media coverage relates to school bullies. While girls can also mistreat each other, most school bullies are in fact, male (Hall, 1999; Talbott, 2002). The traditional social pecking order in schools tends to be based on physical size and the appearance of toughness (Kindlon & Thompson, 2000). The boys who committed school shootings were all described as skinny, chubby, or small—not the "masculine" characteristics that win respect; thus, these boys were bullied relentlessly by the more dominant boys in their school and then tragically retaliated (Klein & Chancer, 2000). Congressional efforts to consider legislation guaranteeing students the right to be free from bullying and harassment in public schools have been undermined by some Christian fundamentalist organizations that suspect these policies are pro-gay propaganda (Morris, 2001).

Many of the boys who have been bullied specifically blamed teachers and parents for supporting the abuse or failing to intervene (Klein & Chancer, 2000). The boys who killed seemed to believe the bullying was wrong and should be changed, either by adults who could protect them or by their own hands. Hannah Arendt (1970) writes: "Only where there is reason to suspect that conditions could be changed and are not does rage arise. Only when our sense of justice is offended do we react with rage" (p. 63).

Cultural Acceptance of Violence

To understand the impact of mass violence on schools and communities, it is necessary to examine the cultural acceptance of violence (Moore, 2002). This includes the bullying experienced by boys and the faculty and parents who may inadvertently collude with these practices. Harris in Colorado in 1999 specifically left a note in his room stating that he acted partly because the adults in his life did not protect him:

> If you are reading this, my mission is complete.... Your children who have ridiculed me, who have chosen not to accept me, who have treated me like I am not worth their time are dead.... I may have taken their lives and my own—but it was your doing. Teachers, parents, LET THIS MASSACRE BE ON YOUR SHOULDERS UNTIL THE DAY YOU DIE. (emphasis in original; MSNBC Staff and Wire Reports, 1999)

Harris' words echoed those of the young boy who killed in Washington in 1996:

> I figured since the principal and the dean weren't doing anything that was making any impression, that I was gonna have to do something, or else I was gonna keep on getting picked on. (Dedman, 2000)

Arendt (1970) argues that when conditions are experienced as unjust, violence can begin to feel intuitive. "To resort to violence when confronted with outrageous events or conditions is enormously tempting because of its inherent immediacy and swiftness" (p. 63). "In this sense, rage and violence that sometimes—not always—goes with it belongs among the 'natural' human emotions," she writes, "and to cure men of them would mean nothing less than to dehumanize or *emasculate* him" (emphasis added) (pp. 64–74). The boys who killed practically articulated these words verbatim. These boys were called *gay, faggot,* and other words associated with females and homosexuals as a means of degradation (Klein & Chancer, 2000). Such words are used to challenge masculinity itself, to suggest a lack of bravery, strength, and male power. Boys are generally taught to fight when their masculinity is questioned.

On April 20, 1999, in Colorado, Eric Harris, age 18, and Dylan Klebold, age 17, took over Columbine High School with high-powered homemade bombs and sophisticated machine guns, killing 15 people, including themselves. This massive slaughter of children was historically unprecedented in the United States, with the highest number of fatalities in a U.S. school shooting to date—but Harris and Klebold were not the first boys to shoot their fellow students. They claimed to have killed for the same reasons reported by previous boys who had killed other students in their schools.

Relatively powerless in their daily lives, Harris and Klebold "were pushed against lockers and had rocks and even lunchroom mashed potatoes thrown in their face," reported one member from their social group, The Trench Coat Mafia (Wilgoren, 1999). The diary of one of the gunmen revealed an explosive rage at ridicule by those "preps" and "jocks" who called him "homosexual" (Barron, 1999).

Luke Woodham, age 16, exhibited a similarly violent reaction when he shot and killed his ex-girlfriend and her best friend at his school in Pearl, Mississippi, on October 1, 1997. He also said he was tired of being called "gay." Woodham explained further: "Throughout my life I was ridiculed. Always beaten. Always hated. Can you, society, truly blame me for what I do" (Teenagers charged with plotting to kill in satanic campaign, 1997, p. 1).

On May 21, 1998, in Springfield, Oregon, Kipland Kinkel, age 15, also killed "jocks" who tormented him for being "small." He shot 4 people dead (2 boys and his parents) and wounded 22 others (Bernstein, 1999; Egan, 1999). A year earlier, Michael Carneal, age 14, killed a girl who didn't return his affections, 2 other girls, and wounded 5 in his school in West Paducah, Kentucky. He also said he was tired of being called a "faggot," and in March 1998, 14-year-old Mitchell Johnson of Jonesboro, Arkansas, proudly publicized his "vow to kill all the girls who had broken up with him" (Bragg, 1998, p. 1).

These cases reveal that sanctioned masculinity expectations, including homophobia, misogyny, and violence itself, are inextricably entwined in the precursors of school violence (Klein & Chancer, 2000). The boys in these cases all seemed to consider it acceptable to violently defend themselves against perceived attacks on their masculinity that associated them with being gay or otherwise feminine.

Impact of Mass Violence in Schools

The impact of mass violence is devastating not just for the individuals involved, but also for larger communities. Understandably, many of those who have experienced school shootings directly are traumatized, still mourning, and living with tremendous despair and anxiety, as most people are after surviving something so devastating (American Psychiatric Association, 1994; Janofsky, 2001). Many others who have only heard of these atrocities or seen the images on television are also scarred, scared, and living with a new and pervasive tension (Piper, 1999). Interviews with children in Colorado following the Columbine school attack found that many students had trouble concentrating in class, reported new difficulties trusting people, or became more dependent on one another, clinging to each other for security and safety (Janofsky, 2000). Students both feared other children might be potential killers and also that they themselves might be perceived as possible perpetrators due to a misinterpreted doodle or comment (School shootings, 2002). Some empathize with the boys who killed, hoping that the bullying they experience might be mitigated as a result of the shootings:

> Once, before Columbine, I was a Chatfield Senior High student who was picked on and harassed to the point of wanting to end it all and taking out all of those who had picked on me and tried to destroy me emotionally and physically only for their amusement, but after the Columbine incident most of the people soon realized that they could not continue treating people the way they did. But still there are people out there who are still bullied and harassed and I pray that they don't follow the same path Eric and Dylan (the school shooters at Columbine High School in Colorado) did. (Lullaby for Columbine, 2002, p. 4)

Parents of victims of school shootings have displayed many different reactions. One mother from Colorado fatally shot herself (Janofsky, 2001). Other parents of victims made it their mission to spread religion or to press for more gun control measures; some just try to make it through each day (Janofsky, 2001). In general, when schools are attacked, parents and other adults often feel incapable of providing comfort and security for their children. Some parents keep their children at home for many weeks or months following a school shooting, further reinforcing their children's fears (Nussbaum, 2000).

Teachers also feel traumatized by recent school shootings. In the United States, 4 teachers and 1 principal were killed and 2 other faculty members were wounded. In Germany, 13 teachers were targeted and killed when a student sought revenge on those he blamed for getting him expelled from school. At the University of Arizona, 3 professors were murdered by a failing student. While teachers previously may have had concerns about being sued by a student who felt a failing grade or bad evaluation was unjustified, now they may fear assassination (Smallwood, 2002).

Expectations for teachers to manage the anxiety students feel relating to school shootings is also a new and difficult challenge. One teacher in a high school expressed concern when principals demanded that teachers go back to the school building to explore a bomb threat. "I didn't want to go back," said the teacher, but the principals said: "There was to be no discussion" (Turley, 1999–2001). A professor held hostage by a bomb threat at Fairfield University said: "Of course any professor caught in such a situation should put the students' welfare first and be alert and respond to their needs" (Dreyer, 2002). But, expectations that teachers give their lives is unrealistic, and their fears, anxieties, and concern for their own families need to be considered. Furthermore, in such situations, teachers are often expected, or expect themselves, to act as the students' social worker, as the above example indicates. This in itself is dangerous and unfair to both teachers and students, as even the most well-meaning teacher is still not trained as a counselor and could inadvertently do more harm than good.

Reactions to school shootings have also provoked draconian security measures. Incidents considered mere pranks five or ten years ago now routinely involve the police and many result in immediate arrests (Nussbaum, 2000). Some schools prohibit book bags, lockers, or even trenchcoats that could potentially hide a weapon; some ban the wearing of clothes of certain color (Brooke, 1999; Verhovek, 1998). Students have been expelled for carrying a nail clipper or put in jail for writing a Halloween essay with violent overtones (Nussbaum, 2000); kindergarten students have been suspended for using their hands as make-believe handguns (School shootings, 2002; Nussbaum, 2000). One superintendent called for authority to allow principals to carry Mace, pepper spray, or stun guns to prepare for potential student-incited violence (Sack, 1999a).

Surveillance cameras in schools serve to monitor student activity and potential misbehavior. Zero-tolerance policies toward violence in many schools mandate that fighting result in immediate expulsion. Widespread use of this type of discipline is "creating as many problems as it is solving," reported Harvard University's Civil Rights Project (Nussbaum, 2000). Furthermore, while most of these policies are instituted in response to school shootings committed primarily by white, suburban, middle- to upper-class students, "African-American, Latino, and disabled children bear the brunt of the consequences of these policies" (Nussbaum, 2000).

While some new school policies may be necessary for creating structure and maintaining civic stability, the trend towards *get-tough* interventions does little to transform destructive social norms and expectations and, in addition to possibly exacerbating racial profiling, may even contribute to the pressure toward unattainable masculinity expectations that could potentially lead to more violence (Sochet, 2000).

Intervention

It is clear that mass violence in schools has a tremendous impact on students, parents, teachers, and members of the immediate and far-reaching communities. Therefore, it is crucial to offer appropriate interventions that support and help heal people, as well as provide prevention methods that ameliorate community and school tensions and build communal and individual coping skills and resources.

Helping Students Recover

In addition to the expected grieving and mourning the loss of teachers and friends after mass violence in schools, some children may experience clinical depression, anxiety, and/or complications of existing mental disorders; some go on to develop posttraumatic stress disorder (PTSD) (American Psychiatric Association, 1994; Janofsky, 2001). One helpful approach that has been used in aiding traumatized children in other countries was originally developed for use with school children affected by terrorism in Israel. Called *BASIC PH* (Lahad & Cohen, 1997), the program is based on the notion that people use many different types of coping skills. It is therefore important to assess students' coping strengths and help them address their stress in a way that is most comfortable and effective for them. The acronym BASIC PH stands for the six different ways of coping that has been applied to helping traumatized children.

"B" stands for "Belief System": Both adults and children rely on beliefs and values, including religious and political beliefs and cultural or familial missions, to guide them through stress and crisis. Such beliefs need to be supported and can be used to organize memorial ceremonies and for self-expression.

"A" stands for "Affect": People use affective coping modes to show emotions, such as crying or laughing, or silent means, such as drawing or writing. Affective intervention may include encouraging students to talk about their feelings, write letters or stories, or use psychodrama to express themselves.

"S" stands for "Social Support": Coping through social supports may include joining a bereavement group or organizing community events that build solidarity and a feeling of belonging among the school, the children, and their families.

"I" stands for "Imagination": Daydreaming, diverting attention, and improvisation are just some of the creative ways to distract oneself from traumatized feelings, or to deal with them in a less scary context. Adaptive use of imagination may include watching or putting on a play, reading stories, or drawing.

"C" stands for "Cognition": People use cognitive approaches to problem solve, gather information, or conceptualize lists of activities. Traumatized students may be encouraged to do a research project together or write relevant articles in school papers.

"PH" stands for "Physical": Physical activities, such as physical exercise or desensitization activities, are useful ways of coping with stress and trauma. Children can be encouraged to play outdoor games, use their bodies in expressive ways, or walk to or around the site of the mass violence.

This multimodal coping model parallels Howard Gardner's conceptualization of *multiple intelligences* (2000) that has become a popular pedagogical tool for engaging diverse groups of students, decreasing alienation, and teaching to students' strengths.

Gardner identifies different intelligence and learning styles and recommends that professionals assess and use students' strengths to get them involved and confident before introducing other new, and possibly less comfortable, approaches. Although using different terms, his approach corresponds with the coping mechanisms described in BASIC PH:

Linguistic (Belief), Visual (Affect), Intrapersonal (Affect), Interpersonal (Social Support), Musical (Imagination), Logical (Cognitive), and Bodily (Physical).

Encouraging the use of different learning styles that reinforce multiple coping mechanisms can also have a positive impact on gender expectations. Emphasizing different pedagogies and coping strategies—*affect* as well as *linguistic, musical* and *visual* as well as *logical*—can encourage an expanded gender continuum. Instead of encouraging boys to rely on their linguistic and logical intelligence, while helping girls by focusing on their emotional and artistic managing abilities, social workers can help students become aware that all the learning and coping styles are important and need to be used by both males and females to develop their full potential.

Social supports are considered an important variable in minimizing the negative consequences of trauma. In *Trauma and Recovery* (1997), Judith Herman charts the essential steps for working through the recovery process. However, some of her core principles, such as maintaining a safe, clinical environment with therapeutic boundaries, are difficult if not impossible to conduct within the current structure of most schools, especially when many if not all members of the community, including social workers and other helping professionals internal to the school, are also traumatized. It is important, then, to adapt her analysis to address the specific needs incurred by schools and also to focus on ways these theories can help to strengthen existing school support services. For example, since the core experiences of psychological trauma are disconnection and disempowerment, recovery is based upon empowering the survivor and creating, maintaining, and strengthening connections with others (Herman, 1997). In schools, then, individual and group counseling and other self-esteem and community-building services are essential. Individuals need to experience self-determination in recovery to regain some sense of control and efficacy. Students can be encouraged to create a peer support group and/or to learn assertive communication skills that they can practice in sessions with their social worker. Students can be helped to advocate for themselves and to help strengthen their other support systems, whether peer, familial, religious, community, or school-based.

Traumatic transference can also complicate the helping process. In traumatic transference the survivor transfers revenge feelings onto the helping professionals in lieu of access to the perpetrator, reducing the counselor to the same feelings of helplessness experienced by the survivor. Consequently, members of the clinical staff also need a support system to deal with the intense reactions evoked in this type of work (Herman, 1997). This is complicated when an entire community experiences a traumatic event and many people require help. In such cases, an external crisis support team may be needed (Straussner & Straussner, 1997). Moreover, it is imperative that schools create strong networks with community-based agencies that can work with students off site and be available to help in the school in the event of a crisis.

However, many adolescents are resistant to getting help even after experiencing mass violence. For boys especially, requesting, or even accepting, help can threaten the masculinity expectations that they are trying so hard to achieve. Some might find the trauma exacerbated by the mere process of asking for help. Counseling, therefore, needs to become a regular part of trauma and violence prevention programs in schools, and students should not need to request such services but have access to them as a matter of course. Schools need to institute their own strong social work programs and also form networks with social work agencies that can serve students year-round. With such familiarity, students will be more open to receiving help and the social worker can more successfully empower the student and help him or her recontexualize the quest for help as an act of courage.

Group and Family Interventions

Groups can help traumatized individuals share their experiences, fostering essential connections that counteract isolation and helping each person establish supports and reengage in ordinary life. Schools provide a natural setting for group counseling. Since adolescents often feel alienated and alone, even prior to a traumatic event, and may often turn to substances as a means of comfort, groups that foster deep and valuable connections among peers become a powerful alternative to more destructive means of coping (Goodman, 1997).

In instances of mass violence, families of grieving students can also be invited to participate in group sessions of various kinds. Parents of the perpetrators and/or victims, as well as grieving siblings, will need help in dealing with their own despair, as well as ways of being supportive. This is a complicated predicament, since adolescents are in the process of separating from their parents, establishing independent identities, and relying more on peer groups for support and guidance (Blos, 1966). Following mass violence, some adolescents regress and cling to their parents in the way they might have as a child, while others withdraw even more dramatically, terrified that their vulnerable feelings will draw them toward their parents indefinitely and prevent an independent existence. Parents need to be made aware of the different kinds of reactions they can expect and be helped to temporarily accept them while everyone finds his or her way toward regaining some kind of normalcy.

A school building that has not been the scene of mass violence can be used as a community center that provides a holding environment and a support system for students, faculty, parents, and other members of the community. Such a safe environment can allow people to process, accept, and integrate the horrific experience that affected them.

Once classes resume, students and teachers need to acknowledge and address the terrible experiences shared by the class before moving on with the curriculum. Traditional leaders like the principal or the student body president may need help from others in the school to offer adequate support and to help build stronger and more constructive relationships in response to the trauma the community faces. It may also be helpful for the school social worker to join with a school parent-teacher association to organize functions that bring people together, to process the experiences and/or to create new opportunities for socializing and thereby supporting one another.

It is important to note, however, that group events need not always be about processing the trauma; discussing the incident of mass violence at large group meetings could interfere with the efforts of some people to cope with the trauma, rather than aid in the process of recovery. Nonetheless, group and community activities can provide opportunities for people to build strong connections, while also providing a means for combating isolation. The PTA president, the school principal, and the student body leader are all in excellent positions to become role models and community healers. This is particularly critical in schools where cliques and bullying were part of the expressed motives for the mass violence.

Prevention of Mass Violence in Schools

In spite of get-tough trends, research on more progressive methods of intervention shows that conflict resolution programs incorporating mediation and negotiation, active listening, assertive communication, community building, and individual and group counseling are effective approaches to reducing violence (Alberti & Emmons, 1992; Fisher & Ury, 1981; Jacobson, 2002, Sareen, 2001; Swets, 1987).

Conflict Resolution and Communication Skill Building

Conflict resolution programs have been implemented in schools across the country, many of them run by social workers. Conflict resolution discussions, group activities, and talks can take many different forms. Mediation involves a neutral third party who facilitates resolution, while negotiation engages only the parties involved in the dispute. Such programs often are effective in helping to resolve conflicts after a fight has occurred, thus preventing retaliation and further escalation of violence. In some schools, students are given the choice between mediation and other forms of school discipline, including suspension—adding an incentive for them to choose to communicate.

While different in character, the various approaches tend to focus on a set of common principles. The challenge is to get the parties involved to move from their specific positions to find their underlying interests, rather than focus on one or the other position that they previously saw as the only solution. An adaptation of Fisher and Ury's (1981) famous "Orange" example typifies this method:

> Two children fight over the last orange. The frazzled parent comes over, hears each child's position, and cuts the orange in half; each child gets half the orange. If the parent, however, had asked the children about their interests—*why* each wanted the orange—it would be revealed that one wanted the peel for an orange cake, while the other wanted to eat the orange. With a little conflict resolution, focusing on their interests, rather than their positions, they both could have had all of what they wanted.

In New York City, all teachers are given the opportunity to receive conflict mediation training as well as information on how to run such programs at their own schools. Teachers can elect to teach mediation techniques to students or teach classes that focus on learning negotiation techniques. In many schools throughout the country, students are trained to be mediators, available for students in conflict with other students, teachers, or parents. Trained to help each party understand the perspective and feelings of the other via "role reversal," they also help the parties focus on resolutions for the future, since the past cannot be changed, and understand the "cost of not settling" (Project SMART, n.d).

Since mediation usually takes only one session, students are exposed to positive communication skills, but do not necessarily learn these skills well enough to practice them after the session itself. Therefore, mediation programs need to be combined with intensive communication skill-building programs that include teaching negotiation skills as well as active listening and assertive communication as a required part of a school curriculum.

Assertive communication is "an alternative to personal powerlessness and manipulation," write Alberti and Emmons (1992, p. 5). Since feelings of powerless are often a catalyst for fights, learning such techniques would seem to have great potential in reducing violence. Assertive behavior is predicated on active listening skills. It is important to understand the interests of the other person when asserting one's own concerns. Active listening involves positive eye contact and other body language, refusing to evaluate or judge the speaker, reflecting back what was heard for further clarification, and finding some part of what the speaker says with which agreement can be declared (Swets, 1983). After listening actively, one can more effectively assert his or her concerns. Recommendations include: speaking with I-statements, refraining from blaming the other, expressing feelings, and describing a specific behavior of concern, rather than attacking the person. The goal is to help the other person feel heard and respected. By addressing behavior and not the person, by using I-statements, rather than blame, and by expressing feelings, rather than presenting opinions as "facts," people are more likely to win the respect of others and ultimately achieve their own ends as well. If students learn these skills, violence escalating from disrespectful communication would certainly be mitigated.

School mediation and conflict resolution programs often fail, however, because violence is so deeply embedded in the fabric of U.S. culture (Aronowitz, 2000; Butterfield, 2002). The pressure to use violence as a means of expressing male gender identity must be addressed in partnerships between parents and schools; a consistent message can begin to undo these destructive expectations. Communication skills as a requirement of a school curriculum could help address some problems related to gender ideologies. Communication skill building could extend the continuum of self-expression for boys, who are often encouraged to communicate aggressively, and for girls, who sometimes feel pressured to speak more passively.

Community Building

Another approach to preventing violence is through community building. Research has shown that small school communities are more supportive to students; large schools and classes increase student alienation and undermine student-teacher relationships and the role that adults play in children's lives (Straussner & Straussner, 1997). In addition, as pointed out by Christopher Stone (1999), director of the Vera Institute of Justice, strong school structure is one of the most important components for preventing school violence: "School structure—by which I mean class size, internal discipline, and leadership by the principal—is more powerful than the disorder, poverty, or violence in a surrounding neighborhood in determining whether a school provides a safe environment for learning" (from an unpublished speech). Consistency and respect among teachers and administrators, and toward students, are integral components for preventing school violence (Sareen, 2001). Top-down school systems can instead cause resentment and bureaucratic goal displacement. Small schools need to build constructive alternatives, while being mindful that policy by consensus (a hallmark of many small school communities) with large groups (i.e., more than nine people) can yield diminishing returns (Gastil, 1993).

Stone (1999) also identified the need for improved student-adult relationships. "Early adolescence is generally characterized by a weakening of adults' place in kids' lives, and the growing importance of peer groups.... Nonetheless, the Vera research suggests that in terms of managing violence and finding safety, the role of adults remains crucial." Parental values also play a significant role. Interviews with school children in New York City found that 68 percent of the students indicated that their parents would want them to defend themselves in a fight (Straussner & Straussner, 1997).

Long-term interagency partnerships with police and probation, mental health, substance abuse, and child welfare agencies are important aspects of violence prevention and community building, helping schools compensate for a lack of resources and more easily address their students' needs (Stone, 1999; Straussner & Straussner, 1997). Building community in this way can help heal the survivors of trauma and work to prevent violence in the future. A supportive community can also be a strong counterforce to unattainable masculinity expectations and defensive manhood battles; such acceptance can be one of the strongest healing forces in a recovery process.

Changing Gender Expectations

Prevention efforts would be greatly improved with stronger emphasis on gender role awareness. The pressures on boys to reject femininity, and especially homosexuality, serve as catalysts for incidents of mass violence in schools, and on smaller scales, for fights that can also regularly take place there. Social workers can be instrumental in helping boys accept these self-disdained aspects of themselves and others.

Harrison Pope documents (in Gwartney, 1998) the escalating pressure toward achieving masculinity expectations and the destructive socialization for men to look increasingly more "male." This training begins when boys are very young. For instance, G. I. Joe dolls marketed for boys are now at least as unrealistic in body shape as Barbie dolls targeted to girls. Pope points out that during the 1960s, G. I. Joe had the equivalent of twelve-inch biceps on an adult male; in 1999, the doll's biceps were the equivalent of twenty-seven inches, as much an anatomical impossibility as Barbie's proportions. Furthermore, the *G. I. Joe Extreme* doll wears an expression of rage that, according to Pope, suggests this emotion is particularly important for young boys (Gwartney, 1998; Klein & Chancer, 2000). As a result of these intensified social pressures, the impact of bullying becomes increasingly devastating and dangerous. With difficulty expressing a range of emotions, and pressure to reject their own and others' "femininity," some boys are willing to fight to the death—using the most symbolically masculine weapons—to prove their manhood.

Gender awareness needs to be an essential aspect of counseling programs and day-to-day life at school. Individual counseling can provide opportunities to explore ways of approaching school conflicts in a context of an expanded awareness of gender possibilities. If a school community reinforces these values, such that boys are encouraged to accept their more emotional, "feminine," aspects of themselves, the many fights instigated from these kinds of attacks may be prevented. To support this culturally transforming paradigm, schools can encourage a more diverse gender identity by providing male role models who are nurturing and by making social workers available to help boys accept themselves more fully.

Changing Social Policy

Programs that are focused on preventing mass violence in schools can only survive if there are social welfare polices and adequate funding in place to support them. In addition, while policy implementation is an essential ingredient for change, attitudes toward social work and psychological intervention are also crucial for successful interventions; it is difficult for social workers to be effective in a school as a host environment if faculty and/or administrators do not support, or are openly negative toward, counseling. The social worker needs to enlist the aid of key community members (i.e., the principal, PTA, and student leaders) to understand and accept these efforts and to help others in the school develop more interest and commitment to these kinds of support systems. In addition, as with many other social change movements, policy change can also be used to preempt prejudice and encourage greater openness to these programs.

Historically, schools were modeled after the prison system; the institutions were a means of containing young people and preventing them from wreaking havoc in the larger society. The militaristic structure was a "masculine" method of control that taught children obedience and conformity to social norms. In some ways, many contemporary schools still emulate these kinds of practices and conditions, at the expense of developing nurturing communities that support academic excellence and foster self-esteem. Metal detectors abound, causing some students to feel like suspected criminals as they enter the school. While it is understandable that people gravitate toward extreme measures to ensure the safety of students given the high level of fear and anxiety raised by recurring experiences of mass violence in recent years, interventions that tend to mimic the prison system can create less, rather than more, trust and security. Most contemporary social work, education, and even criminology research on violence prevention recommends more nurturing communities and cautions against the more militaristic style (Feld, 1998; Goodman, 1997; Jacobson, 2002; Sochet, 2000).

In studies of model initiatives in schools in Austin, Boston, and Charlotte, the Vera Institute of Justice (1999) found that interagency collaboration, community and empowerment skill building, conflict resolution programs, community participation, and healthy budgets were essential components of all the models that were successful in reducing violence. Government funds need to be allocated to schools to support these kinds of initiatives. Changing policy is not the only ingredient in preventing mass school violence and transforming destructive gender expectations, but it can be used as a substantive catalyst for change.

Conclusion

Feeling powerless and helpless is not just upsetting; in some circumstances, it can become a stimulus for mass violence. Young men who feel impotent in some way use violence to make others feel oppressed instead. A cycle of using violence to overcome the experience of powerlessness can be perpetuated indefinitely.

Healing from violence entails empowerment and connection with others; preventing school violence is also based on these principles. Gender awareness and transformation is one component necessary for building healthy communities. Teaching the difference between power hierarchies and community and individual empowerment is crucial for creating peaceful environments safe from the cycle of violence and the devastation and trauma it incurs. As a significant social force, schools that make it a priority to empower all members of the community, support connections, and discourage divisiveness will not only prevent violence in their immediate environment, they will also contribute significantly to a more peaceful picture of the twenty-first century. Government response to mass violence in schools must not only support programs to prevent violence and promote self-esteem, but also sustain an adequate recovery process in the event of tragedy.

References

Alberti, R., & Emmons, M. L. (1992). *Your perfect right: A guide to assertive living.* San Luis Obispo, CA: Impact Publishers.

American Psychiatric Association. (1994). *Diagnostic and statistical manual of mental disorders* (4th ed.). Washington, DC: Author.

Angier, N. (1998, December 22). Drugs, sports, body image and G. I. Joe. *New York Times.* Retrieved June 16, 1999 from www.nytimes.com.

Arendt, H. (1970). *On violence.* New York: Harcourt Brace Jovanovich.

Aronowitz, S. (2000). Essay on violence. In S. Spina (Ed.), *Smoke and mirrors: The hidden context of violence in schools and society* (pp. 211–228). New York: Rowman & Littlefield.

Associated Press. (2001, March 5). Bush condemns school shooting. TCPalm.com/news. Retrieved July 17, 2001, from www.tcpalm.com/newsnational.aba.html.

Barron, J. (1999, May 1). Warnings from a student turned killer. *New York Times,* p. A12.

Bernstein, M. (1999, May 30). Kinkel's boyhood troubles explode in rage, destruction. *The Oregonian.* Retrieved May 30, 1999, from www.oregonlive.com/todaysnews/9898/st083003.html.

Blank, J. (1998, October 12). The kid no one noticed, guns would get his classmates' attention. *U.S. News.* Retrieved July 11, 2001, from www.usnews.com.

Blos, P. (1966). *On adolescence: A psychoanalytic interpretation.* New York: Free Press.

Bragg, R. (1998, May 25). Five are killed at school: Boys eleven and thirteen are held. Retrieved March 6, 1999, via Proquest.

Brooke, J. (1999, April 25). Terror in Littleton: The details; Attack at school planned a year, authorities say. *New York Times,* p. A1.

Butterfield, F. (2002, January 26). Father in killing at hockey rink receives 6 to 10 year sentence. *New York Times.* Retrieved December 21, 2002, from www.nytimes.com.

CBC News Online. (2002). 18 die in German school shooting. CBC News. Retrieved September 22, 2002, from http://www.cbc.ca/stories/2002/04/26/germany_shooting020426.

Dedman, B. (1999, June 21). Secret Service is seeking pattern for school killers. *New York Times,* p. A10.

Dob, J. (1998, October 16). D'Amato cites storm aid and Schumer gun control. *New York Times,* p. B5.

Dreyer, E. (2002, March 29). Held hostage. *Chronicle Review,* p. B20.

Fisher, R., & Ury, W. (1981). *Getting to yes: Negotiating agreement without giving in.* New York: Penguin.

Flannigan, S. (1999, August 5). America's Alabama gunman kills three. BBC News Online Network. Retrieved Dec. 14, 2002, from www.news.bbc.co.uk/1/hi/world/americas/413032.stm.

Gardner, H. (2000). *Multiple intelligences: The theory in practice.* New York: Basic Books.

Gastil, J. (1993). *Democracy in small groups: Participation, decision making, and communication.* Philadelphia: New Society Publisher.

Goodman, H. (1997). Social group work in community corrections. *Social Work with Groups, 1,* 51–64.

Gwartney, D. (1998, Oct. 17). Double bind of boys concerns psychologist. *The Oregonian* 2, via Proquest, May 30, 1999.

Hall, S. (1999, 22 August). The bully in the mirror. *New York Times Magazine,* p. 31.

Herman, J. (1997). *Trauma and recovery.* New York: Basic Books.

Holland, G. (1997, October 3). I am not insane, I am angry; Suspect in pearl handed classmate a chilling note. *Sun Herald.* Retrieved October 31, 1999, from www.newslibrary.com/dekuver.com/deliverccdoc.asp?SMH=133002.

Jacobson, M. (2002, May 8). Interview with former Commissioner for New York City Department of Corrections (1995–1998) and Former Commissioner for New York City Department of Probation (1992–1996), New York City.

Janofsky, M. (2001, March 19). Bill on student bullying is considered in Colorado. *New York Times.* Retrieved December 18, 2002, from www.nytimes.com.

Janofsky, M. (2000, April 17). Year later, Columbine is learning to cope while still searching for answers. *New York Times.* Retrieved December 17, 2002, from www.nytimes.com.

Klein, J., & Chancer, L. (2000). Masculinity matters: The role of gender in high-profile school violence cases. In S. Spina (Ed.), *Smoke and mirrors: The hidden context of violence in schools and society* (pp. 129–162). New York: Rowman & Littlefield.

Kindlon, D. J., & Thompson, M. (2000). *Raising Cain: Protecting the emotional life of boys.* New York: Ballantine Books.

Lahad, M., & Cohen, A. (Eds.). (1997). *Community stress prevention, Volumes 1 & 2.* Kiryat Shmona, Israel: CSPC.

Leibovich, L. (1998, March 30). Making sense of Jonesboro. *Salon Magazine: Mothers Who Think.* Retrieved October 31, 1999, from www.salonivorytower.com/nwt/hot/199803/30hot.html.

Lullaby for Columbine. (2002, November 4). *Columbine-Lullaby for Columbine.* Retrieved November 10, 2002, from www.columbinecd.com/guestbook/guestlist.html.

McCurry, M. (1999). School shooting address. Retrieved April 27, 1999, from www.UnitedStatesGovernment/Information/Resource.

Moore, M. (2002). *Bowling for Columbine.* Film. United Artists Alliance Atlantis and Dog Eat Dog Films.

Morris, K. (2001, 24 May). Anti-bully laws are only first step, child experts say. Seattletimes.com. Retrieved May 27, 2001, from http.seattletimes.nwsource.com/html/localnews/134398754 bullying24m0.html.

MSNBC Staff and Wire Reports. (1999, April 24). Note from gunman warns of more violence to come. MSNBC Home. Retrieved April 24, 1999, from www.msnbc.com/news/261055.asp.

Nussbaum, D. (2000, September 3). Becoming fed up with zero tolerance. *New York Times.* Retrieved December 18, 2002, from www.nytimes.com.

Piper, G. (1999, April 20). Crisis teams respond to school shootings. Current News, Disaster News Network. Retrieved November 21, 2002, from www.disasternews.net/news/news.php?articleid=1011.

Popyk, L. (1998, November 9). I knew it wouldn't be right. *Cincinnati Post.* Retrieved June 12, 1999, from www.cincypost.com.

Project SMART (School Mediation and Rehabilitation Through Knowledge). (n.d.). (Training materials from 1989). Victim Services Agency. Community Board Organization funded in part by the New York City Board of Education.

Rodriguez, R. (1998, March 29). The Jonesboro tragedy: Consequences teach a chilling truth. *Los Angeles Times,* Opinion Desk. Retrieved April 23, 1999, via Proquest.

Sack, K. (1999a, May 24). Schools look hard at lockers, shirts, bags and manners. *New York Times.* Retrieved December 17, 2002, from www.nytimes.com.

Sack, K. (1999b, 30 July). Bloody day in Atlanta. *Wichita Eagle.* Retrieved Sept. 19, 1999, from www.witchitaeagle.com/news/nation-world/atlantashoot0730.htm.

Sareen, H. (2001, October). *Reinforcing positive student behavior to prevent school violence.* New York: Vera Institute of Social Justice.

Schiraldi, V. (1998, May 26). Media misleading on school shootings. *The Progressive.* Madison, WI.

School shootings. (2002). Holology, Department of Research. Retrieved November 21, 2002, from www.holology.com/shooting.html.

Schor, M. (2000, September 11). We like to watch: Violent media and violent behavior: What's the link? ABCNews.com. Retrieved July 11, 2001, from www.abcnews.go.com/sections/living/DailyNews/violenceresearch000911.html.

Smallwood, S. (2002, November 15). The deadly risk of giving an F: Murder of 3 professors by a failing student horrifies University of Arizona. *Chronicle of Higher Education, 49,* A12.

Sochet, M. (2000, November). *The nuts and bolts of implementing school safety programs.* Report under contract with the New York City Board of Education. New York: Vera Institute of Justice.

Stolberg, S. G. (1999, May 9). Science looks at Littleton and shrugs. *New York Times,* Week in Review, p. 1.

Stone, C. (1999, November). *Ten rules for making schools safe harbors for learning.* Speech to Annual Institute for Governor's Education Policy Advisors. New York: Vera Institute for Social Justice.

Straussner, J. H., & Straussner, S. L. A. (1997). Impact of community and school violence on children. In N. K. Phillips & S. L. A. Straussner (Eds.), *Children in the urban environment* (pp. 61–77). Springfield, IL: Charles C Thomas.

Swets, P. W. (1987). *The art of talking so that people will listen.* New York: Simon & Schuster.

Talbot, M. (2002, February 24). Girls just want to be mean. *New York Times.* Retrieved December 18, 2002, from www.nytimes.com.

Teenagers charged with plotting to kill in satanic campaign. (1997, October 17). *New York Times.* Retrieved December 21, 2002, from www.nytimes.com.

Thomas, C. (1998, April 1). Revenge of the children in Denver. *Denver Post,* B9.

Turley, L. (1999–2001). Bomb threats and apathy. America Online. Retrieved December 17, 2002, from www.care-nurse.com/columbine/.

U.S. Department of Justice, Bureau of Justice Statistics. *School violence* Retrieved May 11, 2002, from www. Ojp.usdoj.gv/bjs/pub/press/iscs00.pr

Vera Institute of Justice. (1999, August). *Approaches to school safety in America's largest cities.* Prepared for the Lieutenant Governor's Task Force on School Safety. New York: Author.

Verhovek, S. H. (1998, April 18). Texas legislator proposes the death penalty for murderers as young as eleven. *New York Times.* Retrieved March 6, 1999, via Proquest.

Wilgoren, J. (1999, April 25). Society of outcasts began with a $99 coat. *New York Times,* p. A20.

Wilson, J. Q. (1974). Violence, pornography, and social science. In V. B. Cline (Ed.), *Where do you draw the line: An exploration into media violence, pornography, and censorship* (pp. 293–308). Provo, UT: Brigham Young University Press.

6

Mass Violence and the Workplace

Jane E. Cranston

Human-caused disasters resulting from mass violence, such as terrorist attacks, shootings, and bombings of innocent people, have become fairly common throughout the world. In the United States, most people who are directly impacted by mass violence are at their place of work when the event occurs—a fact that is generally overlooked.

In addition to loss of life for some, mass violence can lead to a great number of losses for others, including loss of employment or place of employment. Besides providing the means of acquiring the basic necessities of life, employment provides a sense of satisfaction and self-worth, a role and status in society, intellectual stimulation, a sense of structure, and social interaction (Kurzman & Akabas, 1993). When work suddenly disappears, relocates, or becomes unmanageable due to trauma, the individual loses emotionally as well as economically. For many, trauma and the resulting grieving process impact everyday coping abilities, including job performance and the possibility of job loss (Paul & Masi, 2002).

During the last decade, important lessons have been learned about the impact of mass violence on employees and on the workplace. Since many fear these types of violent incidents will occur again, it is imperative that social workers and other mental health professionals understand the impact of mass violence on the workplace and develop strategies to help employees and employers in times of trauma.

This chapter discusses the reactions of employees and organizations to workplace disaster and the interventions that need to be taken by mental health professionals, employers, and supervisors in order to help people affected by workplace trauma. The term *workplace* will be applied in its broadest sense to include locations where individuals and groups gather to perform tasks and assignments for monetary compensation or other types of rewards. The term *employees* refers to all those who were performing their jobs when disaster struck or in its aftermath. In addition to employees in a specific workplace, it also applies to secondary victims, such as first responders, medical and mental health workers, clergy, volunteers, and those covering the events for the mass media.

The Meaning and Importance of Work

Work provides not only income, but also enhanced feelings of self-worth and social recognition. It adds structure and activity to daily life and provides satisfaction and a sense of accomplishment. Co-workers often become part of one's community and social support system (Kahn, 1981). Profound losses occur when an individual can no longer work because of illness or disability, layoffs, or, as may be the case in incidents of mass violence, when one's place of employment no longer exists. People worry about the lack of income and about their careers. Just as entering the workforce is an important developmental phase, so is being out of work, particularly when unemployment occurs involuntarily (Straussner & Phillips, 1999). It is not unusual for people to reexamine their priorities and career aspirations during such transitional periods.

The events of September 11, 2001, have had a great impact on attitudes toward work and the workplace. The role of one's work and its worth in the scheme of the larger picture of life has become a discussion point around the office water cooler, in the mass media, and in the therapist's office. There has been a greater appreciation of the work of first responders, such as firefighters, police officers, and emergency medical personnel, as well as mental health workers. The workplace environment has also become less naïve. Physical barricades and other visible security measures have become established, and many workers are required to provide identification in order to enter their workplace. While some see these measures as an inconvenience, others feel that they offer a greater sense of security and comfort while at work.

Violence in the Workplace

The Department of Justice estimates that there are more than one million episodes of occupational violent crime each year (Jossi, 1999; Kelleher, 1996), costing the consumer over $36 billion annually (Jossi, 1999). Assaults in the workplace account for almost 15 percent of all violent acts in the country (Valliere, 2001). According to the U.S. Department of Labor, Bureau of Labor Statistics (2002) there were 5,900 work-related fatalities in the year 2001 (this number does not include those killed as a result of the attacks of September 11, 2001). Eleven percent of all workplace fatalities (639 persons) were homicides, second only to transportation accidents (roadway, air, and rail) among work-related deaths. The leading motive for workplace murder was robbery, with workers in the retail industry comprising one-half of all the homicide victims (Occupational Safety and Health Administration, 2002). Although women comprise almost half of the United States workforce, men, because of the nature of the industries in which they work, such as transportation and construction, are more than ten times as likely to be killed on the job. Despite the fact that women are less likely to be killed in the workplace, more than 30 percent of the 471 job-related fatalities among women were the results of assault or violent acts, making murder the leading killer of women on the job (OSHA, 2002).

While the numbers of those killed in the workplace during any given year are high, they pale in relation to the over 3,000 people who were killed in less than two hours on

September 11, 2001. Most of those killed were at work, en route to their place of employment, or working as first responders. This one-day tragedy represented more than half of all the workplace deaths for the entire previous year in the United States. In New York City alone, nearly 2,900 people were killed, and an additional 25,000 workers in the buildings were evacuated and survived these attacks. At the same time, the striking of the Pentagon in Washington, DC, killed 189 people in the airplane and on the ground. Soon after, 53 passengers, many of them traveling on business, and 6 crewmembers on United Airlines Flight 93, en route from Newark Airport to San Francisco, crashed in Shanksville, Pennsylvania, in an aborted hijacking attempt to crash the plane into the White House.

Previous incidents, such as the 1993 bombing in the basement of one of the towers of the World Trade Center that killed six people and forced the evacuation of 50,000 individuals (U.S. Fire Administration [USFA], 1993), and the 1995 bombing of the Alfred P. Murrah Federal Building in Oklahoma City, when 168 of the building's occupants were killed and 853 injured, would later be viewed as missed opportunities to prepare for future catastrophes in the workplace.

Typologies of Workplace Violence

Violence in the workplace is often classified into two categories: *internal violence*—employee versus employee—and *external violence*—violence initiated by those outside the organization (Liou, 1999). While most incidents of workplace violence occur between individuals known to each other, mass violence is primarily, but not exclusively, external.

Kurtz and Turbin (1999) have developed a typology that describes the most common types of work environment violence from the perspective of the perpetrator's relationship to the company, business, school, or other workplace. It is divided into four categories:

- Type I: The violence is accidental and occurs while an individual is in the process of committing another crime. There is no known connection between the perpetrator, the workers, or the organization. For example, a homicide might occur when a store robbery "goes wrong" and the robber kills the victim(s) in the process of stealing money or merchandise. This type of violence places store workers and customers at high risk. In the year 2000, almost one-half of all homicides occurred in retail businesses (OSHA, 2002).
- Type II: The perpetrator has some relationship with the business or organization, but is not an employee. He or she may be a client in a clinic or company, a patient of a hospital (nearly two-thirds of all nonfatal assaults occur in the health care industry) (Jossi, 1999), or an inmate in a correctional facility. An example of this type of violence can be seen in the 1971 uprising in Attica, a New York State prison, in which 42 people, including 10 prison employees who were held as hostages, were killed.
- Type III: The perpetrator is a disgruntled current or past employee of the business. Although this type of violence receives significant media attention, it is not common, and only 5 to 7 percent of all on-the-job homicides involve a disgruntled employee (DeLaurier, 2001). Mass killings in U.S. Postal Service facilities are often cited as examples, in spite of the fact that studies indicate that post office facilities

are some of the safest places to work, with postal workers being only one-third as likely to be murdered on the job as other workers (National Center on Addiction and Substance Abuse at Columbia University [CASA], 2000). However, media coverage of these occurrences have resulted in a skewed perception of post offices as dangerous workplaces—so much so that "doing a postal" and "going postal" have entered the vernacular as a way to describe the behavior of an employee who shoots his or her current or former co-workers and/or supervisor.

- Type IV: The perpetrator knows his or her victim but has no connection to the workplace or organization. This type of violence is often a continuation of chaos in the worker's life; over 25 percent of female victims of workplace homicide are assaulted by people they know, be it a partner, former partner, family member, or co-worker. Domestic violence that is carried into the workplace, often referred to as intimate partner violence and described as an assault by a current or former husband or boyfriend, accounts for 16 percent of female victims of job-related homicides (NIOSH, n.d.). Typically, the male perpetrator comes to his partner's place of employment seeking revenge or attempting to harass and in the process kills. While the target of the attack may be the spouse or partner, co-workers and supervisors are often harmed, especially when they attempt to intervene. Such incidents are often minimized and receive little public attention because employers want to avoid publicity. Fewer than half of violent acts in the workplace are reported to the police (Valliere, 2001) and, as is often the case with domestic violence, the victim is often held responsible for the outcome.

None of the above four types accurately describe the perpetrators of mass violence in the workplace. Therefore, an additional category, analogous to Liou's category of external violence, is needed. This category would include deliberate and purposeful acts from those outside the organization, aimed at a workplace that has specific symbolic significance, such as the attack on the Pentagon in Washington, DC, on September 11, 2001. This form of violence generally results in the highest number of victims and has greater social impact than other forms of workplace violence.

Reactions to Workplace Violence

Mass violence generally occurs without warning, presents serious threats to personal and organization safety, and is gruesome in its results. In order to provide appropriate interventions, it is important to understand not only the reactions of individuals to such violence, but also the reactions of the organizations and the community.

Reactions of Individuals

A research study, funded by the National Institute of Mental Health (NIMH), of 182 adult survivors directly exposed (within 200 meters of the explosion) to the April 1995 Oklahoma City bombing who were interviewed between four and nine months after the incident, found that 45 percent of the subjects had a "postdisaster psychiatric disorder" (North et al. 1999, p. 1). Thirty-four percent of those surveyed were diagnosed with posttraumatic stress disorder, and 22.5 percent with a major depressive episode. Anxiety and/or substance abuse were also seen in percentages significantly above the general population (North et al., 1999). A nationwide telephone survey conducted by Schuster et al. (2002) within five to seven days after September 11, 2001, interviewed 768 randomly selected adults using five screening questions based on information gained from survivors of the Oklahoma City bombing. The Schuster survey found that 44 percent of adults reported at least one of the five most common symptoms: (1) experiencing distress with reminders of the event, (2) trouble concentrating, (3) vivid memories of the event, (4) difficulty sleeping, and (5) feeling irritable. People who were in close proximity to the event site, those with fear of another attack—younger individuals, women, and persons with high levels of television viewing hours of the events—were more likely to report symptoms (Marshall, 2001). The fact that so many people were able to witness the events of September 11, 2001, live and repeatedly on television contributed to the magnitude and geographic breath of trauma not seen previously with other disasters (Schuster et al., 2001; Marshall, 2002).

Some typical reactions experienced by adult survivors, witnesses, and rescue and relief workers involved in mass violence in the workplace include:

- *Emotional reactions,* such as sorrow, shock, a sense of hopelessness, powerlessness, and emptiness, anhedonia, and disinterest.
- *Cognitive reactions,* including difficulty concentrating, confusion, worry, short-term memory loss, or intrusive memories.
- *Physical reactions,* such as fatigue, insomnia, changes in appetite, and aches and pain.
- *Interpersonal reactions,* including conflict, withdrawal, high need for control, and feelings of rejection. (Lewis, 1994)

Impact of Mass Violence on First Responders. Each of the above four reactions interferes with one's ability to work. However, their impact becomes particularly apparent when they affect those people working as first responders to the scene of the incident. Often the needs of first responders get lost in the drama of their heroic acts. Yet, these workers may experience conflicts between their survival instinct to flee and their sense of commitment to do their job helping others. It is interesting to note that while firefighters working at the Oklahoma City disaster site were less likely than either survivors or witnesses to suffer from PTSD, the incidents of alcohol abuse for the firefighters prior to, during, and following the bombing was significantly higher than among survivors or other witnesses of the bombing (North, 2002).

Impact of Mass Violence on Employees in the Workplace. Witnessing the behavior of co-workers or supervisors during an incident of mass violence may impact future relationships among workers and between the worker and the organization. Residual positive or guilt feelings may persist if a person has seen a co-worker risk his or her own life in a valiant attempt to help others. On the other hand, seeing a co-worker push others aside in an attempt to escape may lead to long-term negative reactions.

Workers may also feel angry at their organizations and management, which, they believe, should have provided better protection for them. Such anger may be expressed directly or it may be acted out in job performance (Fitzgerald, 1999). Workers may feel anger about poor or missed communication by management or about limited or delayed compensation and benefits to victims and survivors. The push to return to work rather than being allowed time to grieve may also impact workers' attitudes toward the employer. Such negative feelings about the workplace may spread to other employees, resulting in a dysfunctional work environment.

A survey described in July/August 2002 *EAP Association Exchange,* a publication of the Employee Assistance Professionals Association, of thirty-six organizations, two-thirds of which had offices located close to the attack sites of September 11, 2001, found increased anxiety among employees with regard to terrorism, unwillingness or fear of travel, and greater expressions of emotions at work as a result of the events of September 11th (Paul & Masi, 2002).

Survivor's Guilt. Survivor's guilt is a common reaction seen in those who have survived a natural or human-caused disaster or atrocity while others died. In the workplace, these individuals may ask themselves, "Why did my friend/colleague die and not me?" They question their self-worth and may feel the burden to make their lives more meaningful (U.S. Department of Health and Human Services, n.d.). People may come to regret not getting to know the deceased better or the lost opportunity to express their feelings to him or her. Others wonder if they should have done more to save those who died, or become angry with colleagues who went back to help and perished.

According to Fitzgerald (1999), "guilt is an isolating emotion" (p. 38). Survivors may feel it inappropriate to feel good and enjoy themselves, so the normal joking or banter in everyday work situations may cease, creating an ongoing solemn, joyless, and depressed atmosphere. Some feel overwhelmed and burdened with the additional work they now have to complete, yet may feel guilty in expressing their resentment. Some employees may find the situation intolerable and choose to resign, while others begin to develop a variety of psychological and/or physical symptoms, including the abuse of alcohol and other drugs, further impacting on their job performance, family cohesiveness, and their sense of self-esteem and well-being (Fitzgerald, 1999).

Gender Differences in Responding to Trauma. When attempting to understand the needs of employees impacted by mass violence, issues of gender must be taken into consideration. Corporate culture, in general, strongly discourages outward expressions of emotion other than controlled, verbal anger. Such dynamics are more suitable to men, who are more likely to adjust to the aftermath of trauma by focusing on work-related goals and who may pressure other employees to resume the task at hand as a way of coping (Ellin, 2001; Staudacher, 1991).

Harper (n.d.) contends that men have developed four coping activities that are acceptable to both them and the male-oriented work environment: (1) keeping their pain to themselves, (2) solitary grieving, (3) attempting to bring control through action—such as physical or legal action, and (4) intense involvement with work or home activities. For example, following the 2001 World Trade Center disaster, many male police officers and firemen attempted to cope with their grief by returning to the disaster site on their days off, going to the homes of fallen co-workers to perform home repairs, or taking on the responsibilities as a surrogate parent for the children of those who died (Ellin, 2001).

Norris (2001) reviewed the research involving 50,000 victims of disaster. It was found that women, in general, showed stronger, and longer lasting, psychological effects of trauma than did men. Women are more likely to seek treatment for their psychological distress from their primary care physicians, mental health workers, or peer support groups (Norris, 2001). Women have "broader and deeper social networks" (Nolen-Hoeksema & Larson, 1999, p. 93), and it is culturally more acceptable for them to express their emotions both verbally and physically, especially with other women. In addition, women demonstrate appreciation and inform others of their gratitude for support more than their male counterparts, thus establishing an ongoing means of connecting through dialogue rather than action (Nolen-Hoeksema & Larson, 1999).

Reactions of Organizations

Communal bereavement (Talbot, 2001), which implies a shared state of distress and diminished sense of well-being and safety, can occur within a workplace community even when the individuals involved may not have had personal ties to victims. Thus, employees of the same or similar organizations in distant cities, with no direct link to the affected employees, may experience grief responses that are similar to individuals who were personally impacted by mass violence. However, they may not have access to the kind of organized supports available to those who are more directly impacted, and consequently their needs may not be addressed without special outreach by their organizations (Talbot, 2001).

Incidence of mass violence in the workplace can produce many types of losses. Besides the most traumatic—the death of a co-worker, supervisor, and/or senior manager—employees may also have to cope with a change in workplace relocation, shifts in leadership, and integration of new members to the team. Separation anxiety is a disorder generally seen in infants, children, and adolescents and described as the cognitive and emotional reaction to impending loss (Astrachan, 1990). Similar coping mechanisms, however, have been observed in the behavior of individual adults and work groups in companies where major shifts have been forced upon organizations due to catastrophic events (Astrachan, 1990). Projection of feelings of anger and resentment onto survivors, company heads, or new hires is not uncommon. Employees may use denial to deal with their grief, sense of betrayal, and loss of trust (Reina & Reina, 1999). Some workers may refuse to come to work, and others are unable to leave or refuse to work alone as conflicts in attachment are felt. A sense of helplessness, with its accompanying loss of productivity and error making, may be visible even in the best of performers. Negative projection—the blaming of others for one's inabilities or shortcomings—and suspiciousness may increase as individuals and groups of people try and find explanations for unfamiliar and intolerable thoughts and behaviors. Stress-caused illnesses and somatization are common.

Organizations need to be prepared for, and respond to, "searching behavior," which is often demonstrated by people in grief (Clark, 1987). Repetitive thoughts of the lost ones and a longing for the sense of community or familiar physical surroundings can lead workers to try to recreate a physical space or an old work routine that is no longer functional. Moreover, in an attempt to remain connected, grieving employees may seek solace from objects that remind them of what was, whether a destroyed structure or individuals who died. Consequently, decisions such as relocation of the business or how long to keep personal property, furniture, or business materials of deceased individuals become highly charged emotionally. Anniversary dates also evoke painful memories and emotions that may disrupt the workplace. Such reactions should be anticipated and addressed appropriately, allowing survivors and families to remember, yet also permitting people to move on. Managers with a "let's get back to work" approach may be using activity as their own way of dealing with the situation, blinding them to the true needs of their staff. Those in positions of authority would serve, and better serve themselves, if they could demonstrate leadership by openly acknowledging the situation and its consequences, continuously take the pulse of the group with a high level of visibility, active listening, and expressions of support and understanding actions (Reina & Reina, 1999).

The events of September 11th presented some unique intellectual and emotional challenges to employers and employees. One workplace culture particularly impacted was the investment community collectively referred to as Wall Street. Known for its fast-paced, quick decision making, "right stuff," never-show-your-hand mentality, this was not a culture that presents itself as compassionate and people-focused. Yet, the magnitude of the trauma during and in the aftermath of that day, with its enormous loss of life, destruction of property and organizations, presented an opportunity for some to push themselves to creative and emotional limits. In the October 2002 issue of the *Harvard Business Review,* Jeffrey Greenberg, Chairman of Marsh & McLennan Companies, a global professional services firm of 58,000 employees headquartered in New York City, recalled standing with co-workers at the windows of their midtown Manhattan office watching the attacks unfold. He and his colleagues were keenly aware that over 1,900 of their company's employees and visitors were in the Towers and on floors very close to the impact sites. Many in this tight-knit business sector also worried about relatives, friends, clients, and former co-workers whom they knew to be in the buildings. Though unspoken at the time, they also were acutely aware of their own vulnerability.

Using the combat term "fog of war," Greenberg (2002, p. 59) described the facts and sensations of being unable to contact his presumably helpless World Trade Center employees. Telephone lines had failed and public access to the area was forbidden. Suddenly people accustomed to relying on hard data to make business decisions were forced to collect sporadic and conflicting information from eyewitnesses, television, and e-mails. A response team was quickly assembled. Seniority and title took a back seat to expertise and availability. Communication with staff became a priority and a communication center was quickly established. Telephone banks and e-mails provided twice a day updates for employees and families, whether there was new news or not. A message wall started to accumulate a list of the missing. It would later record the loss of 295 people. Two days later an offsite family assistance center was opened. Human Resources professionals from other locations arrived at headquarters. Retirees, directors, and members of the business community volunteered. All the while the onsite clinical staff noted the employees' hypervigilant responses, with those present testing their knowledge of fire stair locations, discovering and using the emergency public address system, and regularly checking the sky for any air traffic.

One year after the events, Mr. Greenberg shared some observations that appear applicable to most workplace environments and useful to social workers assisting organizations, working within Employee Assistance Plans (EAPs) or in private practice. He ranks an organization's commitment to its people, employees, and customers as the essence of the organization and the key to its survival. He stresses the need for a voice of authority—someone visibly in charge—who has a group of advisors willing and able to assess the circumstances and make decisions. He also stressed the importance of a company culture and tapping into strength of that culture in times of crisis. This means following the established standards of behavior, using a common vocabulary, and emphasizing a sense of belonging, regardless of employee location or position. The ability to adapt is seen as essential. This can mean openness to alter crisis management plans to meet the immediate needs, such as increasing the levels and methods of communication, as well as a willingness to recognize poor or inappropriate decisions. In the case of Marsh & McLennan, it involved rethinking and adjusting victims' family health benefits after many families expressed discontent. The firm also provided some very concrete services to the families of victims, including the assignment of a relationship manager for each family, counseling through the EAP, extended compensation and health benefits, financial assistance and counseling, advocacy with government agencies and the Congress, remembrance in the form of a memorial service, an electronic message board and web site, as well as plans for a permanent memorial.

Interventions

As pointed out by Naomi Naierman, President of the American Hospice Foundation, "We never quite get over grief; the point is how we manage it" (quoted in Duff, 1999, p. 1). Following mass trauma, there is a need to normalize the grieving process by publicly acknowledging it as a healthy and acceptable response, and by validating what people are feeling and the way they are behaving (Weick, 2001). Naierman is again quoted as saying "in an era when personal matters are aired freely at work, grieving remains in the closet" (Duff, 1999, p. 2). This was vividly illustrated when the CEO of an investment organization that lost 700 of its one thousand employees in the 2001 World Trade Center tragedy, cried openly on national television. His extraordinary behavior became front-page news. Surviving employees and the public seemed grateful for a voice for their emotions. Such openness by a high-level executive often creates a new organizational value and a context that allows people to talk about what happened, share their sorrow, acknowledge loss, and express concerns and fears (Dutton et al., 2002).

Open and honest responses also lead to a shift in the perception of the value of mental health services by the workforce. The stigma of talking with a counselor in an EAP, attending a critical incident debriefing session, or revealing that one was seeking professional help lessens as organizations provide, and openly encourage, people to seek professional help. As a striking example, following the attacks on September 11th, the New York City Police Department required all of its 55,000 employees to attend mental health counseling sessions. Group sessions, some in "town hall" settings or informal discussion groups, co-led by professionals and peer counselors, were supplemented with a confidential telephone helpline and referral service for employees and their families. In addition, the Police Department sponsored a health fair for families where issues and concerns could be aired and addressed (Jones, 2001).

Organizational Responses

In cases of mass trauma, organizations must assume responsibility not only for the survival of their institution, but also for the well-being of their employees. As indicated by Paul and Masi (2002), companies are often ill prepared to communicate with their employees in a rapid and effective manner and need to better understand and deal with people's responses and reactions to traumatic events. Companies need assistance in formal planning for future terrorist attacks, how best to delegate responsibilities for internal services, and how to best support staff.

Structures to Provide Mental Health Services in the Workplace. Organizations that have experienced acts of violence or other traumatic events often turn to their existing Employee Assistance Programs (EAPs), Member Assistance Programs (MAPs), and Human Resources (HR) departments for help with the emotional and concrete needs of their employees. All of these service providers play a crucial role during mass violence.

An *Employee Assistance Program, or EAP,* can be an internal component of an organization or operate as an external, contractual service. Their purpose is to assist employees with work and personal concerns that interfere with their job performance (Straussner, 1990). These programs are often staffed with social workers, psychologists, or other professionals, as well as substance abuse counselors. EA programs and services, which are usually short-term in nature, are funded or paid for by the company and are free to the employees, and sometimes to their immediate family members. Although sponsored by the organization, the services delivered by EAPs are confidential and information about the employee is generally not shared with the employer (Straussner, 1990). EAPs may also provide consulting services to supervisors and the work organization.

Member or Union Assistance Programs (MAPs or UAPs) are funded by unions and/or membership organizations and offer similar services to their members and their families as those provided by the EAPs. Many MAPs/UAPs are staffed with members who may or may not be professionally trained in the field of mental health, thus the quality of service provision may vary.

Human Resources departments administer the hiring, termination, and performance measurement process of employees. In addition, they may determine and administer death, disability, and other benefits to employees and their beneficiaries—a crucial, and often emotionally difficult, service following incidents of mass violence.

The Critical Incident Stress Debriefing (CISD) Model of Intervention. During times of mass violence, staffs of the EAP, MAP/UAP, or HR department, as well as staff of outside consulting firms hired to assist in special or emergency situations, are often called upon to provide immediate help to employees and management. One of the most frequently used interventions during such circumstances is the Critical Incident Stress Debriefing (CISD) model. Although the efficacy of one session, or the immediate use of the psychological or stress debriefing, a more generic term, or critical incident stress debriefings, a specific model, is being questioned, it remains a popular intervention tool (American Psychiatric Association, n.d.).

Among the specific clinical challenges experienced by social workers and other clinicians in responding to incidents of mass violence is the use of single debriefing sessions with large numbers of participants. Since the attacks of September 11th, the debate regarding the short-term value and efficacy of CISD interventions has escalated. Those who advocate for its use speak to the benefits of immediate intervention, education, and the sharing experience as well as the practicality of reaching large numbers of people in a short amount of time (NCPTSD, 2001). Opponents point out that the CISD model was originally developed for first responders, and its widespread use may be inappropriate for some survivors and secondary witnesses. Some claim that debriefing may hinder natural recovery and actually heighten arousal (Mayou, Ehlers, & Hobbs, 2000). Concern is expressed that the professionals delivering the program are not always properly or sufficiently trained in it and that participants may not be suitable, the timing maybe inappropriate, or employers may see the technique as a substitute for needed counseling or psychotherapy (NCPTSD, 2001).

Specific training and skills in the CISD model, defusing techniques, and similar crisis management skills are necessary for providing these interventions. Social workers and other professionals need to work with department heads and staffs to ensure that the needs of individuals are met while respecting the role and culture of the organization. In addition to working with employees, the professionals are often simultaneously training supervisors and management on the signs and symptoms of trauma and grief, helping leaders with their own trauma, as well as coaching them in assisting reluctant employees to seek the services they need.

A clinical social worker employed by an external EAP, who provided mental health services to survivors and families in both Oklahoma City and the 2001 World Trade Center attacks, pointed out how different this type of clinical work is from the type and manner of services generally given by an EAP. For example, because of the high and immediate demand, debriefing and support groups are generally led by a single clinician rather than having the traditionally recommended co-leaders. Moreover, there is limited time for clinicians to debrief one another before returning to lead additional groups and less chance for them to refresh themselves physically and emotionally. These circumstances can contribute to emotional burnout or compassion fatigue for the clinician (Gillespie, 1987).

Clinicians based in the workplace may experience additional challenges. For example, a social worker in a Human Resources department found herself facilitating a debriefing group in which her immediate supervisor was a participant. The resulting mutual discomfort may have deprived the supervisor of the sense of privacy she deserved and certainly placed added performance pressure on the group leader. Another social worker had to deal with his own trauma of having barely survived a terrorist attack while at the same time facilitating the debriefing process of his co-workers.

Clinicians need to be aware that some employees and managers may be reluctant to show vulnerability, especially in a group setting, for fear of being seen as weak or incompetent. For many, this is their first experience with professional mental health services, and the stigma of being viewed as needy or mentally ill if they accept such help prevails. Referring to group sessions as "debriefing," "support groups," or "counseling," rather than "therapy," and having a detailed script or role-play before an actual session, enhanced with printed educational materials, provides an extra level of structure and security for clients and clinicians (Taffel, 2001).

Organizational Compassion. Studies done by the CompassionLab (n.d.), a research collaboration between the University of Michigan and the University of British Columbia, show the enormous impact of "organizational compassion" (Dutton et al., 2002). Those organizations that openly acknowledge the challenges of dealing with trauma, show good faith effort, and engage employees in finding solutions are rewarded with a high level of commitment and sense of duty from their employees (Hoffman, 2001). Following mass violence, organizations need to keep survivors and their families informed and connected through extensive, round-the-clock communication efforts and provide survivor helplines via e-mail, websites, and television and radio spots (Fitzgerald, 1999). Time off to attend wakes, funerals, and memorial services needs to be made available. Symbolic gestures and rituals, such as onsite religious services, memorials, and remembrance days help survivors say goodbye and have powerful and long-lasting effects (Griffin, 2001). Such expressions of compassion help to strengthen employees' resolve and establish connections among the staff members as well as with the organization (Dutton et al., 2002).

On the other hand, organizations that do not handle this responsibility in a manner acceptable to its employees are faced with unforgiving workers who will not forget and often respond with lower productivity, higher turnover, reduced loyalty, and the incursion of increased medical and mental health expenses for the company (Duff, 1999; Hoffman, 2001; Tyler, 2000).

Facilitating Remembrances. Employees and management need to anticipate, tolerate, and encourage references and remembrances of lost individuals. For example, when faced with the enormous challenge of writing about those killed in the 2001 World Trade Center attack, the editors of the *New York Times* Metro Section designed "Portraits of Grief." This daily presentation, in the form of 200-word sketches, remembered over 2,000 of those who died. No person's life received more or less prominence, and personal characteristics and anecdotes were featured over professional accomplishments. During a radio interview, Executive Editor Howell Raines told of the enormous response the newspaper received for this remembrance, not only from its readers but also from other staff members. The newspaper would receive the Pulitzer Prize for its efforts. The work proved so powerful that over 180 of the newspaper's writers, including some of its most notable figures, volunteered as contributors without a byline. In addition to honoring those who died and providing information to a grieving public, the project allowed staff members at the newspaper a means of using their talents to express their own grief. It proved to be cathartic for this group of people who prided themselves as "objective, professional observers," while providing them with a meaningful "way to give back to the community" (Cotter, 2002, p. E33).

Other forms of creative and artistic expressions can also be useful to express individual and communal grief. These may include writings in company newsletters, murals, photography exhibits, volunteer days, and quilt projects. They can serve to help people to continue to remember while also moving on with their lives (Cotter, 2002).

Formation of Internal Response Teams. Some corporations and government agencies have taken it upon themselves to develop their own internal crisis response teams. For example, in 1996, Eastman Kodak, an organization with a domestic workforce of 45,000 employees, formed an internal Critical Incident Stress Management team, consisting of an emergency medical technician, occupational nurse, security professional, EAP counselor, and a physician (Volpe, 2001). The team is prepared to assist co-workers in the event of an incident of mass violence, as well as provide help if there is a death of an employee at work or following an industrial accident. It is also prepared to assist and educate supervisors and managers during the aftermath.

Social workers and other helping professionals providing workplace interventions to victims and survivors of mass violence must be mindful of the challenges to take care of themselves in order to help others. They also need to establish clear reporting relationships so that clients understand who the social worker is and their relationship with the organization by stating "I am a social worker hired by your organization" or " I work for your Member Assistance Program." Knowing sources of referral within companies, understanding the organization's hierarchy, learning which department is in charge of providing services (it could be Human Resources, the Employee Assistance Program, or top management), being trained in debriefing, trauma, and grief work, and obtaining clinical supervision during and after working with trauma survivors are all essential aspects of workplace intervention.

The role that the American Psychiatric Association has played in launching the National Partnership for Workplace Mental Health with leading U.S. employers (National Partnership for Workplace Mental Health, n.d.) needs to be examined and possibly duplicated from a social work perspective. We need to look for new opportunities to serve, as well as continue the work to help remove the stigma placed on the use of social and mental health services in the world of work.

Government Responses

The day of the Murrah Building bombing in Oklahoma City, the Oklahoma City Compassion Center, a family assistance program locally known as "The Center," was established for a period of sixteen days. Initially, The Center served as the conduit for death notification of next of kin, as well as a means of providing information—the Medical Examiner's Office instructed loved ones as to the types of information that would be required to identify the dead and search for the missing, and funeral directors were present to assist family members of victims with making arrangements. Officials attempted to protect families from the media deluge that was quickly forming. Soon after, the American Red Cross became the administrator of the program, adding mental health counselors, emergency relief services, comfort, and support. Families were kept informed of rescue and recovery efforts with updates twice a day. A "family room" acted as a safe haven, meal station, and telephone service for grieving survivors and families.

The efforts later evolved into Project Heartland, a multidiscipline, multiphased program that provided both immediate and long-term crisis intervention, support, education, and outreach services to survivors and their families, medical and rescue workers, volunteers, and others requesting help. This project was funded by the Federal Emergency Management Agency (FEMA). Functioning as part of Oklahoma's Department of Mental Health and Substance Abuse Services, Project Heartland was "the first community mental health response to a large-scale terrorist event in the United States" (U.S. Department of Justice, 2000, p. 8). In its first year, Project Heartland provided direct counseling services and group education to 40,000 specific cases (Flynn, 1996). Policy recommendations were developed and published addressing the roles and responsibilities of federal, state, and local governments with regard to victim assistance.

This experience with successful interventions following the Oklahoma City tragedy was helpful to professionals in their response to the shootings at Columbine High School (Owens, 2001) and with the preparations of family members observing the trial of the accused bombers of Pan Am Flight 103 (USDJ, 2000). In the publication "Responding to Terrorism Victims: Oklahoma City and Beyond" (USDJ, 2000), specific recommendations were made and adapted, including a protocol for viewing the trial, supporting victims who were to testify and assisting them with the aftermath of legal decisions, separating families from defendants, and developing ways of keeping survivors updated on proceeding and decisions.

Oklahoma City's Project Heartland also developed recommendations to assist workers with their reintegration into the workplace following the mass trauma. Among the suggestions was the need to include supervisors and EAPs in creating a plan for impacted workers "with special attention given to the types of assignments, the work environment, and timing" (USDJ, 2000, p. 36). The Project staff found that just because people return to the workplace does not necessarily mean they are capable of performing at the same level as they did prior to the trauma. Consequently, the division of tasks may have to be rearranged, deadlines reassessed, and the environment adjusted, particularly if the worksite is near the site of the traumatic incident. Contact and communication from management needs to increase, along with opportunities for privacy. Supervisors must be alert to employees who seem depressed, and while it is not the supervisors' responsibility to diagnoses employees, they do need to encourage staff members to seek help.

Workplace Policies

Among the many lessons learned from the incidents of mass violence is the need for trauma-related policies and explicit organizational procedures. Most organizations have elaborate plans for the protection of property, but few organizations imagine, no less prepare for, the havoc wreaked by incidents of mass violence (USDJ, 2000).

Numerous questions have been raised following September 11, 2001: Should all employees of an organization be located at a single site? Are there safety plans for people with disabilities, from the physically handicapped to the developmentally disabled? How does the organization deal with what Pauline Boss (1999) refers to as "ambiguous loss"—when there is no evidence that the person is alive or dead? When the fate of victims is unknown, or there are numerous losses, current employee procedures may not adequately meet the needs. Plans must be established to determine who will contact the missing or deceased's family members, and in what manner, and how to inform or update co-workers in order to reduce rumor or speculation. Organizations, moreover, have to question their traditional procedures. For example, since the World Trade Center disaster, the New York City Fire Department is questioning its "First In, Last Out" tradition where the highest-ranking member of a unit is the first to enter the scene of a disaster and is the last to leave. Does the leader always have to be in the most danger, or does this type of policy actually put everyone at greater risk? they ask. Should off-duty personnel be allowed to participate, or does their presence only contribute to the chaos and ultimately result in additional lives lost?

Many organizations lack bereavement policies to address multiple deaths (Fitzgerald, 1999). For example, how is the "immediate family" defined for purposes of providing benefits ranging from bereavement leave to emergency funds and other compensation? Tyler (2000) found that while many bereavement leave policies of government organizations and private businesses included domestic partners, most did not address what is generally referred to as "common law marriages" or persons raised by friends or relatives other than their biological parents. Tyler (2000) has suggested that all policies add provisions allowing for some flexibility by stating, "bereavement leave may also be granted because of the death of an individual whose close association with the employee is the equivalent of a family relationship." She found that where such leave privileges exist, their abuse "is virtually nonexistent" (p. 4).

Conclusion

The Chinese ideogram for "crisis" is the joining of the words "disaster" and "opportunity." The pain and loss caused by incidents of mass violence have greatly impacted the social fiber of the local, national, and global community. In the past, citizens of the United States, for the most part, have been isolated from acts of terrorism and the long-term consequences that result. High levels of personal freedom, an unquestioned sense of physical security, along with an extraordinary level of privacy, are basic tenets of the American way of life. Going to work may have involved the hassles of commuting, the stress of competition, demand for high productivity, and a need to keep pace with technology, but it was never cause for uneasiness that one might be harmed, or worse, killed. The workplace was a safe haven, for some even safer than the home or neighborhood in which they lived. It took incidents of mass proportions to shake these fundamental assumptions and to radically change the everyday activities at places of employment. It has also provided a rare opportunity to recalibrate priorities and adjust perspectives.

Following the mass violence of September 11, 2001, mental health services have been offered in the workplace in record numbers and utilized by a broad segment of the workforce with less stigma and a greater appreciation of their value. Public grieving, open responses to trauma, and questioning of one's purpose and direction have become somewhat more acceptable office topics. Leaders in the workplace have come to realize that their responsibilities to their workers are shifting; cutting a paycheck is not enough. The concept of what constitutes a safe workplace has been expanded, with violence prevention given an even higher priority. The issue of ethnic and racial diversity in the workplace has been forced into the open as people look to blame and scapegoat in order to cope with their anger and grief.

The role of social workers in dealing with mass trauma in the workplace is to help the individuals and the workplace communities move forward, but also not to forget. Even in the midst of our personal grieving we must help others feel their losses and rebuild. There is opportunity for mental health services to join together as a high functioning, well-integrated community with a full menu of complementary services. Social work needs to continue to build relationships with the business community, unions, and other organizations in order to become an integral part of the workplace. Social workers have an opportunity to remain present in the workplace and influence policy and procedures.

References

American Psychiatric Association. (n.d.) Public Information. The Debriefing Debate. Retrieved January 3, 2002, from www.psych.org/public_info/debriefingdebate92801.cfm.

Astrachan, J. H. (1990). *Mergers, acquisitions and employee anxiety: A study of separation anxiety in a corporate context.* New York: Greenwood.

Boss, P. (May 1999). *Ambiguous loss: Learning to live with unresolved grief.* Cambridge, MA: Harvard University Press.

Clark, E. J. (1987). Bereaved persons have rights that should be respected [Electronic version]. In A. Kutscher, A. Carr, & L. Kutscher (Eds.), *Principles of thanatology* (pp. 82–96). New York: Columbia University. Retrieved January 22, 2002, from www.naswdc.org/t/clark.htm.

CompassionLab. (n.d.). *Leadership and compassion.* Retrieved January 10, 2002, from www.bus.umich.edu/learning/Leadership_and_Compassion.htm

Cotter, H. (2002, February 1,). Amid the ashes, creativity. *New York Times,* p. E33.

DeLaurier, G. F. (2001). Dying to serve you: Violence in the retail workplace [Electronic version]. *Dollars & Sense, 237,* 27–29.

Duff, S. (1999, July 1999). Unresolved grief can be costly. *Employee Benefit News, 13,* 1–2.

Dutton, J. E., Frost, P. J., Worline, M. C., Lilius, J. M., & Kanov, J. M. (2002). Leading in times of trauma. *Harvard Business Review, 78,* 54–61.

Ellin, A. (2001, September 30). Traumatized workers look for healing on the job. *New York Times,* p. 32.

Fitzgerald, H. (1999). *Grief at work: A manual of policies and practices.* Washington, DC: American Hospice Foundation.

Flynn, B. W. (1996, April 24–25). *Psychological aspects of terrorism.* The Center for Mental Health Services. Presented at First Harvard Symposium on the Medical Consequences of Terrorism. Retrieved December 18, 2001, from www.mentalhealth.org/newsroom/speeches/terrorispeech.asp

Gillespie, D. (1987). *Burn-out among social workers.* New York: Haworth.

Greenberg, J. (2002). September 11, 2001—a CEO's story. *Harvard Business Review, 80,* 58–64.

Griffin, P. Y. (2001). After disaster: Helping with personal recovery. *Consulting Today,* Special edition, 1–2.

Harper, J. M. (n.d.). Men and grief. Retrieved January 22, 2002, from www.griefnet.org/library/mengrief.html.

Hoffman, C. (2001). Responding to workplace trauma. *Trauma Response, VII,* 14–15.

Jones, L. (2001, Nov. 30). A national challenge: The New York police; All in Police Dept. face counseling. *New York Times,* Sec. A, p. 1.

Kahn, R. (1981).*Work and health.* New York: John Wiley.

Kelleher, M. (1996). *New arenas for violence: Homicide in the American workplace.* Westport, CT: Greenwood.

Kurtz, L., & Turpin, J. (Eds.). (1999). *Encyclopedia of violence, peace and conflict.* San Diego: Academic Press.

Kurzman, P., & Akabas, S. (Eds.). (1993). *Work and well-being: The occupational social work advantage.* Washington, DC: NASW Press.

Lewis, G. (1994). *Critical incident stress and trauma in the workplace.* Muncie, IN: Accelerated Development Inc.

Liou, K. (1999, April 3). Understanding violence in the workplace: Social and managerial perspectives. *Public Administration and Management Journal.* Retrieved December 12, 2001, from www.pamij.com/99_4_3_Liou.html.

Marshall, R. (2002). The scientist's role in the community: What we have learned from 9/11. Retrieved September 16, 2002, from www.ncptsd.org.

Mayou, R., Ehlers, A., & Hobbs, M. (2000). Psychological debriefing for road traffic accident victims. *The British Journal of Psychiatry, 176,* 589–593.

National Center on Addiction and Substance Abuse at Columbia University (CASA). (2000, August 31). Postal Commission releases groundbreaking report on workplace violence. Retrieved January 23, 2002, from www.casacolumbia.org/newsletter_show.htm?doc_id=34000

National Center for Post-Traumatic Stress Disorder (NCPTSD), Department of Veterans Affairs (2001). What are the traumatic stress effects of terrorism? Retrieved January 21, 2002, from www.ncptsd.org/facts/disasters/fs_terrorism.html

National Institute for Occupational Safety and Health (NIOSH) (n.d). Women's safety and health issues at work. Retrieved September 10, 2001, from www.cdc.gov/niosh/womsaft.html.

National Partnership for Workplace Mental Health (n.d.). Disaster, terror, trauma in the workplace: What did we know before 9/11 and what have we learned since? Retrieved February 21, 2001, from www.workplacementalhealth.org

Nolen-Hoeksema, S., & Larson, J. (1999). *Coping with loss.* Mahwah, NJ: Lawrence Erlman Associates.

Norris, F. (2001). *50,000 disaster victims speak: An empirical review of the empirical literature, 1981–2001.* For the National Center for PTSD and The Center for Mental Health Services. Retrieved January 11, 2002, from http://www.istss.org/terrorism/victims_speak.htm

North, C. (2002). Researchers predict problems for survivors of terrorist attacks [Electronic version]. Washington University News & Information. Retrieved August 14, 2002, from www.news-info.wus1/ed/tips/2002/culturliving/north/html

North, C., Nixon, S. J., Shariat, S., Mallonee, S., McMillen, C. J., Spitznagel, E. L., & Smith, E. M. (1999). Psychiatric disorders among survivors of the Oklahoma City bombing [Electronic version]. *Journal of the American Medical Association, 282,* 755–762.

Occupational Safety and Health Administration (OSHA) (2002). Workplace violence. Retrieved October 1, 2002, from www.osha.gov.

Owens, B. (2001). The report of Governor Bill Owens, Columbine Review Commission. Denver: Office of the Governor.

Paul, R., & Masi, D. (July/August 2002). Organizational impact assessing the needs of employers. *Exchange: The Magazine of the Employee Assistance Professionals Association, 32,* 13–16.

Reina, D., & Reina, M. (1999). *Trust and betrayal in the workplace: Building effective relationships in your organization.* Berkeley, CA: Publishers Group West.

Schuster, M. A., Caddell, J. M., Ebert, L., Jordan, B. K., Rourke, K. M., Wilson, D., Thalji, L., Dennis, J. M., Fairband, J. A., & Kulka, R. A. (2002). Psychological reactions to terrorist attacks: Findings from the national study of Americans' reactions to September 11. *New England Journal of Medicine, 345,* 1507–1516.

Staudacher, C. (1991). *Men and grief: A guide for men surviving the death of a loved one: A resource for caregivers and mental health professionals.* Oakland, CA: New Harbinger.

Straussner, S. L. A. (1990). Occupational social work today: An overview. In Straussner, S. (Ed.), *Occupational social work today* (pp. 1–17). New York: Haworth Press.

Straussner, S. L. A., & Phillips, N. K. (1999) The impact of job loss on professional and managerial employees and their families. *Families in Society, 80,* 642–648.

Taffel, R. (2001, November/December). From crucible to community—Renewal in the midst of calamity. *Psychotherapy Networker, 25,* 23–40.

Talbot, M. (2001, December 9). Communal bereavement. *New York Times Magazine,* p. 62.

Tyler, T. (2000). Giving time to grieve: Compassionate bereavement leave policies and procedures provide support to employees when they need it most. Retrieved January 21, 2002, from www.kathryntyler.com/giving time to grieve.htm.

U.S. Department of Health and Human Services, Substance Abuse and Mental Health Services Administration. Knowledge Exchange Network. (n.d.). *Training manual for mental health and human service workers in major disasters,* Sec. 2, p. 1. Retrieved February 1, 2002, from www.mentalhealth.org/publications/allppubs/ADM90-538/tmsection2.asp.

U.S. Department of Labor, Bureau of Labor Statistics (2002). Fatal occupational injuries. Retrieved September 25, 2002, from www.data.bls.gov/cgi-bin.surveymost.

U.S. Department of Justice. (2000). *Responding to terrorism victims: Oklahoma City and beyond* (NCJ 183949). Washington, DC: Office for Victims of Crime.

U.S. Fire Administration, Federal Fire Management, Federal Emergency Management Agency. (1993). *World Trade Center bombing: Report and analysis* (USFA-TR-076). Emmitsburg, MD: Author.

Valliere, R. (2001). Massachusetts panel seeks zero tolerance, humane policies to reduce violence at work. Retrieved January 14, 2002, from Society of Human Resource Management *www.shrm.org/hrnews/articles/default.asp?page=bna07501c.htm.*

Volpe, J. (2001). Eastman Kodak critical incident stress management (CISM) team. *Trauma Response, VII,* 10–13.

Weick, K. E. (2001). Leadership when events don't play by the rules. Retrieved January 10, 2002, www.bus.umich.edu/leading/when_events.htm.

7

Interventions with Communities Affected by Mass Violence

Marygrace Berberian, Linda Lausell Bryant, and Gerald Landsberg

As stated by Norris (2001), "disasters impact whole communities, not just sole individuals" (p. 8). The social supports that communities provide to individuals, families, and even to the community as a whole are often crucial to the healing process following a disaster. This was seen in the case of survivors of the bombing of the Alfred P. Murrah Federal Building in Oklahoma City in 1995 (Sitterle & Gurwitch, 1999); it was also seen in New York City immediately following the September 11, 2001, attacks on the World Trade Center. For example, while relatively few people in New York sought the individual therapeutic help that was made widely available (Goode, 2002), thousands turned out en masse to support local firefighters. In many communities—particularly, but not exclusively, in those communities that lost firefighters—people spontaneously gathered at the local firehouse evening after evening in order to bring cakes and cookies, donate money, and talk to the firemen. The resulting sense of connection helped both the firefighters and the surrounding communities deal with this tragedy.

Unfortunately, since the "heady" days of the 1960s and early 1970s, when the social work profession focused on community organizing, there has been a markedly diminished attention to the role of community building in social work education. This trend reflected the increased attention given to psychopathology and work with individuals and families, mirroring a larger societal focus on the individual, rather than the community. At a time when a growing number of people are affected by mass violence, it is essential that social workers relearn the lessons of community building.

This chapter focuses on the various roles of communities in recovery from mass violence and provides background and selected examples of responses of different types of communities. While the specific examples reflect the recent experiences of the authors following the attacks of September 11th in New York City, the lessons learned can be generalized to other places and times where mass violence is experienced.

Communities and Their Responses to Mass Disasters

According to the American Red Cross (2002), there are an estimated 67,000 disasters in the United States each year, and during the year 2000, natural and human-made disasters affected 256 million people throughout the world—more than in any year over the past decade. The overwhelming percentages of these disasters were natural, such as floods, hurricanes, and tornadoes (International Federation of the Red Cross and Red Crescent Societies, 2001).

Although there had been previous human-made horrific events in the United States—the first World Trade Center bombing in 1993 and the Oklahoma City bombing in 1995—the nature and scope of the September 11th attacks fundamentally changed our perspectives on vulnerability and the importance of communities in the United States. Terrorist acts were no longer limited to the Middle East, Spain, or Northern Ireland, but happened in two large metropolitan areas of the United States, New York City and Washington, DC. The nature of the events—planes used as weapons of mass destruction—pierced a deeply held sense of security.

Communities responded in unique and caring ways. Makeshift memorials emerged offering families, friends, and strangers opportunities to reflect, pray, and benefit from the comfort of others. Countless vigils were held for those lost, and organized collections of money and services, as well as blood donations, were quickly established.

The communities affected by the disaster went far beyond New York City. People everywhere were affected by the trauma and were comforted by the commonality of the experience. People remember exactly what they were doing and where they were located when hearing about or, for those nearby in New York City, witnessing the tragedy. They can clearly remember whom they reached out to, whom they contacted first or who contacted them. Thus, while people remember the devastation, they also remember the social connections—the feeling of being part of a community—that helped them through the experience.

Norris (2001), in her comprehensive study of disasters, found that the impact on communities and individuals is most severe and long lasting when a number of factors are present in the disaster, including:

- Extreme and widespread damage to property
- Serious and ongoing financial consequences for the community
- Disaster caused by human intent
- High prevalence of trauma as a consequence of loss of life, injuries, and threat to life (p. 5)

The ability of a community to respond to mass violence is impacted by its existing social resources, the strength of the community's inherent social supports, its level of cohesiveness, and available social networks. Naturally occurring social resources are particularly vital for survivors of mass violence. Professionals and outsiders are important sources of assistance when the level of need is high, particularly in communities with low economic resources; however, they cannot supplant natural helping networks. More than ever, survivors of mass trauma need to continue their routine social activities in their communities, since these provide natural forums for sharing experiences and preserve a sense of social embeddedness that is easily destroyed during times of mass violence (Norris, 2001).

Types of Communities

The concept of "community" has various meanings. It may refer to *neighborhood communities* that often, although not always, have clearly defined geographic boundaries. Neighborhoods tend to be stable and long lasting, although they may be changed by radical physical actions, such as tearing down buildings for urban renewal or building a new highway. There are also what Rubin and Rubin (1992) refer to as *solidarity communities,* in which "people share a common interest, whether ethnic, national, cultural, or religious, that promotes shared values" (p. 84). These solidarity communities, which may include religious or cultural institutions, or groups that are formed to advocate for or are engaged in special interests, can be stable and last as long as the particular interests and goals of community members are maintained. Finally, there are *communities of interest* (Rubin & Rubin, 1992) that are formed as a direct result of individuals being thrown together to address or deal with a specific situation, such as escaping from a disaster. These communities are fleeting in duration and exist only as long as the immediacy of the situation.

The nature of responses to mass violence by each of these three types of communities differ and are reflected in the following case examples.

Agency Initiative in a Community Defined by Neighborhood

The Lower East Side of Manhattan represents the geographic neighborhood definition of community. It is a neighborhood of substantial duration and has served as a gateway community for millions of immigrants arriving during the eighteenth, nineteenth, and twentieth centuries. Currently, it remains an ethnically and culturally diverse community of over 200,000 people. The southern part of the community is only blocks from the World Trade Center, and its northern boundary is within one mile of the World Trade Center.

The *Educational Alliance* is a comprehensive, multiservice settlement house that has been serving the Lower East Side community since the late 1800s. Among its ongoing services are day care programs for children, Head Start programs, mental health services, substance abuse services, senior programs, art programs, and recreational programs. The community and the agency were greatly impacted by the events of September 11, 2001, and the agency has been actively engaged in developing community responses to the disaster and its aftermath. The following description of the agency's response to the disaster is provided by Dr. Gerald Landsberg and is based on conversations with Ms. Marion Lazer, Executive Deputy Director of the Educational Alliance, and Ms. Cheryl Fuller, Director of NORC Senior Services for the Alliance.

> On September 11, 2001, the Educational Alliance was faced with the immediate need to respond to the residents of the community and to the many people passing outside the agency

as they were fleeing from the World Trade Center after the attacks. The Alliance, which operates food programs, as well as having an auditorium and gym space, became a place where people could stop, sit down and rest, and be given food and water before continuing their journey home. Its staff operated both inside its building and outside on the street, providing physical comfort and emotional support. From the time immediately after the attack until late in the evening its doors were open to all. For that day, the Educational Alliance became a safe haven where at least 400–500 people found refuge and assistance. In the days and months that followed, the Alliance became a catalyst for the surrounding community and its residents to begin healing.

During the days immediately after the attacks, the Alliance responded in multiple ways to the community's needs. It became a drop-in center where people could find physical and emotional support, and became a location in which neighbors could help neighbors. Due to heightened security, the flow of food to neighborhood supermarkets stopped. Supplies to the Alliance and other agencies that housed and fed clients also stopped, creating major hardships for many community residents who depended on these services. Utilizing their connections to politicians, executives of the Alliance reached out to key state and city representatives to arrange for emergency delivery of food supplies to the supermarkets, service centers, and other key agencies, so that the community could be ensured of having sufficient food.

The numerous elderly people in the community were particularly at risk. Due to lack of transportation and the demands of coping with their own losses, many home attendants could not come to provide services to their clients. In addition, some of the seniors ran out of necessary medications. The Educational Alliance organized its staff and volunteers to help those seniors who were homebound and without assistance. This crucial short-term response supported large numbers of seniors through the initial crisis.

In the first few weeks that followed the attacks the Alliance organized community events, such as a number of "pot luck" dinners, so that the community members could come together and support each other. It also supported local rescuers, including firefighters and police, by holding ceremonies to "honor the heroes." During the chaotic period immediately after the disaster, showing concern, providing opportunities for community members to connect with each other, and offering concrete and emotional support were the key functions of the agency.

Over time, as the chaos faded, the Alliance began to use both its regular and newly developed programs to support all age groups, especially the elderly and children. As a major provider of senior citizen programs in the community, the Alliance reoriented these programs to assist the elderly population in addressing issues created by the events of September 11th. Care management took on a new focus of assisting the seniors with practical and emotional needs. Further, using its arts and language programs, seniors had the opportunity to share their reactions to the disaster with each other using art, poetry, short stories, and discussion groups. Such groups, together with other modalities, became important tools in reinforcing community support. It was found that this support was especially crucial for seniors who had been previously traumatized, such as those who experienced the Holocaust, or those who were coping with the death of a spouse.

The Alliance also provided innovative programs to assist adolescents. One particularly meaningful effort was focused on the two high schools that were in close proximity to the World Trade Center. Many of the students witnessed the attacks, they all had been evacuated from their schools, and most felt traumatized by the events. While initially welcoming the numerous professional counselors who came into the schools to help, after a brief time the principals of both schools began to feel overwhelmed by the constant stream of helpers and they finally said "No more therapists." Some other approach to help was needed. The staff at the Alliance decided to reach out to a faculty member at the Tisch School of the Arts at nearby New York University, and a video project was developed to help students channel their feelings into a creative project. The students, with the assistance of the University, developed a highly effective 30-minute video, "Student Responses to 9/11," in which they discussed their September 11th experiences and the trauma of returning to the schools and completing the academic year. The extremely positive impact of this activity on the students and the schools encouraged the participants to make the video available to other school throughout New York City and nationally to help adolescents deal with their complex responses to mass violence.

Artistic Expression in a Solidarity Community

It has been noted that rather than passively experiencing victimization in traumatizing environments, individuals tend to try to actively overcome their difficulties (Quota, Punamaki, & El Sarraj, 1995). In dealing with the events of September 11th, the New York City community as a whole expressed the same inclination. Individuals felt compelled to join together in solidarity in order to try to help others. In spite of their own suffering, people generously offered whatever help they could. Some chose to bring food to Ground Zero or volunteered in other ways. Some held signs with words of praise on the roadsides to encourage rescue workers. Countless others simply prayed. Many expressed their feeling through the use of arts.

Artistic expression is a powerful tool in alleviating the pain of a community struggling to cope and make sense of an illogical sequence of events. The use of artistic creativity allows for describing, building, and reconfiguring an injured object so that mourning can begin. According to Hanna Segal (1952), "It is when the world within is destroyed, when it is dead and loveless, when our loved ones are in fragments, and we ourselves in deepest despair, it is then that we must recreate our world anew, reassemble the pieces, infuse life into dead fragments, re-create life" (p. 492). While there were numerous concrete and creative ways for adults to form communities to address their common response to this mass violence in order to "re-create life," there were few venues for young children to become involved in community actions that were appropriate for their age.

The World Trade Center Children's Mural Project represents a solidarity community of adults desiring to help traumatized children cope with their fears and regain their sense of mastery, and a worldwide community of children identifying with and supporting each other. The description of this project is provided by Marygrace Berberian.

> On the morning of September 11, 2001, I got off at the World Trade Center train stop on my way to work in a building across the street, when the first plane plunged into the World Trade Center. Unaware of what was happening, I stopped to buy fruits at the Green Market set up directly in front of the Towers. Hot debris began falling and the blue sky was littered with slowly descending papers. In a moment, people ran toward me screaming, one woman with her head covered with blood. People screamed that there was a fire in the World Trade Center. Trying to find shelter, I ran across the street to my building and went to my office on the 30th floor. My head and shopping bags were covered with debris.

After the second plane hit, the building I was in rumbled, windows blew out, and all the occupants were evacuated. People seemed paralyzed on the streets. My colleagues and I boarded one of the last trains out of the city. We were stuck temporarily in the tunnel as the train lost power. People cried, screamed, and some fainted. I was fortunate to find my way home safely.

Despite my distressed state, three days later I returned to my job working with children. As a social worker and art therapist, I develop and implement art therapy programs in public schools and community-based organizations throughout New York City and work with a school-based art therapy program in a public school in midtown Manhattan. Still significantly traumatized, I spent the school day wandering aimlessly through classrooms to assess students who were in need of intervention. I saw the letters that students wrote to police officers and firefighters—almost every student had spontaneously included a drawing of the Twin Towers in their letters. As an art therapist, I realized that the children needed to symbolically rebuild the Twin Towers—they needed to rebuild what was destroyed.

Parents and teachers spoke to me about the children's responses. They themselves were overwhelmed and unsure how to respond to the children. Their ability to protect the children seemed to have disintegrated, as the whole community was vulnerable to massive destruction. Adults shared that they themselves felt more equipped to cope with the circumstances after they spent time with their children. It was the children who provided a sense of hope and encouraged the adults to mobilize resources for survival.

At the end of the school day, I went home exhausted. Friends who were displaced from their homes in Battery Park City, just across from the Towers, were staying in my apartment. The days immediately following the profound losses of September 11th were a warp of time and space, a disturbing cycle of mourning, exhaustion, and lapses of memory.

As I replayed my observations from the day at the school, I felt driven to respond. I decided to provide young people with the prospect of symbolically rebuilding the Towers, offering an opportunity to gain mastery amidst profound feelings of helplessness. I conceived a project that came to be known as "The World Trade Center Children's Mural Project." Children would draw self-portraits, depicting their own responses to the tragedy. The focus of the drawing was on the face. As noted by Machover (1949), the face, the most expressive part of the body and center of communication, is often depicted in drawings as a completed image of the person, even without any other parts. It is the human face that most fascinates infants early in their development as it represents the configuration involved in eating, talking, hearing, and smiling (DiLeo, 1973). Moreover, drawing a face is a skill all children master early on that does not require any advanced artistic training. Finally, it also reflects ethnic and cultural attributes. I felt that cultural awareness and cultural acceptance needed to be emphasized since anti-Arab sentiments were emerging.

The completed portrait was a validation of the self and a testament of each individual child's connection to the larger community. The art served as a means to communicate the harsh realities and hopeful fantasies present in that moment. I envisioned mounting the faces together on a large mural of a new cityscape for New York. Murals have been identified in the literature as a way of memorializing lost loved ones and lost heroes and role models (Delgado, 2000), and now such a mural could be used not only to memorialize what children felt they had lost in this disaster, but also to give them the opportunity to symbolically rebuild. Information about this project was sent to schools and community-based organizations. Flyers were posted at groceries, libraries, and laundromats. In a short time, the response was overwhelming. Schools, community-based organizations, religious groups, residential treatment facilities, and shelters responded. Professions representing all disciplines seemed eager to offer young people the opportunity to process what happened, but many were apprehensive to approach the subject with young people, and some educators were resistant to have the children talk about their feelings. Since they needed hands-on guidelines to do so, facilitators' guidelines were quickly developed.

The World Trade Center Children's Mural Project was designed to be easily facilitated. First, groups of children shared what they knew about the events. Adults then had the opportunity to respond to the children's concerns and to dispel false perceptions about what had happened. For example, some children became hypervigilant about the cracks in their school buildings, wondering if their school had been hit or was going to fall down. This gave the adults the opportunity to explain the situation clearly and in a manner in which children could understand. In order to address their concerns about safety, the children were then asked to brainstorm and name their favorite places in New York City. This ensured them that their immediate environment was still safe. Many children tended to name Central Park and McDonald's as their favorite places. Facilitators confirmed that these places were indeed still safe in the city.

Children then compared hands to examine skin colors and share countries of origin. Since New York is such a diverse city, it was important to acknowledge cultural differences during this period of international conflict. Facilitators then organized a vote of the children to determine whether each ethnic group wanted New York City to be a peaceful place; the votes were unanimously positive. Project facilitators emphasized that a community's wishes for peace were not dependent solely on the basis of skin color or culture, but as a community, we all wished for peace. When offered the opportunity to use drawings to rebuild New York with others, the children became excited. Children drew self-portraits to rebuild New York City using their faces. Since art materials are often limited at schools and community organizations, children were asked to use any media (crayons, markers, paints, or pencils) to draw their faces on a standard sheet of paper. Each portrait produced was unique and represented the mood and level of resiliency of the child at the time. Some children drew themselves in sorrow, with tears and saddened mouths. Others were joyful, proudly drawn with American flags. Some children placed themselves between the Towers, seemingly in an effort to hold them up. Other children identified with leaders in the city, namely fireman and former Mayor Guiliani. Despite the basic and modest directive, children's artistic expressions were quite complex.

Representatives of the Christian Children's Fund (CCF), which supports children's programs in territories exposed to war and terrorism, arrived in New York to provide assistance and partnered with the project. CCF translated the World Trade Center Children's Mural Project's guidelines into twelve different languages and distributed it to participating countries. Children in twenty-two countries, such Uganda, Kosovo, and Colombia, sent portraits and written messages of hope to encourage survival of New York City's children. The portraits of these international faces symbolize profound resiliency and offer solidarity for world peace. It was incredibly poignant to see a child who was living in the harsh conditions of Kosovo send a message of hope to a child living in New York City.

On March 19, 2002, the montage mural, compromised of over 3,100 portraits, was unveiled in New York City, directly across from Ground Zero. Upon completion of the mural, it was realized that the total number of portraits contributed by children around the world was close to the total number of lives destroyed by the attacks of September 11th. The children had filled the city with hope by paying homage to each life that had been lost in the attacks. The creation of this mural served to lessen feelings of isolation and helplessness felt among those children who had difficulty understanding the complexity of this tragedy.

Children around the world collaborated and were empowered to utilize skills and energies toward positive solutions. The World Trade Center Children's Mural Project enhanced individual strengths, celebrated cultural diversity, and empowered children to work collectively toward peace.

Thousands of adults, many who lived or worked in the World Trade Center area, and tourists from around the United States and other countries viewed the exhibition and were deeply moved by the message that had been delivered by children throughout the world. Many responded with a reverence similar to that observed at the sites established for missing persons. The mural had become a symbol both for mourning and of profound positive feelings for and connectedness to New York City. The conception and development of the project inspired many to believe that when children are offered support and opportunity, they can readily be helped as well as help others in the community to heal.

Transitory Community of Interest

The many bridges that connect the island of Manhattan to the surrounding New York City boroughs delivered many desperate individuals to safety on September 11, 2001. While the bridges served as concrete structures to safely connect those who were separated from home, they also provided for the development of spontaneous, transitory communities as unfamiliar people helped each other on their dusty paths. Following is an example of a transitory community that evolved as people were attempting to escape the area of the World Trade Center, as described by Linda Lausell Bryant.

As I look back on my experiences on September 11, 2001, they served as a social work practicum on the importance, and also the effectiveness, of community in times of crisis.

At about 8:45 in the morning of September 11th, I escorted my 4-year-old daughter Jasmine into her preschool less than a block away from the World Trade Center. In the minute or so that we waited for the elevator, I noticed what looked like ticker tape raining down along with what looked like crushed soda cans on fire, falling from the sky and littering the sidewalk in front of the preschool. I attributed this to a deranged person on the roof of the building igniting gasoline-filled soda cans and throwing them onto the street.

We took the elevator up to the preschool and shortly after, we heard an explosion and our building shook. The caring and courageous preschool staff made sure that the children were moved away from windows and subsequently into a sub-basement playroom thought to be the safest place in the building. The children played as parents made futile attempts to make calls on cell phones, and the preschool staff tried to keep us informed and calm. Suddenly, there was a loud, crashing noise, like thunder. This rumbling shook the building, and within moments the basement filled with ash and smoke. I would later learn that what we heard was the first tower collapsing. Like so many of the parents, I grabbed my daughter and got down on the floor with her, covering her face with a wet wipe. My daughter knew that something was very wrong; she became quiet and protective of a classmate who did not have a parent there. We were told that we could not leave because everything outside was pitch dark. Moments later, however, the building security ordered us to evacuate immediately.

As we exited, I could not reconcile the incomprehensible scenes before me with anything I knew previously. Everything was covered in inches of ash and visibility was poor. My daughter asked, "Mommy, what happened?" Of course, I had no answer and as my mouth filled with ash, I said that we shouldn't talk now so that she could keep the wipe over her nose and mouth and try not to breathe the smoke. We walked quickly, unsure of where we were headed except that it was south. As we walked, the second tower collapsed and pandemonium broke out.

Still unable to figure out what was happening, I assumed from the sounds that a bomb had been dropped. People ran in every direction. I scooped Jasmine up and began to run. A priest ran past me and with his arms outstretched. He told me to give him my daughter so he could get her to safety faster than I could run. In a split second, I had to decide whether to let my daughter go to increase her chances of getting to safety, or whether to keep her with me and protect her the best way I could. I took one look behind me and realizing that the cloud of debris was gaining on us, I decided that I had to give my child the best chance at surviving. I placed her in the arms of the priest, running behind them and telling Jasmine that I would catch up with her. Jasmine did not protest and I could tell by her face that she was scared.

After a short time, I found the priest who had taken Jasmine to the relative safety of the South Ferry terminal at the very tip of Manhattan where many of the preschool teachers and children also had taken cover. I also met up with my mother, who was in the area on that day. We wanted to get home across the river, and with thousands of others began our trek toward the Brooklyn Bridge in front of us. Yet we feared that the bridge would be bombed and we were scared to make our descent across. It was hard to know which way to go and in which direction we would find safety. Eager to ask someone for direction, I soon realized that no one had any answers. Our direction could only come from a higher source. Standing on the Brooklyn Bridge, I held my daughter and my mother's hands and began to pray to God for guidance and direction. Secure in the belief that God was with us, we began our journey across the bridge as the slow and painful realization of what had happened set in.

By this time, I was limping from a sharp pain in my right heel as I carried my daughter and tried to support my mother. Torn between concern for my mother's asthma and heart condition and the strong maternal urge to get my child to safety, I tried to push my mother along. A young South Asian man offered to carry my daughter for me. As he carried Jasmine, he stayed close to me. Suddenly we heard rumbling sounds and everyone began walking faster. I urged my mother to walk faster but I could see that she was struggling to breathe. I began to feel desperate. I didn't want to leave her behind and I didn't want to linger on the bridge. I had to get my child to safety. I noticed that the young man who was carrying Jasmine was getting tired and I offered to take Jasmine back, thanking him for helping.

We were then approached by an older man who also appeared to be of South Asian descent. He took charge of my mother, telling her that he would take care of her. He took her by the arm and motioned for me to walk ahead with my child. This kind gentleman also gave us masks to cover our mouths and gave water to my mother.

Relieved that my mother was receiving assistance, I began to pick up speed. A young man of Latino descent offered to carry Jasmine, and again, walked close to me. As I was limping, a petite woman approached me offering to carry my heavy backpack for me, but I didn't let her, though I thanked her for offering. Finally, after what seemed like an eternity, we made it over the bridge. I looked back and saw my mother slowly making her way; someone had draped a wet towel over her head making it easier for her to breathe. The South Asian man was holding her hand tightly, helping her along. I waited on the Brooklyn side for them to cross over and when they did, I thanked the man for taking care of my mother. He told us that he has been married for thirty years and in all that time he had never touched another woman's hand. In his culture, men are not allowed to touch other women. He told my mother that he had made an exception so that he could take care of her. I asked him for his name so that I could pray for him and thank God for what he had done. His name was Jamal.

We made our way to a cement bench in front of an apartment complex and sat there to catch our breath and figure out how to get home. We were exhausted. We started walking again, hoping to find a working payphone, when a car pulled up and an African American woman in the car asked if she could give us a ride to a bus or subway. We could hardly believe our blessings! We had crossed one bridge and this woman would help us to cross another one and get closer to home. She took us several blocks away to an intersection where we could get a bus home. Miraculously, I was able to get a brief signal on my cell phone and reached my father, who picked us up.

Conclusion

As pointed out by Williams, Zinner, and Ellis (1999), "whatever their origin or purpose, members of a community have a common focus which brings them together" (p. 7). It is this commonality and the social support offered by communities that plays a crucial role in the promotion of emotional healing following mass violence.

Looking at the history of social work, one can see that social work is rooted in work with communities. As a profession, social work is committed to build on the client system's natural strengths and to work with people in the context of their environment, including their community. Situations of mass violence require that professionals recognize the importance of communities and respond immediately to develop innovative programs that help to build and rebuild communities. During this era of increased threat of mass violence, the social work profession must be poised to mobilize, strengthen, and support the potential of communities to help themselves and to use the lessons learned thus far to develop effective models of community intervention.

References

American Red Cross. (2002). Disaster services. Retrieved December 2, 2002, from www.redcross.org/services/disaster.

Delgado, M. (2000). *Community social work practice in an urban context: The potential of a capacity-enhancement perspective.* New York: Oxford University Press.

DiLeo, J. (1973). *Children's drawings as diagnostic aids.* Philadelphia: Brunner/Mazel.

Goode, I. (2002, August 2). Program to cover psychiatric help for 9/11 families. *New York Times,* p. 1.

International Federation of Red Cross and Red Crescent Societies. (2001). *World disasters report 2001.* Bloomfield, CT: Kumarian Press.

Machover, K. (1949). *Personality projection in the drawing of human figure.* Springfield, IL: Charles C. Thomas.

Norris, F. H. (2001). *50,000 disaster victims speak: An empirical review of the empirical literature, 1981–2001.* National Center for PTSD and The Center for Mental Health Services (SAMHSA).

Quota, S., Punamaki, R., & El Sarraj, E. (1995). The relations between traumatic experiences, activity, and cognitive and emotional responses among Palestinian children. *International Journal of Psychology, 30,* 289–304.

Rubin, H., & Rubin, I. (1992). *Community organizing and development.* New York: Macmillan.

Segal, H. (1952). A psychoanalytic approach to aesthetics. In R. Frankiel (Ed.), *Essential papers on object loss* (pp. 486–507). New York: New York University Press.

Sitterle, K. A., & Gurwitch, R. H. (1999). The terrorist bombing in Oklahoma City. In E. S. Zinner & M. B. Williams (Eds.), *When a community weeps: Case studies in group survivorship* (pp. 161–189). Philadelphia: Brunner/Mazel.

Williams, M. B., Zinner, E. S., & Ellis, R. R. (1999). The connection between grief and trauma: An overview. In E. S. Zinner & M. B. Williams (Eds.), *When a community weeps: Case studies in group survivorship* (pp. 3–17). Philadelphia: Brunner/Mazel.

8

Mass Violence and Law Enforcement Personnel

George T. Patterson and Grace A. Telesco

During and following situations of mass violence, law enforcement personnel, firefighters, and emergency service personnel are among the first to respond at the scene. Other agencies, such as the American Red Cross and the Federal Emergency Management Agency (FEMA), also may be called in order to assist survivors. Each of these first responder agencies has a specific role and specialized tasks at the site of mass violence incidents.

On September 11, 2001, during the first few minutes of the attack on the World Trade Center in New York City, police officers from the New York City Police Department, members of Port Authority police, Emergency Medical personnel, and the Fire Department all responded en masse to the scene. All these first responders hurried into the burning buildings to rescue those who were still alive. Typically, the jurisdiction at the scene of a fire or explosion is with the fire department, while police and emergency medical personnel assist in the rescue efforts. In the World Trade Center attacks, both police and fire department personnel helped to evacuate thousands of people from the buildings, while police officers were also responsible for getting the survivors as far away from the scene of the incident as possible. As the minutes turned into hours and as the towers fell, the rescue attempt became even more critical. At the same time, the need to provide emotional support to the traumatized population became apparent.

However, it is not just those who are the victims or survivors of mass violence who may need help and emotional support. Among those who may be traumatized in incidents of mass violence are the first responders themselves. To provide effective social work services to first responders and their families, it is important to understand the functions of the organizations in which first responders work and the unique stressors that impact on them. As an example of a group of first responders, this chapter will highlight the response of law enforcement personnel to mass violence, the impact of mass violence on law enforcement personnel and their families, and their needs for help in dealing with trauma.

Role of First Responders in Situations of Mass Violence

At the scene of mass violence, the specific roles and responsibilities of law enforcement, emergency rescue, and medical personnel will largely depend on the unique requirements of the event. For example, at the scene of the Columbine school shooting in Colorado, certain key pieces of criminal intelligence relative to this crime scene were unknown at first. It was uncertain whether the perpetrators of the shooting were still posing a threat, if they were holding hostages, and how many students and faculty were injured or possibly dead. Consequently, it became clear that jurisdiction over this situation belonged to law enforcement. In this kind of situation, rescue functions provided by firefighters and emergency medical personnel can only commence once it has been established that the perpetrators no longer pose any danger and that the presence of first responders would not compound the threat level, placing more lives at risk.

In general, because of its criminal nature, it is law enforcement that possesses and maintains jurisdiction and authority over the scene of a critical incident involving mass violence. A collaboration and coordination of all rescue and medical services will be implemented, while the responsibility to ascertain intelligence, engage in threat assessment, and the removal of the actual threat lies with the law enforcement agency in charge. Once the law enforcement agency determines the immediate potential of threat, and elements of imminent danger are seen as no longer existing, other resources and agencies will be requested. It is at this point that outside volunteer rescue agencies, such as the American Red Cross or Salvation Army, may be called upon to provide concrete and emotional assistance to survivors.

Characteristics of Law Enforcement Organizations

Wilson (1968) identified the two main functions of law enforcement agencies: *law enforcement* and *order maintenance.* Law enforcement functions include situations involving a law violation in which officers need to resolve the situation formally, according to the law. Order maintenance functions include situations that may or may not involve a law violation, and officers can exercise discretion to manage the situation informally. As pointed out by Goldstein (1990), the term "law enforcement officer" is a misnomer because it only refers to the law enforcement function of an officer's occupational tasks. Law enforcement comprises much more than arresting individuals and enforcing the law. What is ignored is a third function in Wilson's typology—the *service function* of the police. This may include responding to the concerns and needs of the community (Greene & Mastrofski, 1988), such as conflict resolution and crisis intervention, which, in cases of mass violence, may involve comforting and aiding the victims. Consequently, the first response provided by law enforcement personnel at the scene of mass violence may affect how victims and survivors experience the situation and may possibly impact their recovery process.

Law enforcement at the scene of mass violence includes some or all of the following activities:

- Request mobilization and deployment of additional forces
- Relinquish authority and responsibility to officer in charge
- Gather intelligence
- Ascertain threat level
- Obtain information about survivors and level of injury
- Coordinate rescue and medical services
- Interview witnesses
- Control the inner perimeter and maintain integrity of any physical evidence
- Maintain control of onlookers and preserve the integrity of the crime scene
- Determine resources and equipment
- Request outside agency response and rescue volunteer involvement
- Determine perpetrator information
- Provide crisis intervention
- Develop and implement a plan of action

For law enforcement officers, the safety of all persons at the scene of a critical incident involving mass violence is of paramount importance. Careful consideration has to be made in determining how and when survivors will be rescued and given the necessary medical attention. Prioritization is critical, and that is usually the responsibility of the officer in charge. Depending on the size of the law enforcement agency, this officer could be the chief of police or a lower-ranking member of the agency. The circumstances at the scene will determine the steps in the response plan and their respective order. The emergency nature of mass violence dictates that prioritization focus on removing imminent danger, rescuing those still in danger, and removing the injured to the hospital. Criminal investigation then follows.

Impact of Mass Violence on Law Enforcement Personnel

Due to the potentially negative psychological effects of traumatic or critical incidents on law enforcement personnel and the necessity for specialized mental health services, such as critical incident debriefing, Patterson (2001) contends that these incidents are an important source of stress. Ordinarily, when police officers respond to the scene of mass violence, they will be confronted with an enormous amount of confusion and chaos. Survivors, witnesses, and onlookers are likely to be demonstrating hysteria, despair, confusion, and apprehension (Bennett & Hess, 2001), and it can be a challenge for the officer at the scene to remain calm and not get caught up in the crisis. In addition, because the nature of mass violence puts first responders themselves at grave risk for injury or death, those in charge must assess risks not only for civilians, but for their officers as well, further adding to their stress level (Paton, Flin & Violanti, 1999). Such psychological and emotional needs are often neglected by law enforcement agencies.

Studies show that although traumatic and dangerous incidents may occur infrequently in law enforcement, these incidents are ranked as very stressful (Coman & Evans, 1991; Cooper, Davidson, & Robinson, 1982; Gudjonsson & Adlam, 1985; Sewell, 1983). Traumatic occupational incidents for law enforcement officers have been described as "those major life experiences which in themselves can create havoc for the individual officer, physically, emotionally, socially, intellectually, and spiritually" (Stratton, 1983, p. 5). Brown and Campbell (1994) identified three kinds of incidents as being the most stressful for officers: incidents involving injury or violence to the officer or others; incidents associated with major disasters, such as mutilated bodies and fatalities; and incidents that require managing public disorder. All three of these highly stressful incidents are commonly found in situations of mass violence, and all were clearly evident following the September 11, 2001, terrorist attack on the World Trade Center in New York.

Westerink (1990) found that within one year after being hired, law enforcement personnel experienced a wide range of traumatic incidents involving the death or injury of children or the removal of body parts. Asserting that such situations are not the usual experiences that people go through in their daily lives, McCafferty, Godofredo, and McCafferty (1990) suggest that law enforcement personnel employed within large urban areas are exposed to the same traumatic situations as military personnel who encounter situations involving booby traps, snipers, and other physical dangers that may lead to psychological trauma and even posttraumatic stress disorder.

Responses to Mass Violence: Compassion Fatigue and Posttraumatic Stress Disorder

The effects on law enforcement personnel responding to mass violence include the risk of vicarious traumatization and compassion fatigue. Figley (1995) and others describe compassion fatigue as an adverse effect of offering assistance to traumatized individuals and to families and communities dealing with grief. The use of empathic responses when dealing with trauma survivors and their families makes police officers vulnerable to developing their own symptoms of vicarious traumatization or vicarious bereavement (McCann & Pearlman, 1990; Rando, 1997; Saakvitne & Pearlman, 1996). A study of police officers working with victims of tragedy conducted by Martin, McKean and Veltkamp (1986) found that 26 percent of the sample met the criteria for posttraumatic stress disorder (PTSD) following exposure to psychologically traumatic events relating to their own victimization or from working with victims.

The following example, in which the second author was a support team leader, illustrates of the kinds of responsibilities of law enforcement personnel that may result in compassion fatigue and PTSD:

> At approximately 1:30 PM on September 11th, when many first responders were immersed in the rescue efforts at the World Trade Center, a mental health team from the New York City Police Department's Community Affairs Division was sent to an auditorium at the City

Department of Health across the street from the city morgue. The role of these officers was to provide crisis intervention and emotional support to many of the family members of the approximately 3,000 dead and missing individuals who came to the morgue searching for their loved ones that first week.

In the week following the attack, because of the enormity of this mass violence and the massive numbers of family members requiring assistance, a large facility, officially known as the Family Assistance Center at Pier 94, was set up and was operational for four months. Law enforcement personnel, with the assistance of volunteer Red Cross mental health service providers from all over the country and mental health practitioners from the New York City Department of Mental Health, provided support and crisis intervention to the bereaved. They were joined by spiritual care teams, pet therapy dogs, family survivors from the Oklahoma City bombing, and law enforcement officers from neighboring states.

The Police Department's Community Affairs Division, whose expertise lies in working closely with the community, was responsible for the safety and security at the Family Assistance Center. It was also responsible for the provision and coordination of support services for the families of the victims. Such services included the preparation of missing person reports, obtaining DNA sampling for proper identification, releasing lists of survivors who were hospitalized and of identified deceased individuals, distributing death certificates and memorial urns, and escorting the families to Ground Zero.

The scene at the Family Assistance Center was extremely emotional. Most people wanted their questions answered and neither the police nor the mental health practitioners could offer a resolution. Some individuals pleaded to be allowed access to Ground Zero and help find their loved one: One woman was screaming in a rage that she wanted to go and "dig her baby brother out of the rubble" (Telesco, 2002). Others believed that their friend, parent, lover, partner, son, or daughter, whose "missing person" photo they carried with them, was unconscious and lay unidentified in a hospital and wanted to know where to look. In most cases, those in crisis screamed in frustration at the lack of information about their loved ones, while others cried in anticipation of the worst or when informed about the identification of a deceased family member or loved one. Some police officers, unsure of how to respond, could only reply with "I'm sorry, it doesn't look as though his name is here," when asked about a missing loved one. For many of the other officers, active listening was the only tool of intervention.

With very few bodies being recovered and no one being rescued alive after the first few days, Mayor Guilliani slowly changed the term "rescue effort" to "recovery," while the families' emotional state turned from pre-mourning to mourning. Comfort rooms where individuals and families could receive private emotional support were set up at the Center. An officer would escort people to these rooms when there was a special need, particularly when remains were recovered and information was required to help identify the individual. Various mental health practitioners and spiritual care providers then offered support to those in need.

One of the services offered at the Family Assistance Center was to escort families by ferry to visit Ground Zero. Giving the families the opportunity to see the place where their loved ones were last alive proved to be one of the most beneficial services provided. Families were also given an opportunity to stop at a temporary memorial site nearby where they could reflect on their loved one and leave flowers, teddy bears, or cards if they desired.

The safety of the families was a major concern to the Community Affairs police officers responsible for this unique and ongoing service that was operational up to three times a day, seven days a week. This support team escorted a total of 4,000 people to the site for three months. In light of the heightened alert and concern of another attack, law enforcement professionals provided additional security.

Unlike service providers from the Red Cross, the city Department of Mental Health, spiritual care providers, and pet therapy handlers, all of whom rotated and changed over the course of the three months, the same police officers were assigned to work at the Family Center 12- to 14-hour shifts, six to seven days a week, and escorted families to the site on a minimum of two boat trips each day. The psychological impact that this work had on the officers who were consistently and empathically working with families was enormous.

Coping Strategies Utilized by Police Officers

Police officers tend to use a variety of defenses in dealing with traumatizing situations. Violanti and Marshall (1983), in a study of 500 full-time officers, examined the psychological outcomes of police job demands and described how officers cope with these stressful situations. The authors found that officers learn to dissociate from their emotions when dealing with unpleasant work experiences. Additionally, they found a strong positive relationship between stress and respondents' use of alcohol. In another study examining how officers handle their emotions in dealing with tragic events, Pogrebin and Poole (1991) found that in order to avoid being perceived as vulnerable in showing emotion, officers tend to diffuse the impact of the tragedy through the use of humor, thereby avoiding dealing with their feelings.

Harvey-Lintz (1997) examined the psychological effects and coping strategies employed by Los Angeles police officers in the aftermath of the civil unrest immediately following the acquittal of those officers involved in the Rodney King incident in 1992. The sample included 141 officers of the Los Angeles Police Department who voluntarily agreed to participate in the study. Findings indicate that 17 percent of the respondents met the criteria for PTSD; moreover, they were twice as likely to use avoidance coping strategies than those who did not meet the criteria for PTSD. These findings illustrate the tendency of officers who respond to mass violence to suppress their feelings and the deleterious effects this has on their psychological well-being.

Mental Health Services with Law Enforcement Personnel and Their Families

The role of the law enforcement agency's leadership in providing support and resources to the responding officers at the rescue and recovery level during incidents of mass violence is of major importance in moderating the deleterious effects of the trauma. Five years following the Bureau of Alcohol, Tobacco, and Firearms raid of the Branch Davidian compound in Waco, Texas, in 1993, a study was conducted to examine how the level of support was related to traumatic stress experienced by law enforcement officers who were at the site. The researchers found that administrative support and concern for officers by the leadership played an important role in their recovery (Solomon & Mastin, 1999).

Some law enforcement agencies have a history of employing social workers and other mental health professionals to staff crisis intervention teams and to provide assistance to law enforcement officers with social problems, such as domestic violence and child abuse. However, to assist officers and their families with the negative psychological and emotional effects of trauma and other forms of occupational stress, many law enforcement agencies hire only psychologists, following the tradition started in 1968 when the Los Angeles Police Department hired a full-time psychologist. This was the first formal recognition of the need for mental health professionals to assist law enforcement officers with social and personal problems (Reese & Hodinko, 1991). The need for law enforcement personnel to receive counseling was also recognized following the attacks on the World Trade Center in 2001.

Intervention with Families of Law Enforcement Personnel

The negative psychological impact of responding to mass violence situations not only affects law enforcement personnel, but also their family members. Psychological defenses, such as detachment, used by law enforcement personnel as a way of dealing with their sense of helplessness in light of massive exposure to human tragedy, do not readily disappear when the officer is at home. Consequently, many police officers become emotionally distant from their families. Emotional detachment from family members may also be due to the family's inability to compete with the job in providing emotional gratification. The pleasurable rush of having real power, of giving orders and compelling others to obey, is lacking at home (Bonifacio, 1991). In addition, the extensive job demands and the many hours of work during situations of mass violence mean that the police officer is unavailable to help his or her own family members cope with the stress of the situation. Finally, police family members often worry that the officer will be hurt or killed while on duty (Johnson, 1991).

These factors contribute to the tremendous stress on both the spouse and children of police officers, and there is a growing recognition of the need to provide services to families of law enforcement personnel. The 1997 National Institute of Justice's Issues and Practices Report, titled *Developing a Law Enforcement Stress Program for Officers and their Families,* recommends that mental health services be extended to family members. This report focuses on the benefits of services for family members to the police officers, as such services make it possible for family members to remain or become sources of support for the officers. In addition, it recognizes that family members are often the first to know when an officer needs help, and they can be in a position to encourage officers to seek help before their problems become too severe (Bonifacio, 1991).

Conclusion

In addition to performing their usual functions, law enforcement personnel do much to respond to the immediate concerns and needs of communities. Their efforts take on vast proportions at the scenes of incidents of mass violence where there has been harm to many people and can continue for a long time after the destruction. Depending on the severity of destruction and the extent of human suffering, law enforcement personnel can become overwhelmed with their multiple functions.

In many communities, current approaches to mass violence and disaster situations involve the formation of mental health crisis teams to respond following incidents of mass violence. Working together with other law enforcement personnel, they provide mental health services to victims. Social workers affiliated with the American Red Cross or the department of mental health and other human service agencies may be called upon to serve as part of such teams. Expanding current crisis intervention teams to assist law enforcement personnel as they respond to mass violence situations represents an important direction for social work.

Because they generally are among the first to be on the scene, much of the initial crisis intervention falls to the first responders. It is important that they be prepared to handle these situations and that they receive the needed help to cope with these extraordinarily difficult and emotionally demanding circumstances. The provision of social work services within the law enforcement community presents a future direction for practice. While the number of social workers and other mental health professionals providing direct services to officers and their families nationwide is unknown, the need for services to this population is recognized, and it is clear that social workers and other mental health professionals have much to contribute.

References

Bennett, W., & Hess, K. (2001). *Criminal investigation.* Belmont, CA: Wadsworth.

Bonifacio, P. (1991). *The psychological effects of police work.* New York: Plenum.

Brown, J. M., & Campbell, E. A. (1994). *Stress and policing: Sources and strategies.* New York: John Wiley.

Coman, G. J., & Evans, B. J. (1991). Stressors facing Australian police in the 1990s. *Police Studies, 14,* 153–165.

Cooper, C. L., Davidson, M. J., & Robinson, P. (1982). Stress in the police service. *Journal of Occupational Medicine, 24,* 30–36.

Goldstein, H. (1990). *Problem-oriented policing.* New York: McGraw-Hill.

Greene, J. R., & Mastrofski, S. D. (1988). *Community policing: Rhetoric or reality.* New York: Praeger.

Gudjonsson, G. H., & Adlam, K. R. (1985). Occupational stressors among British police officers. *The Police Journal, 58,* 73–80.

Figley, C. R. (1995). *Compassion fatigue: Coping with secondary stress disorder in those who treat the traumatized.* Psychological Series No. 23. Philadelphia: Brunner/Mazel.

Harvey-Lintz, T. (1997). Effects of the 1992 Los Angeles civil unrest: Post traumatic stress disorder symptomatology among law enforcement officers. *Social Science Journal, 34,* 171–183.

Johnson, L. B. (1991). Job strain among police officers: Gender comparisons. *Police Studies, 14,* 12–16.

Martin, C., McKean, H., & Veltkamp, L. (1986). Post-traumatic stress disorder in police and working with victims: A pilot study. *Journal of Police Science and Administration, 14,* 98–101.

McCafferty, F. L., Godofredo, D. D., & McCafferty, E. A. (1990). Posttraumatic stress disorder in the police officer: Paradigm of occupational stress. *Southern Medical Journal, 83,* 543–547.

McCann, I. L., & Pearlman, L. A. (1990). Vicarious traumatization: A framework for understanding the psychological effects of working with victims. *Journal of Traumatic Stress, 3,* 131–149.

Paton, D., Flin, R., & Violanti, J. (1999). Incident response and recovery management. In J. Violanti & D. Paton (Eds.). *Police trauma: Psychological aftermath of civilian combat* (pp. 113–123). Springfield, IL: Thomas.

Patterson, G. T. (2001). Reconceptualizing traumatic incidents experienced by law enforcement personnel. *The Australasian Journal of Disaster and Trauma Studies.* Retrieved November 12, 2001, from www. massey.ac.nz/~trauma/.

Pogrebin, M., & Poole, E. (1991). Police and tragic events: The management of emotions. *Journal of Criminal Justice, 19,* 395–403.

Rando, T. (1997). Vicarious bereavement. In S. Strack (Ed.), *Death and the quest for meaning: Essays in honor of Herman Feifel* (pp. 257–274). Northvale, NJ: Jason Aronson.

Reese, J. T., & Hodinko, B. M. (1991). Police psychological services: A history. In J. T. Reese, J. M. Horn, & C. Dunning (Eds.), *Critical incidents in policing* (pp. 297–309). Washington, DC: Government Printing Office.

Saakvitne, K. W., & Pearlman, L. A. (1996). *Transforming the pain: A workbook on vicarious tramatization.* New York: W. W. Norton.

Sewell, J. D. (1983). The development of a critical life events scale for law enforcement. *Journal of Police Science and Administration, 11,* 109–116.

Solomon, R., & Mastin, P. (1999). The emotional aftermath of the Waco Raid: Five years revisited. In J. Violanti & D. Paton (Eds.), *Police trauma: Psychological aftermath of civilian combat* (pp. 113–123). Springfield, IL: Thomas.

Stratton, J. G. (1983). Traumatic incidents and the police. *Police Stress, 6,* 4–7.

Telesco, G. (2002, Summer). Rescue and recovery: Providing crisis intervention to the families of the victims of the world trade center. *Reflections,* 12–18.

Violanti, J. M., & Marshall, J. R. (1983). The police stress process. *Journal of Police Science and Administration, 11,* 389–394.

Westerink, J. (1990). Stress and coping mechanisms in young police officers. *Australian Police Journal, 44,* 109–113.

Wilson, J. Q. (1968). *Varieties of police behavior.* Cambridge, MA: Harvard University Press.

Section IV

Issues for Social Work Practice

9

Helping People Retraumatized by Mass Violence

Graciela M. Castex

When a client has suffered a trauma, particularly when the person is a survivor of mass violence and the treatment is conducted in a crisis atmosphere, it may be easy to overlook the client's previous history. In some cases, this may not be the first severe trauma the client has experienced, and in such situations, reactions to that earlier trauma may partially affect responses to the more recent trauma. This later traumatization is, in effect, a retraumatization.

Identifying, assessing, and dealing with the reactions to an earlier trauma can be a challenging task for the social worker, especially if the client's painful reactions and memories of earlier traumas may have been partly or wholly suppressed and therefore might no longer be consciously accessible. This chapter examines the impact of retraumatization resulting from human-induced violence and introduces key issues for social workers providing services to retraumatized clients.

The Case of Laura

The intersection between massive, immediate trauma and traumatic memories may exert tremendous force on the client, as the following example illustrates:

> Early for a morning appointment, Laura, a 27-year-old woman, leaves the subway two stops early, hoping to enjoy the sun warming her bare shoulders while she strolls along, sipping her morning coffee. Straightening up and walking free, she adjusts the strap of her small backpack.
>
> Date: September 11, 2001
>
> Location: Lower Manhattan, New York City
>
> Time: 8:45 A.M.
>
> There's a huge blast, instantly followed by a percussion wave that violently shoves Laura to one side; moments later debris starts crashing to the pavement around her. At first

she is paralyzed, uncomprehending, then instinct urges her to flee toward safety. A wave of fear sweeps through her; she feels desperately alone and struggles to save herself.

Then, Laura feels a forceful tap grabbing at her bare shoulder and, for an instant, feels comforted by this connection to another human being. She turns to acknowledge her companion in flight and sees a woman's hand. To her horror, it is *only* a hand; no arm, no body, no whole being was attached. She began frantically brushing away at it, trying to get it off, but the hand had become entangled in the straps of her backpack. She has begun gasping for air, and her frantic efforts to rid herself of the human remains seem only to jostle the clutching fingers lower onto her blouse. As she runs, her lungs labor for oxygen, sucking in some of the smoke and dust swept into the air by the yet mysterious explosion.

A stranger, also running for her life, notices Laura's predicament, tears the hand off Laura's body, and tosses it aside. Supporting each other, the two women escape to safety.

This incident was reported by Laura several days later. Concerned about her, Laura's mother urged her to call someone she trusted to talk about the incident. Laura, a former student and now a CSW social worker, called the author.

Except for her excessive focus on her difficulties breathing, Laura's feelings of shock and fear, her hypervigilance and isolation, and her difficulty sleeping, lack of appetite, and difficulty even leaving the house—she had missed two days of work—seemed appropriate, especially since she had to deal with the burden of seeing and handling human remains. It was Laura's descriptions of her difficulty breathing that were at the center of her discussion. This was unusual, since for most survivors of this tragedy breathing difficulties due to the dust clouds became serious at least 45 minutes after the first plane struck, by which time Laura had already reached safety.

As it turned out, the September 11th event had *retraumatized* Laura, triggering feelings around an earlier sexual assault; she had been raped fifteen years earlier when she was about 12 years old—the memory of which she had totally repressed. When her surprising focus on her inability to breathe was offered as an observation during a second interview, this repressed memory flashed into her consciousness. Laura remembered that her breathing difficulties during her September 11th experience started once she realized that it was the hand, alone, that was clutching at her. She then recalled her panic when, during the rape, the rapist had placed his hand over her mouth and nose, partially smothering and gagging her. At that time, her conscious focus was on her fear that she would suffocate. The hand, and the obviously frightening experiences of September 11th, triggered the repressed memories of the assault years earlier.

How was it that the association between these two traumas was so immediate and intense, with the emotions of the first transfusing into and potentiating the emotions engendered by the trauma of September 11th?

Nature of Retraumatization

Retraumatization involves an evocation of an earlier trauma. The American Psychiatric Association [APA] defines psychological trauma as "an event or events that involved actual or threatened death or serious injury, or a threat to the physical integrity of the self or others" (APA, 2000, p. 494). To be severely traumatized is "to have the untenable happen," explain Lizabeth Roemer and Leslie Lebowitz (1998): "A victim is left with the almost insurmountable task of making sense of and coping with something that is overwhelming, beyond comprehension, inherently unacceptable" (p. 2). Examples of traumatic events caused by human actions might include kidnapping, military combat, torture in a Latin American prison, the Chernobyl nuclear disaster, ethnic cleansing in Bosnia and Kosovo, school violence, sniper attacks in the nation's capital, child abuse, or other situations in which safety has been compromised.

The effects of traumas induced by mass violence are often stark: A refugee from armed conflict now living in the United States might flash back to explosions and flames that he or she may have witnessed—a symptom of posttraumatic stress disorder (PTSD)—if he or she becomes trapped, however briefly, in a burning room or is injured when a water heater bursts. In instances when the second trauma touches upon issues engendered by mass violence, such as physical injury, manifold emotional and economic losses, threat to safety, and perceived loss of security, long dormant responses to an earlier trauma may be triggered. Or the experience of immigration, with its manifold emotional and economic losses, might itself be a source of trauma. Eviction from an apartment in, say, Chicago might evoke flashbacks to the violent destruction of one's home in wartime Bosnia (Perez Foster, 2001; Weine, Kuc, Dzudza, Razzano, & Pavkovic, 2001).

This is the essence of retraumatization. While this term is relatively new and not always referred to as such in the literature, the impact of retraumatization has been widely recognized. For example, in discussing the consequences of the sniper attacks around Washington during the fall of 2002, Zaslow (2002) includes several recommendations from the Montgomery County, Maryland, Victim Assistance Program, directed toward people dealing with grief due to the shootings. The first recommendation states, "Be prepared for a past trauma to resurface in your mind, especially if you never got help [for the first trauma] then" (p. D1).

Trauma, Retrauma, and Neurology

All components of the individual's experience, including biological, psychological, and social aspects, can affect brain function and structures, especially if the person has been physically and/or psychologically traumatized. A second trauma triggers not only some of the psychological effects of the earlier trauma, but also some of the same physical reactions experienced previously, such as a fast heartbeat and sweating. This new trauma activates memories that may "generate heightened emotional reactions to stimuli reminiscent of their previous trauma" (Fischman, 2001). In fact, retraumatization follows an earlier trauma that has already *literally* changed the brain.

While the human brain is as unique as every person's unique experiences, there is much about the brain and its responses that is common among all individuals and defines us as human beings. The general responses to severe threats and trauma do not depend on the stage of the life cycle that the traumatized person is passing through, the specific event, his or her ethnic or racial group or nationality, or cultural experiences. The mechanism by which a suite of biological reactions of the brain and endocrine system are triggered by psychological trauma is no different for a male Vietnam War veteran, a female survivor of sexual abuse in Pakistan, or for a 12-year-old child in Cambodia who watched while his parents were killed by a land mine. The behaviors and responses a particular trauma evoke or elicit will, of course, vary with the experiences, physiology, and temperament of each individual. While variation in the content or causation of a trauma may modulate cognitive responses to that experience, we all share in common the brain's physiological response to psychological trauma: the creation and potentiation of pathways and connections among memories, the endocrine system, and the structures controlling such basic physiological housekeeping functions as respiration and heartbeat rates (Elbert & Schauer, 2002; McNew & Abell, 1995). A brief outline of some of the neurochemical responses to threat may illuminate common symptoms and concerns expressed by retraumatized victims of mass violence.

The human brain, even in adulthood, is more plastic—that is, it can be structurally altered by experience—than was once believed (Azmitia, 2001). During and immediately following a severely traumatic episode, the structure and interconnections of various electrochemical neuronal systems are altered into new patterns. In other words, when treating retraumatized clients, it is important to remember that the physical and emotional responses of the client cannot be immediately controlled by the individual but are due to reactions of a changed pathway in the brain. To oversimplify complex and as yet imperfectly understood biological/biochemical processes, a severe trauma results in profound changes in how the brain is "wired" and in the way it controls other physiological systems in response to a later threat.

Normally, our cortex, where our functioning and reasoning takes place, modulates our responses to stimuli from the environment. You check to see if a roadway is clear of cars before you decide to cross the street. If it seems that a bus is about to veer into you, however, most likely you will leap to safety first without considering the pros and cons of the best action. In other words, sometimes it is really better to leap first and look later; this is an example of a fight-or-flight response in which the higher regulatory functions of the brain's circuits are short circuited for an immediate, potentially life-saving response (Roemer & Lebowitz, 1998). An extreme threat, such as a gun pointed at one's head or being nearly run down by a car, often triggers this "fight/flight/freeze" response (Matsakis, 1999, pp. 75–78). In a fight or flight response, a number of stress hormones are released into the bloodstream, the most prominent among them being norepinephrine. Its breakdown product, epinephrine (commonly called adrenaline), leads to exceptional strength and speed to either fight off an "aggressive" threat or to flee danger quickly. Epinephrine strongly activates a number of brain and body systems, among them memory; during the fight-or-flight response, for example, intense events may be remembered more vividly (if not always more accurately) than ordinary events. Epinephrine also activates many functions of the sympathetic nervous system, among them heart rate, blood pressure, sweating, and respiration rate. At first, epinephrine release increases heart and respiration rates, while relaxing the blood vessels in the arms and legs and sending blood supplies with energy and oxygen reserves rushing into the muscles, preparing them for quick bursts of movement. The body is in a state of hyperarousal that interferes with reasoned thought (Roemer & Lebowitz, 1998).

A strong memory trace is laid down, comprising truly deep learning. With neuronal pathways connecting memory and the body's various physiological reactions to terror, the body will react even more quickly next time a similar threat is repeated. Thus the body "remembers" what has frightened it so it can prepare for action even more quickly the next time around without even bothering to call on the reasoning/thinking part of the brain for advice (Elbert & Schauer, 2002).

The symptoms of posttraumatic stress are in this sense a "learned" response. The reactions associated with extreme threat appear to have evolved as survival mechanisms over millions of years. It can save one's life to be able to run away fast, to be stronger if one has to fight off some attacking animal, or to move a heavy limb that has fallen on top of a friend. At times, however, a "freeze" response may be the safer and a more adaptive behavior. So while today an attack by a wolf pack is unlikely, if a robber threatens one with a gun, for example, a freeze response will likely be safer than fighting or running away. Discretion is often truly better than valor—and leads to more offspring.

In a typical freeze response, the threat is so extreme that *very large* amounts of norepinephrine are released, inducing a seemingly paradoxical response (actually, a second set of receptor sites begins to be triggered): a drop in blood flow to the extremities and muscles in the legs and arms, causing a feeling of weakness and various other neurological reactions that tend to immobilize the threatened person. This can be seen when an individual relating his or her reaction in an extremely threatening situation comments that "I couldn't move." Physiologically, this literally may have been the case. In addition to the inability to move, the individual may feel numbed, less sensitive to physical pain, and his or her memory may be imperfect or blurred. Some rape victims have reported this response, finding themselves completely unable to act to fend off an assailant during an attack. When the threat is perceived as ended, the alarm reaction shuts down and the levels of activating chemicals move toward normal. However, by this point the body is often depleted of its reserves of energy, leading to a sense of lassitude, fatigue, trembling, and a whole range of posttraumatic physiological reactions (Matsakis, 1999; Silove, 1998).

In a stress disorder, not only is the traumatized person often hypervigilant, but many different stimuli may also evoke a sense of threat; the survivor lives in a state of constant readiness. "High levels of arousal and hypervigilance, and schemas regarding the lack of safety in the world, combine to create a style of processing information that is exquisitely sensitive to the slightest indication of threat and often overlooks evidence of safety" (Roemer & Lebowitz, 1998). A sound, image, odor, or an event may stimulate a flashback to the original trauma, which is then followed by a threat response. "Traumatic experience," Roemer and Lebowitz add, "[disrupts] attentional and organizational abilities, so that...parts of the memory may be fragmented or separated so that the emotions are separated from the thoughts, the pictures separate from the words, parts of the events separate from each other, and the meaning of the event may be distorted or nonexistent" (Roemer & Lebowitz, 1998).

When many different stimuli evoke the traumatic event, the body may be in a frequent state of arousal and shock, each of which may be followed by exhaustion or fatigue, and, not surprising, mood swings. Among the chemicals produced as a response to threat is cortisol, which, among many other effects, may inhibit the formation of long-term memories. Consequently, some victims may not even remember portions of the traumatizing event, while other aspects of the event seem indelibly imprinted. The entanglement of physiology and psychological repression clearly is highly complex. In a sense, the feedback of evoked memories creates a neurological pathway, strengthened and conditioned over time, to memories of the earlier trauma. In retraumatization, a subsequent traumatic event is traveling a pathway, already well worn, to an earlier trauma. It is thus evident that the intrusion of a memory, a flashback, or the emotional content related to the earlier trauma into the current situation is not voluntary. Instead, the later trauma, the retraumatization, follows a direct course, a physiologically conditioned pathway, to the sometimes fragmented memory of the earlier event, which is then re-experienced either consciously or unconsciously (Bremner, 2001; Downing, 1994; Whybrow, 1997).

Symptoms of Retraumatization

Clinicians working with traumatized clients should be alert to the possibility that a trauma may evoke experiences and feelings rooted in an earlier trauma. Sometimes the signs of retraumatization are subtle, sometimes blatant. There is no typical manifestation of retraumatization; symptoms are determined by an individual's physiology and prior history of trauma.

September 11th will no doubt become a date to be remembered in the United States, a remembrance of horror, disaster, and of a surprise attack; perhaps somewhat like December 7, 1941. The United States will not be alone in remembering this date; September 11th also marks the date of the violent coup de etat in 1973 that brought General Pinochet to power in Chile. In the aftermath, thousands were slaughtered by the army, and Chile is not a populous country. Far more were arrested, never knowing whether in the next moment they would be pulled aside and shot at the whim of their captors or perhaps only tortured, and then released. This was the story frame for Mrs. Martin, an elderly immigrant from Chile, widowed several years ago:

> On September 11, 2001, Mrs. Martin, a generally healthy Chilean woman in her 80s, sits in her Florida living room, transfixed in horror as the events unfolding in New York, Washington, DC, and Pennsylvania are displayed on her TV. While watching, she begins to experience anxiety, stomach pains, difficulty breathing, cold sweats, a slight dizziness, and later seems depressed and withdrawn. Her son-in-law takes her to the doctor, fearing heart problems, which fortunately were ruled out. The physician offers reassurances in Spanish. Hearing her native language triggers Mrs. Martin's *memories* of the events of 1973. Mrs. Martin begins to cry as she recalls the anniversary and its aftermath, standing on a bridge in the capital, Santiago, desperate that she *not* recognize her missing husband among the bodies floating down the river. Once aware of this association, Mrs. Martin became much calmer and her physical distress resolved quickly.

Mrs. Martin's symptoms are consistent with the psychological and physiological manifestations associated with retraumatization, although they were fairly mild and resolved quickly. Perhaps this was so because her family had been relatively lucky; her husband had, eventually, been released from prison in good condition. Her reactions to the trauma of her husband's imprisonment had never become disabling for her, and after September 11th, the somatization (the expression of a psychological state in overt physiological symptoms) of her anxiety ceased quickly after she had identified their source in the history of her earlier trauma. It is important to note, however, how language—a vehicle of both thought and emotional expression, with almost every utterance evoking, and intending to evoke, myriad associations—may also serve to trigger emotions and memories in complex ways. The affect or feelings related to painful memories, and, at times, even the memories themselves, are associated with the linguistic environment in which the trauma was embedded and may not be easily accessed when using a second language (Perez Foster, 2001). It is, therefore, not surprising that it was only after hearing her doctor speak to her in Spanish that Mrs. Martin's memories and the emotions attached to them become overt.

But also imagine Mrs. Martin's frustration; she thought she had dealt with her feelings about the Pinochet coup in Chile and felt that she had moved forward. Now, on this dreadful anniversary, she felt thrown back in time. Frank Ochberg (2002), speaking about PTSD and anniversaries, and September 11ths in particular, explains that such anniversaries can be particularly difficult as people might feel that they are actually reliving the traumatizing event.

Reactions to Trauma

Reactions to what might indicate retraumatization may at first seem similar to those experienced at the onset of a new trauma. Such reactions may include frustration, anger, sadness, irritability, avoidance of usual activities, decreased desire or ability to communicate or relate to others, and attempts to self-medicate through alcohol or drugs. It is the *intensity* of the symptoms, fed by dormant emotions associated with the original trauma, and clues in the narrative storytelling, that often cues the social worker that this individual has traumatic imprints of previous violent experiences. Examples include:

- *Persistent nightmares and/or flashbacks.* A Vietnam veteran suffers minor injuries as he is assaulted and robbed while walking down the street. He flashes back to the experience and terror of combat in Vietnam, not solely to his fear while being punched and having his wallet stolen.
- *Aggressive or risk-taking behavior, directed toward self or others.* Enraged, a refugee high school student from Kosovo begins viciously punching and kicking another boy following a slightly off-color remark to the refugee's teenage sister. After being pulled off the hapless verbal offender, it emerges that the sister had been raped by Serbian hooligans in Kosovo, evoking the extreme overreaction to the remark in defense of his sister's honor. The issue was not cultural since the same remark might otherwise have been ignored in his homeland.
- *Persistent irritability.* A normally patient person who experiences trauma might develop a lightning-strike temper, for example, or might begin making out-of-character cutting comments about other persons.

- *Family discord or deterioration of vocational and/or social functioning.* Discord may take many forms, perhaps fueled by an increased irritability or obsessiveness. How is the client getting along with others? How have the relationships changed? How have vocational and social functioning changed?
- *Any type of serious and/or persistent deterioration of normal functioning.* Laura, in the case discussed previously, for example, had difficulty leaving her home.
- *Serious problems with self-medication.* Alcohol or other substances may be used to blot out, however temporarily, anxiety and painful memories. While self-medication through substance abuse is notoriously common among trauma victims, the relationships among trauma, retraumatization, and self-medication may be difficult to tease apart (Langer, 1998; Roy, 1983). A change in behavior is sometimes an important signal: Having a stiff drink to "settle the nerves" after being narrowly missed by a falling beam, for example, may not be significant; drinking on a daily basis, especially if the client has not done so in the recent past, is a different matter.
- *Any threat, direct or indirect, of suicidal intent.* Betty Cohen (1991) describes crises that were triggered for Holocaust survivors upon institutionalization in a nursing home or hospitalization. "The sick and the infirm were murdered by the Nazis, along with the very young and old. Thus sickness and old age may be associated with certain and violent death" (p. 227). A woman admitted to a nursing home in Miami once became extremely depressed with suicidal ideation. It emerged that she was a survivor who wanted to die rather than suffer the restricted freedom and physical indignities associated with care in the institution.

Reactions to trauma vary throughout the life cycle, with differing psychological and physical reactions seen at different ages—all of which can offer hints signaling retraumatization. For example, a specific trauma might induce thumbsucking in a preschooler; depression in an adolescent; withdrawal, suspicion, and/or irritability in an adult; and apathy in an older adult. Following are examples of reactions in various life-cycle stages.

Preschool reactions: Crying, whimpering, screaming; thumbsucking; fear of being left alone or of strangers; fear of crowds; fear of darkness or animals; excessive clinging; loss of bowel/bladder control; irritability; confusion; immobility; difficulty going to sleep; nightmares.

Latency age reactions: Headaches or other physical complaints; depression; fears about weather or safety; confusion; inability to concentrate, poor performance, fighting, reluctance to leave home or go to school; behavior problems or poor academic performance.

Preadolescent and adolescent reactions: Headaches; depression; confusion; poor performance; aggressive behaviors; changes in peer group and friends; drug or alcohol use.

Adult reactions: Psychosomatic problems such as racing heart, ulcer-like symptoms; withdrawal, suspicion, irritability; anger; sleep disturbances; loss of interest in everyday activities; difficulty in communicating thoughts; increased use of alcohol or other drugs; mood swings; feelings of hopelessness; colds or flulike symptoms; confusion; crying easily; overwhelming guilt or self-doubt; fear of crowds, strangers, or being alone; and difficulty concentrating.

Reactions of older adults: Depression, withdrawal; apathy; agitation, anger; disorientation/confusion; memory loss; accelerated physical decline; increased number of somatic complaints, irritability/suspicion. (Lystad, 1985; SAMHSA, 1997, 2001; Thames & Thompson, 2002)

Survivor Guilt: A Special Indicator

Survivor guilt is particularly pervasive for severe trauma sufferers, particularly among survivors of mass, human-induced traumas such as war veterans. In one study, 55 percent of Vietnam War veterans with posttraumatic stress disorder suffered survivor guilt (Langer, 1998). Unresolved or untreated survivor guilt can warp and shape lives; it leaves sufferers particularly vulnerable to subsequent traumas and thus retraumatization.

Guilt can take both "normal" and neurotic forms. As May and Yalom (1989) explain, "Neurotic guilt feelings (generally called *guilt*) often arise out of fantasized transgressions. Other forms of guilt, which we call *normal guilt,* sensitize us to the ethical aspects of our behavior" (p. 365). Normal guilt, in this scheme, is necessary for social life. The individual incapable of feeling normal guilt would tend towards Antisocial Personality Disorder. May and Yalom (1989) also identify a third form of guilt, one toward ourselves for failure to live up to our potentialities, or, adopting the terminology of Medard Boss, for "forgetting being" (p. 365).

As recounted by Roemer and Lebowitz (1998), a boy who had watched as his mother was beaten and raped now experiences debilitating fear as well as incapacitating shame and guilt for not having rescued her. In reality, as one would expect, any attempt by the child to help his mother would have been futile at best and possibly quite dangerous for him. "He may be left with a profound sense of danger in the world," they warn, "along with a malignant sense of self that may preclude his ability to form mutually satisfying relationships, [and/or] find meaningful work. The potentially devastating impact of trauma cannot be overemphasized."

In neurotic guilt, part of the torment comes from the irrational feeling that the individual could have prevented the death, injury, or mistreatment of another person or, at least, should have faced the same fate. "If I had only..." and "Why me?" are common expressions in neurotic guilt. "On an irrational level [these survivors] wince at their privileged escape from death's clutches" (Hass, 1995, p. 163). Survivor guilt sometimes results from the trauma of witnessing a trauma inflicted upon another. Commonly, these are examples of fantasized transgressions; there was usually nothing the survivor could have reasonably done, or the decision made was the best the survivor knew how to make with the information available at the time. For example, consider the common reaction "Why me?," which exemplifies Boss's concept of "forgetting being" (May & Yalom, 1989, p. 365); one almost literally loses oneself and a sense of one's innate value by obsessively thinking that one could have made a difference, "If only I had...." In addition, the evaluation that there were others more deserving of survival (they were more religious, talented, smarter, stronger, more educated, younger) is likewise irrational (Matsakis, 1999). This very easily translates to "Why them?" for the observer of mass trauma, and the experience of witnessing a traumatic event courses into the same psychic pathways as the original trauma, and thus retraumatizes.

Sometimes reality sharing may provide some beginning framework for therapeutic intervention. Who is to say that you could have made a difference? What role did chance play? What unrecognized strengths may have facilitated survival? Here, too, unearned shame or guilt felt by the survivor results from the loss of a sense of oneself and one's separate worth as an individual. One common reaction is to take on a sometimes unrealistic burden, demanding a level of achievement that compensates for the loss of what is seen as the more deserving person. Survivors may experience retraumatization when these unrealistic goals cannot be achieved—when they have "failed" yet again to be deserving. Persons experiencing survivor guilt are particularly prone to repeated intrusive thoughts and images in which the experiences are relived again and again (May & Yalom, 1989).

One Holocaust survivor, for example, alleviated her survivor guilt (perceived as having beaten the odds and the feeling that someone else died in her place) by finding a meaningful purpose in life—she would replenish the Jewish people (Hass, 1995). Unfortunately, she now feels she has been stripped of her reason for being, her identity: "Her son is a 40-year-old drug addict and her unmarried 38-year-old daughter suffers from panic attacks whenever she leaves her parents' house" (Haas, 1995, p. 174). There is an inauthenticity at the core of her being; she would have to do what is impossible to do—to control her children's behavior for her own life to have meaning. The fact that her children could not or do not live as she needs them to has severely retraumatized this mother. Recognition of neurotic survival guilt might be the base point for intervention with her.

Implications for Social Work Interventions

Work with retraumatized victims is delicate and demanding—after all, intense emotions are themselves being fed by often obscure and/or as yet unidentified intense emotions. As with any client, social workers establishing a trusting relationship with a trauma victim need to be empathetic, nonjudgmental, and attending carefully to any signs, verbal and nonverbal, of retraumatization. The establishment of trust, vital in any therapeutic relationship, is of particular importance when dealing with those who have been retraumatized by mass violence, since the individual's loss of trust in others during the original trauma is compounded by a new sense of betrayal.

Recognition that the client may be experiencing retraumatization is often based on professional intuition. While the memory, or emotional content of a memory, is repressed, and the second trauma is an activator, the association may not be obvious or "logical." It is particularly useful for the social worker to attend to the client's dreams, symbols, flashbacks, and body movements or motions because they may provide vital clues. The client may seem to be attending to portions of the later trauma that seem unusual, such as Laura's primary focus on breathing difficulties rather than the handling of human remains, or reactions may seem more strongly infused with emotions than one might expect. Any tentative thoughts along these lines must be explored with great sensitivity. Not only might one's intuition or clues be incorrect but, as Mrs. Martin's experience suggests, even well-intended debriefing interventions may be damaging, triggering a flashback to the original trauma. A worker must be especially careful not to add to the trauma being experienced.

It is also helpful to keep in mind that traumas bond people. Social workers who were not part of the trauma are "outsiders" and have no right to be "in" except by invitation; they are guests. In cases of mass violence, disempowerment and insecurity are usually among the objective ends of a perpetrator and are at the heart of the trauma. One therefore must be very conscious that as a therapist one might be seen as an authority figure; thus, in these situations the therapist must take great care that one's offering of help should not be experienced as an intrusive or oppressive act and thereby in itself be potentially retraumatizing (Snelgrove, 2001).

Snelgrove suggests that the practitioner empower people with choices—in contracting, respect the fact that the client may choose not to debrief the experience, even if you disagree. Honor and respect who they are (perhaps, the client may not be loquacious). With retraumatized clients—and this certainly includes traumatized emergency workers and/or war veterans—social workers may well be guests in more than a single trauma.

There are a number of reasons why clients might have difficulty describing traumatic events. Not only might these descriptions evoke painful memories that the victim may have been trying to repress or avoid, but traumatic events may also "engender shame due to the degradation and utter helplessness the individual [may have been] subject to during victimization as well as the social stigma of victimization [and, in addition,] trauma victims often accurately perceive that others do not want to hear about the horrible things they have lived through. They fear rejection, incredulity, and invalidation" (Roemer & Leibowitz, 1998).

Other intervention approaches might include the use of open-ended questions, such as "Can you tell me more?" and "What is the significance of this for you?" These help create a physically and psychologically safe environment for the social work relationship and encourage a discussion of the nature of confidentiality. It is important to ascertain and develop the client's previous coping skills and to offer techniques, such as muscle relaxation and breathing exercises, that might lessen states of arousal. Finally, it is helpful to normalize the client's reactions ("Most people would be upset").

Sometimes the client is "stuck " in the traumatic experience, for example, ruminating about it (obsessively reliving the experience in one's thoughts) to such a degree that it is difficult to attend to much else. It may be possible to break the cycle by urging a return to typical routines and social interactions and developing cognitive strategies of self-awareness. And in all interactions, the advisability of a referral for evaluation for antidepressant, anxiety, or other medications should be considered. These can be very helpful in breaking ruminative cycles, depressive ideation, and pervasive anxiety, thus facilitating other helpful interventions such as cognitive approaches and analytical insight.

The National Mental Health Information Center of the Substance Abuse and Mental Health Services Administration (SAMHSA, 1997) offers these "do say" suggestions for anyone debriefing individuals after a disaster: *These are normal reactions to a disaster. It is understandable that you feel this way. No one who sees a disaster is untouched by it. You are not going crazy. It wasn't your fault; you did the best you could. It is normal to feel anxious about yourself and your family's safety.* These statements help the clients normalize and ground their feelings in a more common reality; the normalization tends to release the pressure of some of the emotions and thus facilitate recovery.

Conclusion

The pervasiveness of the impacts of severe trauma cannot be overemphasized; it affects every aspect of a client's bio/psycho/social environment.

> *Trauma disrupts our biological equilibrium, affecting the body's housekeeping functions.* These functions are generally outside our cognitive control, and the resulting disequilibrium may result in headaches, pounding heart, fatigue, restlessness, insomnia and other sleep disorders, and heightened startle responses.
>
> *Trauma overwhelms our psychological constructs of reality.* The content of severe psychological trauma challenges the cognitive map of our world. We're unsure what is safe, what is not, and our assumptions about the relative value of things, which had previously given meaning to one's life and to the world, may now seem unreliable or false. Problems with psychological functioning might be manifested cognitively through forgetfulness, difficulty concentrating, confusion, boredom, pessimistic or negative attitudes, and ruminative thoughts. Emotional manifestations might include anxiety, panic attacks, mood swings, depression, irritability, crying spells, obsessive worry or other obsessive behaviors, lack of perseverance, and hypervigilance.
>
> *Traumatic effects on biology and psychology also pervade our social interactions.* These social effects might be signaled by a client's isolation, expressed resentments, loneliness, lashing out, nagging, withdrawing from contacts with friends, exploiting people, clamming up, or a diminished sex drive (Roemer & Lebowitz, 1998; Thames & Thomason, 2002).

Traumatic reactions pervade every aspect of a person's life, and the symptoms of trauma do not always disappear—particularly those that are induced by some form of human-caused mass violence. Trauma can be treated and the pain can be relieved, but as the case of Mrs. Martin demonstrates, some impact of trauma will always be with the victim. Thus the danger of retraumatization will also be present. As pointed out by Frank Ochberg, a former Associate Director of the National Institute of Mental Health, "Closure is a bad word.... It falsely implies the end to something that doesn't end. You don't get closure on trauma, tragedy, the impact of human cruelty, but you do grow, you do get sadder and wiser.... Closure is a myth, but progress is not" (Ochberg, 2002).

References

American Psychiatric Association. (1994). *Diagnostic and statistical manual of mental disorders* (4th ed.). Washington, DC: Author.

Azmitia, E. C. (2001). Impact of drugs and alcohol on the brain through the life cycle: Knowledge for social workers. In R. T. Spence, D. DiNitto, & S. L. A. Straussner (Eds.), *Neurobiology of addictions: Implications for clinical practice* (pp. 41–63). New York: Haworth.

Bremner, J. D. (2001). A biological model of delayed recall of childhood abuse. *Journal of Aggression, Maltreatment & Trauma, 4,* 165–83.

Cohen, B. B. (1991). Holocaust survivors and the crisis of aging. *Families in Society: The Journal of Contemporary Human Services, 72,* 226–232.

Downing, R. (1994). *What are traumatic memories?* The Sidran Foundation. Retrieved February 1, 2002, from www.sidran.org/traumabr.html.

Elbert, E., & Schauer, M. (2002). Psychological trauma: Burnt into memory. *Nature, 419,* 883.

Fischman,Y. (2001). Understanding terror-induced trauma. *Dialogus, 6,* Retrieved March 29, 2002, from <http://home.earthlink.net/~circlepoint/health0702.html>.

Hass, A. (1995). Survivor guilt in holocaust survivors and their children. In J. Lemberger (Ed.), *A global perspective on working with holocaust survivors and the second generation.* Proceedings of the Preconference Institute on Working with Holocaust Survivors and the Second Generation, Jerusalem, July 3–4, 1994 (pp. 163–183). Jerusalem: AMCHA, Brookdale Institute, & World Council of Jewish Communal Services (co-publishers).

Langer, E. (1998). PTSD: A diagnostic report on war veterans. Retrieved January 31, 2002, from www.geocities.com/SouthBeach/Shores/6052/ptsd2.html.

Lystad, M. (1985). *Innovations in mental health services to disaster victims.* U.S. Department of Health and Human Services, Public Health Service, Alcohol, Drug Abuse, and Mental Health Administration: National Institute of Mental Health. Washington, DC: U.S. Government Printing Office.

Matsakis, A. (1999). *Survivor guilt.* Oakland, CA: New Harbinger Publications.

May, R., & Yalom, I. (1989). Existential psychotherapies. In R. J. Corini & D. Wedding (Eds.), *Current psychotherapies* (4th ed.; pp. 363–401). Itasca, IL: Peacock.

McNew, J. A., & Abell, N. (1995). Posttraumatic Stress Syndrome symptomatology: Similarities and differences between Vietnam veterans and adult survivors of childhood sexual abuse. *Social Work, 40,* 115–126.

Ochberg, F. M. (2002). An interview with Frank M. Ochberg, M. D. Retrieved December 4, 2002, from www.mental-health-matters.com/articles/gfw001.php?artID=294.

Perez Foster, R. (2001). When immigration is trauma: Guidelines for the individual and the family clinician. *American Journal of Orthopsychiatry, 71,* 153–170.

Roemer, L., & Lebowitz, L. (1998). Understanding severe traumatization. *Advocate, 20* (1). Retrieved November 31, 2002, from http://dpa.state.ky.us/library/advocate/january98/trauma.htm.

Roy, R. E. (1983). Alcohol and posttraumatic stress disorder (delayed): An alternative interpretation of the data. *Journal of Studies on Alcohol, 44,* 198–202.

Silove, D. (1998). Is posttraumatic stress disorder an overlearned survival response? An evolutionary-learning hypothesis. *Psychiatry: Interpersonal & Biological Processes, 6,* 181–190.

Snelgrove, T. (2001). Psychological-educational debriefings and outcome assessment: A point of view. Retrieved December 6, 2002, from www.ctsn-rcst.ca/PsychoEd.html.

Speyrer, J. (2001). Can re-living a trauma be a retraumatization? Retrieved January 31, 2002, from www.webpages.charter.net/jspeyrer/retrauma.htm.

Substance Abuse and Mental Health Services Administration [SAMHSA]. (1997). After a disaster: Self-care tips for dealing stress. Retrieved December 2, 2002, from www.mentalhealth.org/publications/allpubs/KEN-01-00095.

Substance Abuse and Mental Health Services Administration [SAMHSA]. (2001). Mental health aspects of terrorism. Retrieved December 2, 2002, from www.mentalhealth.org/publications/allpubs/KEN-01-0097.

Thames, B. J., & Thomason, D. J. (2002). Stress management for the health of it: Self-study lesson. Clemson Extension [South Caroline Agricultural Extension Service]. Retrieved December 3, 2002, from the National Agricultural Safety Database [NASD] www.cdc.gov/nasd/docs/d001201-d001300/d001245.html.

Weine, S., Kuc, G., Dzudza, E., Razzano, L., & Pavkovic, I. (2001). PTSD among Bosnian refugees: A survey of providers' knowledge, attitudes and service patterns. *Community Mental Health Journal, 37,* 261–271.

Whybrow, P. C. (1997). *A mood apart.* New York: Basic Books.

Zaslow, J. (2002, October 16). The sniper's other victims: Going back to work at the scene of a tragedy. *Wall Street Journal,* p. D1.

10

The Role of Spirituality and Religion in Responding to Mass Violence

Arlene Gellman and Barbara Dane

A person's religious and spiritual commitments can have a profound impact on how he or she will respond to mass violence. While some people do not hold strong religious or spiritual beliefs, during times of mass violence they may turn to religious and spiritual rituals for solace (Rosner, 2001). Many survivors of mass violence remain receptive and trusting in the notion of a higher power; they remain unshaken in their faith that those who died or survived did so by the "grace of God." Some, however, may rely more on an inner sense of spirituality that is not connected with organized religion. For others, witnessing mass violence and dealing with its effects creates a dilemma because their religious and spiritual beliefs are challenged by the terrible reality. They question the nature of good and evil and the nature of God, asking the age-old question—How can a benevolent God allow such suffering? Consequently, some people turn away from their previously held beliefs and from the potential support of their families and religious communities, leaving themselves more vulnerable to isolation and despair.

Social workers working with people traumatized by mass violence need to recognize the wide range of religious and spiritual views held by survivors, the impact of the trauma on these beliefs, and the supports that may be available through their religious or spiritual communities. This may be unfamiliar territory for many clinicians, as social work practice has developed in a secular, social science context that does not typically consider the spiritual realm.

This chapter will discuss the roles of religion and spirituality on the lives of clients affected by mass violence and offer assessment and intervention approaches that can be particularly useful in working with traumatized clients.

Distinguishing between Religion and Spirituality

Religion and spirituality are multifaceted, overlapping constructs whose specific definitions remain a subject of debate. According to Hood, Spilka, Hunsberger, and Gorsich (1996), "any definition of religion is likely to be acceptable only to its author" (p. 4). The concept of *religion* is viewed as a societal phenomenon, involving social institutions whose values are defined by rules, rituals, covenants, and formal procedures. Some of the common components of religious practice include theological beliefs, commitments, practices, and congregational activities by an organized institution. Spiritual practice has a more personal focus that may include prayer, developing a sense of meaning in life, reading and contemplation, meditation, feeling a sense of closeness to a higher being or to nature, interactions with others based on the commonality of beliefs and practices, and other individual or communal experiences (Carson, 1993; Pargament, 1997). Walsh and Vaughn (1985) have defined *spirituality* in terms of personal views and behaviors that express a sense of relatedness to a transcendent dimension or to something greater than the self. Spirituality is, at its core, intensely personal and experiential (Plante & Sherman, 2001).

Thoresen, Harris, and Oman (2001) summarize the following assumptions about spirituality and religion:

- Religiousness and spirituality as concepts represent primarily functional or process-oriented phenomena, such as coping or social integration, rather than fixed structural characteristics, such as religious denomination. They are concerned with the changing nature of what the person does, thinks, feels, and subjectively experiences within particular social and cultural contexts.
- Both religion and spirituality are multidimensional in nature. Some dimensions can be easily observed, such as attending services, and some dimensions have latent qualities that are not readily observed, such as feeling closeness to God. In this way they are much like the concepts of personality, health, and love. Just as personality is more than behavior, health more than blood pressure, and love more than sexual arousal, spirituality is more than feeling connected to life, and religiousness is more than attending church services.
- An individual's spiritual and religious commitments may change with time and circumstances. Also, such commitments cannot be adequately assessed through the use of questionnaires only or by relying exclusively on personal accounts or narratives, but require multiple assessments tools.

Different terms have been used to describe religion and spirituality, with some overlap in meaning. As a consequence of the increasing disillusionment with organized religion in the 1960s and 1970s, spirituality began to acquire meaning and connotations that separated it from religion (Zinnbauer & Pargament, 1996). Spirituality and spiritual care are more inclusive terms; spirituality is the essence of one's human nature that may or may not be expressed through religious practices or beliefs. "Religion is a search for significance in ways related to the sacred" (Pargament, 1997, p. 11). Religion may have and often does have a powerful spiritual component; however, spirituality is no longer seen as an exclusive offspring of religious practice.

Religion and Spirituality in Social Work Practice

As an academically supported social science discipline, social work severed its historic religious and spiritual roots in the 1940s, and the profession began to refer to the spiritual needs of people in nonsectarian terms, such as human needs of the individual (Bullis, 1996; Canda & Furman, 1999; Joseph, 1987). Social work thus developed as a secular profession, and models of law, socialism, Freudianism, and behaviorism became more influential than theology. In the 1970s and 1980s the guidelines of Council on Social Work Education (CSWE) further eliminated even the nonsectarian references to spirituality (Marshal, 1991). According to Loewenberg (1988), this process of secularization caused social workers with religious and spiritual beliefs to separate their work from their own beliefs. Wilson (1982) stated that "some social workers may at times seek answers or reassurance from religious sources, but even for them religion has become a private, part-time institution which has relatively little bearing on their professional lives" (p. 70). While many social workers did not personally reject religion, some raised doubts about the usefulness of religion and spirituality to the problem-solving process and maintained that religious beliefs solve neither concrete nor emotional problems. Still others suggested that religion and social work are two incompatible systems and it made little sense to unite them (Loewenberg, 1988).

Nonetheless, many social workers maintained their religious and spiritual beliefs, and the disjuncture between the practice of social work and spirituality and religion did not go unchallenged. Some social workers posited that social work is fundamentally a spiritual profession—one that sets its reason for existence and its highest priorities at the spiritual level (Biestek, 1953; Siporin, 1985). A 1995 survey of 56 Mormon and Protestant social workers in Utah found that 89 percent of respondents felt that spirituality is an important part of social work practice, and 91 percent reported spirituality to be a topic raised by their clients (Derezotes & Evans, 1995). Another study of 142 social workers in North Dakota (Furman, 1994) found that 33 percent indicated that they frequently encountered issues of religion and spirituality with clients in their practice.

In recent years, the recognition of the relevance of spirituality to social work practice has grown, and current revisions to the Council on Social Work Education's curriculum guidelines support the inclusion of this content in both master's and bachelor's level social work courses (Canda & Furman, 1999). In addition, the National Association of Social Workers' *Code of Ethics* now requires social workers to be culturally competent in several areas, including spirituality and religion (Staral, 1999), and social workers are prohibited from discriminating in their professional practice on the basis of religious diversity (Standard 1.05).

As the social work literature has broadened its focus in the effort to understand the "whole person" (Bullis, 1996; Canda, 1998), a growing array of new and professionally sanctioned conceptual models incorporating spiritual beliefs and practices has been developed (Canda, 1998; Canda & Furman, 1999; Carroll, 1998). These approaches, including the strengths-based practice perspective (Saleebey, 1997), feminist theory (Van Den Berg, 1995), and constructionist approaches (Fleck & Carter, 1981), have challenged social workers to expand their assessment tools and their repertoire of skills as they attempt to provide help to diverse clients. One such new paradigm is *transpersonal theory* (Wilber, 1995), which supports Maslow's (1970) view that behaviorists have erroneously ignored the inner world of people, while focusing on the external, mechanistic nature of human activity. The new theoretical views and the focus on providing holistic treatment for clients have reopened the question of the place of spirituality in social work theory and practice in general and its role in dealing with grief and trauma in particular.

Spirituality and Trauma

Trauma has a profound and pervasive impact on all aspects of the self. The healthy development from childhood into adulthood involves the capacity to maintain an inner sense of connection with benign others who can be counted on to gratify one's needs and the internalization of others who are experienced as separate and stable sources of support (Pearlman & Saakvitne, 1998). The experience of mass violence can lead to the loss of such an internalized protective presence.

Witnessing death and experiencing losses as a result of mass violence propels us into appreciating what we had, what we lost, and what we now have. For some, the rawness one experiences from mass violence may evoke utter despair. For those with religious and spiritual ties, one's religion and/or spirituality can provide needed guidance and support to process the initial shock and the subsequent grief. According to Canda and Furman (1999), "Spiritual emergency in the form of a debilitating crisis as trauma, imposes a serious risk for physical illness, psychopathology, and social disruption" (p. 225). Such traumatic events often lead to dramatic change in survivors' worldviews, creating negative shifts in a person's fundamental assumptions about meaningfulness, goodness, and safety. For those whose core values are theologically founded, traumatic events often give rise to questions about the fundamental nature of the relationship between the Creator and humankind (Pearlman & Saakivtne, 1998).

Atchley (1995) suggests that deficiencies of vocabulary and conspiracies of silence about inner experiences, common in social work practice, have a particular significance for professional work with individuals experiencing trauma. For those clients who have spiritual and religious beliefs, these systems can be a rich source of strength and insight, while keeping these beliefs beyond the scope of consideration limits the social worker's understanding of a client and his or her strengths. Frankl (1969) asserted that those who "ignore man's spiritual side are giving away one of his most valuable assets" (p. 16). Even Freud (1907), who thought of religion as a form of mass neurosis, viewed it as critical in understanding a patient's human and social consciousness. The challenge to the profession is to realize that spirituality is not a realm separate from daily life or relegated to religious places or rituals.

The Interaction of Trauma and Spirituality

Trauma can initially call into question one's religious and spiritual commitments, leading to a sense of alienation from a Supreme Being or Higher Power. This can be manifested by feelings of emptiness, disappointment, and betrayal. An immediate isolation from one's self, family, others, and God may occur. However, the deep shock that survivors of massive trauma suffer can also "transform the human spirit from extreme diminution of the will to an existential transcendence which is spiritual in nature (Wilson, 1982, p. 8). According to Jung (1954), "as long as all goes well and there are no uncertainties or doubts, an individual can feel secure. When one's 'river of psychic energy' is dammed up, one's spiritual walk has been blocked" (p. 294). This loss of personal wholeness is often experienced during mass violence and in its aftermath.

Spirituality and the Immediate Effects of Trauma

In the initial phase of disaster people often feel intense social disorganization. The initial numbness yields to feeling overwhelmed, with people feeling a lack of control over their world as they struggle to make sense of incomprehensible events. For the newly traumatized, their religious values and spiritual needs may be interconnected with their emotional, cognitive, and even physiological needs. Various tasks and opportunities present themselves in the early days following a disaster that invite people to explore the meaning of religion and spirituality for themselves. These include the following issues:

Burying the Dead. As survivors experience the pain of loss, many try to maintain their defenses through denial and disbelief. However, family members are also called upon to make immediate and essential decisions about burial arrangements. This task requires that they confront their religious attitudes toward death, the rites of burial, and approaches to mourning (Cullinan, 1993; Rando, 1986).

When there is no body to bury, as may occur in mass trauma, grievers feel "disenfranchised." Such disenfranchised losses may place survivors in a double bind—while the loss raises strong issues related to mortality and meaning, sources of support based on religious belief or ritual may not be forthcoming or helpful (Doka & Morgan, 1993). Bettelheim remarked that in the absence of the evidence of death, and without a "definite point in time when mourning could have started, and with it no date at which it could be expected to end (according to Jewish tradition)...mourning seemed impossible to complete and one is apt to suffer all one's life from its continuation" (p. 172). Despite these challenges, grievers of victims of mass violence bring themselves to eventually reframe the meaning of the trauma and take necessary steps to cope and grieve. Awareness and sensitivity of the impact of the violence and the loss and questioning one's religion and spiritual life constitute first steps to ameliorate the feelings of disconnectedness.

Coping with Survivor's Guilt. Survivors experience trauma "like an earthquake, shaking the soul to its very being" (Doka & Morgan, 1993, p. 247). Trauma can occur even if the individual is not at the actual event; hearing the story can result in visual imaging of the event and intensify the response pattern involving physical, emotional, cognitive, and spiritual parts of the person.

It is not uncommon for survivors to feel guilty for not having done things differently. According to Danielle (1985), "the most agonizing instances of self-reproach and self-blame are generated in cases of sudden death and of violence" (p. 51). It is also common for survivors to become obsessed with the suffering experienced by their loved one in the process of dying (Knapp, 1986). Many times survivors utilize destructive or dysfunctional strategies to deal with survivors' guilt, such as emotional repression, use of chemicals, or denial of their feelings of vulnerability. Integration and recovery involve the survivor's ability to develop a realistic perspective of what happened, by whom, to whom, and to accept the reality that it happened the way it did; what was and was not under his or her control, what could not be, and why. Accepting the impersonality of the events also removes the need to attribute personal causality with the consequent sense of guilt and false responsibility (Danielle, 1988).

The Quest for Meaning. During the aftermath of a disaster, many individuals share a quest for meaning that is religious or spiritual in nature. Many seek solace not only from family and friends, but also from the clergy. Some begin to question their belief systems and feel angry at God; others become frantically immersed in religious or church-related activities or feel resigned to the situation they feel was willed by God. Still others expect clergy magically to take the pain away.

Shapiro (1994) contends that people search for the cause of death in an attempt to integrate the death in their lives and to regain a sense of safety and order in the world. According to Frankl (1969), when people get in touch with their spirituality, they might find sustenance and resilience in the face of tragedy. Some families try to make sense of the death of a loved one by projecting religious meaning onto coincidental events. For example, one family took the sudden availability of a previously unavailable cemetery plot as a sign that a Higher Power was involved. In another case, a woman patient reported that after she had prayed again and again for God to let her know where her sister was, the song "I'm in Heaven" came on the radio (Winchester-Nadeau, 1998).

In contrast, some families do not believe that a disaster was a calling to heaven or part of God's master plan and can find no spiritual meaning in their loss. They see the death as senseless (Lofland & Lofland, 1984). Frankl (1969) suggested that comments such as "God let us down," "I'm mad at God," or "I blame God" point out that although most grieving individuals may search for meaning in their suffering, the meaning is not always positive. Therefore, it is not helpful to suggest to grievers that they should be able to find a positive meaning and purpose in their loss and suffering, but rather to assess each individual's religious and spiritual feelings as they relate to the specific event.

Finding meaning in adversity is one possible way of coping. Suffering can invite one into a spiritual domain (Wright, 1996) where, gradually, integration and healing occurs. The ability to integrate transpersonal religious insights into one's daily life results in what Maslow (1970) referred to as a "plateau experience." He felt it is a way of being that is oriented toward compassion, beauty, wisdom, creativity, profundity, and responsibility (Canda & Furman, 1999).

Spirituality and the Long-Term Effects of Trauma

Dealing with trauma over time can result in people questioning their long-held spiritual beliefs; it may also launch a quest for a new dimension to their faith (Walsh, 1999). Werner and Smith (1982) have found that meaningfulness in terms of spiritual connection was important for long-term resilience.

Long-term effects of trauma can include survivors' questioning of the overall meaning of life. While this can lead to a renewed commitment to life, it may also result in temporarily giving up on ideals, on one's belief in God, and even on life itself. Bitterness and resentment toward God and "the world" can become deeply rooted and remain for the rest of one's life. For a great many people, mourning continues throughout their lives; this does not constitute pathology, but rather a lifetime response to massive losses. It might bring with it an ongoing questioning of the circumstance, a lack of feeling of the presence of God, and anger, which may take many forms, including rage directed first at the medical community, at the clergy, and then self-blame and withdrawal. Long-term intervention by clinicians and the clergy can be effective in helping individuals triumph over what may at first seem to be an insurmountable adversity.

Social Work Interventions

Clinical social work interventions with people affected by mass violence have begun to embrace some techniques that enable people to draw on their spiritual and religious beliefs to aid the healing process. Techniques that have been found to be effective include the use of

- Rituals and meditation
- Mental imagery and metaphors

For millennia and in various locations around the globe, the uses of mental imagery and metaphors have been essential facets of the healing process. As noted by Foote (1996), "both yoga and tantric Buddhism use an elaborate system of internal imagery. Similarly, vision quest and sand paintings of Native Americans involve images, as do techniques of the Australian aborigines" (p. 355). Recently, the field of psychoneuroimmunology (PNI), which includes guided imagery, hypnosis, relaxation, and meditative techniques, has shown promise in supporting traditional mental health interventions (Naparstek, 1994). Clinical social work interventions during and after mass violence and traumatic life events have begun to embrace some alternative techniques that have historically complemented one's spiritual journey during times of crisis (Achterberg, 1985; Naparstek, 1994).

Guided imagery is a deliberate creation of sensory images in altered states of consciousness during which one remains both relaxed and highly focused. Sights, smells, sounds, tastes, and feelings can be experienced in our imagination in order to create positive physical and emotional changes in the entire mind-body system (Naparstek, 1994). Imagery has been known to affect some aspects of involuntary responses of the body, including the release of adrenalin. Recent studies have demonstrated encouraging effects of guided imagery on self-esteem, coping, disruptive behavior, depression, and anxiety in traumatized adolescent boys (Gellman, 2001) and on the functioning of the immune system and physical healing (Holden-Lund, 1988). It has also been found to be effective for performance enhancement, self-esteem, self-regulation, and problem solving (Sommers-Flanagan, 1966; Taylor, Pham, Rivkin, & Armor, 1998), improvement in coping (Ott, 1996), stress and anxiety reduction (Gruber et al., 1993; Thompson & Coppens, 1994; Weber, 1996), and depression (Leja, 1991).

Use of Rituals and Meditation

The use of rituals can lead to significant healing. *Rituals* requiring a retelling of stories about the deceased seem conducive to resolving grief and helping survivors feel less isolated. Families and communities involved in a ritual can gain emotional support from one another, provide clarity to each individual, and infuse meaning into the collective experience. Achterberg (1985) cites several benefits of ritual, not the least of which is that through ritual, "the patient can sense relief through believing that harmony between himself/herself and the spirit world is established" (p. 157). The same sentiment is echoed by Powell (1998) with regard to meditation. He posits that "the soul finds direct expression in human consciousness the same the world over. In contemplation, meditation, and quiet reflection, regardless of culture, we are intuitively drawn to images of beauty, truth and peace" (p. 102). He further claims that when the soul is engaged during therapeutic work, there is an expansion of one's reality that he refers to as "spiritual object relations" (p. 103). Powell (1998) believes that "the drama of the internal object world that we know so well from life in the body is no less lively in spirit" (p. 103) and that perhaps our object-seeking behavior throughout our lifetime is a continuation of the feeling and acting on the joy of being in union with the soul of another (p. 103).

The importance of ritual and meditation to a client affected by mass violence is illustrated by the case of Sy:

> Sy is an emergency medical technician (EMT) who, on September 11, 2001, was called to the scene of the World Trade Center attacks in New York City. He entered a building with his fellow EMT worker and cherished friend, Burt. In the chaos that ensued at the scene they lost track of one another and Burt never found his way out.
>
> Sy was not a religious man, attending worship only as a tradition during religious holidays. However, in treatment, he described moments of spiritual clarity during his lifetime. When his mother passed away, he recalled feeling her presence for moments of time in the week following her death, a sensation he described as a total physical calm that came over his body—an awareness not easily communicable. He continued to feel his mother's presence during significant celebratory events over the course of his life. Sy was asked if he had felt Burt's presence since his disappearance and he said he had not, which made him feel that Burt might still be alive, although he conceded that his survival was unlikely.

It is evident here that Sy utilizes ritualized life events as a medium for sustaining a feeling of connection with those who have passed on. While in a meditative state, the comfort and cultural spirituality with which such events are infused transcend the boundaries of life and death to create for the meditating client a tangible location for spiritual feelings. While Sy's awareness of such feelings had been unconscious, he was able to employ imagery as his tool for harnessing the power of the spiritual-ritual realm, creating a stability that would inform his conscious mind. It was therefore necessary for Sy, during therapy, to engage in a ritual practice of a spiritual object-relations nature with Burt in order that he may resolve the confusion surrounding Burt's death.

During a session, while in an altered state of consciousness, Sy was asked to locate a place in which he might meet Burt. He said that he was entering the baseball stadium that they had often gone to together. After a few moments, he said he could see Burt sitting in "some great seats behind home plate." Sy smiled as he described walking up to and sitting down with Burt, who was, perhaps, "waiting for him." Sy reported that he and Burt remained verbally quiet with one another, but that in looking at each other and experiencing the other's presence, they knew exactly what the other was feeling, and in those moments together he relayed his love and devotion to Burt, as did Burt to him. He felt the same bodily calm that he had experienced after his mother's passing.

By bringing to mind a baseball game as a symbol of connectedness to Burt, together with his recollection of the ritual of attending baseball games together, Sy was able to make contact with the spirit of a union that gave him joy, strength, and relief—much the same way as family ritual events returned the spirit of his mother to a palpable location, so too did a baseball game, which as both a culturally and personally significant cue provided a destination where Sy and Burt could be reunited. In this place, Sy began his healing.

Use of Mental Imagery and Metaphors

The therapeutic interventions in Sy's case also included guided imagery. As noted, guided imagery occurs in an induced altered state of consciousness. For Sy, imagery permitted him to engage with and resolve an event in the past. However, imagery can also allow one to practice for situations and events that have not yet occurred, thereby enabling the individual to respond to difficult situations with confidence. This practice can provide access to the unconscious and its symbolic images so that individuals can utilize these symbols to restore purpose and meaning to their lives.

In the context of spirituality, imagery has served as a gateway to healing by accessing subtle levels of consciousness through *preverbal* and *transpersonal* modes of communication. Achterberg (1985) notes that in the preverbal context, imagery impacts tissues, organs, and cells to assist in creating change. This mind/body connection was forged before words and transmits information through differing neural pathways. For example, when children experience traumatic events, a disruption between internal process and external systems arises that can result in major developmental derailments as the child moves into "modes of survival and self-protection" (Everstine & Everstine, 1993, p. 113). There is a particularly urgent need to find a sense of security during times when an individual experiences trauma or retraumatization. If trauma initiates a departure from expectation and normalcy, ritual and symbol are the vehicles by which the client can return to a place of safety. These techniques are illustrated in the following case of Danal:

> Following the events of September 11th, Danal, a very bright, introspective 13-year-old, began to have an increasing number of frustrated outbursts at home and fights and disruptive behavior at school. When he saw a social worker, Danal began his treatment by

> acknowledging this anger. "People don't feel safe any more," he said, and he proceeded over time to express his own feelings of insecurity.
>
> Danal had been taught progressive relaxation techniques and a breathing meditation while participating in therapy previously with the same therapist; now time was spent getting reacquainted with these techniques. During one session, Danal was asked if he might consider finding ways of feeling safe and empowered. He was asked to describe a place where he felt comfortable, at which point he described a chair in his grandmother's living room that he would often sit in and watch TV while engaging in conversation with his grandmother. The social worker suggested that the TV could be a place where he could watch thoughts that come to his mind, and if anything were to give him discomfort, he could change the channel or use the remote control to turn the TV off. It was further suggested that he create a TV show about himself meeting a person, place, or object that was wise and strong and could listen and advise him on anything he might need to know.
>
> Danal sat quietly for a few moments with his eyes closed, and then proceeded to turn on the imaginary TV with the remote. He saw a very tall tree and described leaving the chair and walking onto the TV screen. He then described sitting under the tree and feeling calm and protected on a quiet, very cloudy day in a time where the tree was full of leaves and the sky was on the verge of rain. He said that the tree "knew everything," specifically "about life and death" and the notion that "when you die you do not go to heaven right away. You have to keep coming back many times until you get it right, and that there is always another chance." When asked what word would bring the tree to his mind, Danal stated "heaven."

Everstine and Everstine (1993) note that often children who suffer the effects of trauma do not have the verbal skills to communicate their subjective experience. They further posit that a traumatic event may leave the defense system so depleted that attempts to cope with the demands of daily life or to learn new things may be too challenging. In the case of Danal, the events of September 11th caused him to display behavior that was typical of an earlier stage of development. His anger served as a means of giving him a sense of empowerment over a situation that was beyond his immediate control. However, he was able to replace this false empowerment with a true empowerment via his communication with the religious-spiritual symbol of the tree, which was able to provide him with answers to the impossible questions that fueled his anger and confusion. Through guided imagery, the conscious searches for answers in the unconscious, similar to the way a congregation might search in the doctrine of their religion in moments where religion acts as a touchstone for emotional control. Hence, the mind becomes both the student and spiritual teacher, with the therapist the facilitator of this education.

Conclusion

After decades of secular orientation, the field of social work increasingly recognizes the powerful role religion and spirituality play in our lives and our culture. To ignore the quest for meaning in life is to relinquish a significant tool in therapeutic intervention.

An important aspect of holistic treatment is to acknowledge the spiritual and religious beliefs of patients and to incorporate the strengths they offer as an integral part of treatment. Fortunately, this awareness is accompanied by a growing body of research that supports the uses of ritual, imagery and metaphors, and meditation as valuable techniques in resolving grief and supporting the healing process in traumatized individuals. Attention to the spiritual needs of the traumatized is intimately connected with attention to their emotional, cognitive, and physiological needs. This promising new realm of treatment options offers new approaches to assessment and intervention to clinicians who treat the survivors of incidents of mass violence.

References

Achterberg, J. (1985). *Imagery in healing.* London: Shambhala.

Atchley, R. C. (1995). The continuity of the spiritual self. In M. A. Kimble, S. H. McFadden, J. W. Ellor, & J. J. Seeber (Eds.), *Aging, spirituality, and religion: A handbook* (pp. 68–73). Minneapolis: Fortress.

Bettelheim, B. (1977). *The uses of enchantment: The meaning and importance.* New York: Vantage Books.

Bettelheim, B. (1993). Foreword. In M. Nyiszli, *Auschwitz: A doctor's eyewitness account* (R. Seaver, Trans.). New York: Arcade.

Biestek, F. P. (1953). The non-judgmental attitude. *Social Casework, 34,* 235–239.

Bowers, M. K. (1969). Psychotherapy of religious conflict. In E. M. Pattison (Ed.), *Clinical psychiatry and religion* (pp. 233–242). Boston: Little Brown.

Bullis, R. (1996). *Spirituality in social work practice.* Washington, DC: Taylor & Francis.

Canda, E., (1998). *Spirituality and social work: New directions.* Binghamton, NY: Haworth Pastoral Press.

Canda, E., & Furman, L. (1999). *Spiritual diversity in social work practice.* New York: Free Press.

Carroll, M. M. (1998). Social work's conceptualization of spirituality. In E. R. Canda (Ed.), *Spirituality and social work: New directions* (pp. 1–13). Binghamton, NY: Haworth Pastoral Press.

Carson, V. B. (1993). Prayer, meditation, exercise and special diets: The hardy persons with HIV/AIDS. *Journal of the Association of Nurses in AIDS Care, 4,* 18–28.

Comstock, G. W., & Tonascia, J. A. (1977). Education and mortality in Washington County, Maryland. *Journal of Health and Social Behavior, 18,* 54–61.

Cornett, C. (1992). Toward a more comprehensive personology: Integrating a spiritual perspective into social work practice. *Social Work, 37,* 101–102.

Cross, D. G., & Kahn, J. A. (1983). The values of three practitioner groups: Religious and moral aspects. *Counseling Values, 28,* 13–19.

Cullinan, A. (1993). Spiritual care of the traumatized: A necessary component. In K. J. Doka & J. D. Morgan (Eds.), *Death and spirituality* (pp. 227–242). Amityville, NY: Baywood.

Danielle, Y. (1985). Separation and loss of families of survivors of the Nazi Holocaust. *Academic Forum, 29,* 7–10.

Danielle, Y. (1988). Treating survivors and children of survivors of the Nazi Holocaust. In F. M. Ochberg (Ed.), *Post-traumatic therapy and victims of violence* (pp. 100–108). Philadelphia: Brunner/Mazel.

Derezotes, D. S., & Evans, K. E. (1995). Spirituality and religiosity in practice: In depth interviews of social work practitioners. *Social Thought, 18,* 39–56.

Doka, K. J., & Morgan, J. D. (Eds.). (1993). *Death and spirituality.* Amityville, NY: Baywood.

Everstine, D. S., & Everstine, L. (1993). *The trauma response: Treatment for emotional injury.* New York: W. W. Norton.

Fetzer Institute/National Institute on Aging. (1999). *Multidimensional measurement of religiousness/ spirituality for use in health research.* Kalamazoo, MI: Author.

Fleck, J. R., & Carter, J. D. (Eds.) (1981). *Psychology and Christianity: Integrative readings.* Nashville, TN: Abingdon.

Foote, W. (1996). Guided imagery therapy. In B. Scotton, A. B. Chinen, & J. R. Battista (Eds.), *Textbook of transpersonal psychiatry and psychology* (pp. 355–365). New York: BasicBooks/Perseus.

Frankl, V. E. (1969). *The will to meaning.* Don Mills, Canada: General.

Freud, S. (1907). *Obsessive acts and religious practices.* London: Hogarth Press.

Furman, L. E. (1994). Religion and spirituality in social work education: Preparing the culturally sensitive practitioners for the future. *Social Work and Christianity: An International Journal, 21,* 103–115.

Gellman, A. R. (2001). *Guided imagery: Exploring an alternative adjunctive intervention with traumatized adolescents in residential foster care.* Unpublished dissertation, NYU School of Social Work.

Gruber, B., Hersh, S., Hall, N., Waletsky, L., Kunz, J., Carpenter, J., Kverno, K., & Weiss, S. (1993). Immunological responses of breast cancer patients to behavioral interventions. *Biofeedback and Self-Regulation, 18,* 1–22.

Hart, T. (1994). *Hidden spring: The spiritual dimension of therapy.* Paramus, NJ: Paulist Press.

Holden-Lund, C. (1988). Effect of relaxation and guided imagery on surgical stress and wound healing. *Research in Nursing and Health, 11,* 235–244.

Hood, R. W., Spilka, B., Hunsberger, B., & Gorsich, R. (1996). *The psychology of religion: An empirical approach* (2nd ed.). New York: Guilford.

Joseph, M. V. (1987). The religious and spiritual aspects of clinical practice: A neglected dimension of social work. *Social Thought, 13,* 12–23.

Joseph, M. V. (1988). Religion and social work practice. *Social Casework, 69,* 443–452.

Jung, C. (1954). *Modern man in search of a soul.* New York: Harvest.

Knapp, R. J. (1986). *Beyond endurance: When a child dies.* New York: Shocken.

Leja, A. (1991). Using guided imagery to combat postsurgical depression. *Journal of Gerontological Nursing,* 15(4): 7–11.

Loewenberg, F. M. (1988). *Religion and social work practice in contemporary American society.* New York: Columbia University Press.

Lofland, J., & Lofland, L. H. (1984). *Analyzing social settings.* Belmont, CA: Wadsworth.

Marshal, J. (1991). The spiritual dimension in social work education. *Spirituality and Social Work Communication, 2,* 12–15.

Maslow, A. (1970). *Religions, values and peak experience.* New York: Viking.

Miller, D. (1994). *Women who hurt themselves: A book of hope and understanding.* New York: Basic Books.

Mol, J. J. (1976). *Identity and the sacred.* Oxford: Blackwell.

Mol, J. J. (1983). *Meaning and place: An introduction to the social scientific study of religion.* New York: Pilgrim.

Naparstek, B. (1994). *Staying well with guided imagery.* New York: Time Warner.

Ott, M. (1996). Imagine the possibilities! Guided imagery with toddlers and pre-schoolers. *Pediatric Nursing, 22,* 34–38.

Pargament, K. I. (1997). *The psychology of religion and coping.* New York: Guilford.

Pearlman, L., & Saakvitne, K. (1998). Constructivist self development approach to treating secondary traumatic stress. In C. R. Figley (Ed.), *Compassion fatigue: Secondary traumatic stress disorder among those who treat the traumatized* (pp. 168–180). New York: Brunner/Mazel.

Plante, T. G., & Sherman, A. C. (2001). *Faith and health: Psychological perspectives.* New York: Guilford.

Powell, A. (1998). Soul consciousness and human suffering: Psychotherapeutic approaches to healing. *The Journal of Alternative Medicine, 4,* 101–108.

Rando, T. A. (1986). *Parental loss of a child.* Champaign, IL: Research Press.

Rosner, H. (2001, November 5). Deliver us from evil. *New York Magazine, 11*(5), 50–56.

Saleebey, D. (Ed.). (1997). *The strengths perspective in social work practice* (2nd ed.). New York: Longman.

Shapiro, E. R. (1994). *Grief as a family process: A developmental approach to clinical practice.* New York: Guilford.

Siporin, M. (1985). Current social work perspectives for clinical practice. *Clinical Social Work Journal, 73,* 198–217.

Sommers-Flanagan, J. C. (1995). Psychotherapeutic techniques with treatment-resistant adolescents. *Psychotherapy, 32,* 131–140.

Spencer, S. (1956). Religion and social work. *Social Work, 1,* 19–26.

Staral, J. M. (1999). Seeking religious and spiritual competence: The perception of BSW students at a private Catholic university. *Social Work and Christianity, 26,* 101–111.

Taylor, S., Pham, L., Rivkin, I., & Armor, D. (1998). Harnessing the imagination: Mental simulation, self-regulation and coping. *American Psychologist, 53,* 429–439.

Thompson, M., & Coppens, N. (1994). The effects of guided imagery on anxiety levels and movement of clients undergoing magnetic resonance imaging. *Holistic Nurse Practitioner, 8,* 59–69.

Thoresen, C. E., Harris, A. H. S., & Oman, D. (2001). Spirituality, religion, and health: Evidence, issues, and concerns. In T. Plante & A. Sherman (Eds.), *Faith and health: Psychological perspectives* (pp. 15–52). New York: Guilford.

Van Den Berg, N. (Ed.). (1995). *Feminist practice in the 21st century.* Washington, DC: NASW Press.

Walsh, F. (1999). *Spiritual resources in family therapy.* New York: Guilford Press.

Weber, S. (1996). The effects of relaxation exercises on anxiety levels in psychiatric inpatients. *Journal of Holistic Nursing, 14,* 196–205.

Werner, E. E., & Smith, R. S. (1982). *Vulnerable but invincible: A longitudinal study of resilient children and youth.* New York: McGraw-Hill.

Walsh, R., & Vaughn, F. (1995). *Paths beyond ego: The transpersonal vision.* New York: Plenum.

Wilber, K. (1995). *Sex, ecology, spirituality.* Boston: Shambhala.

Wilson, J. P. (1986). *Trauma, transformation, healing.* Philadelphia: Brunner/Mazel.

Wilson, S. R. (1982). In pursuit of spiritual energy: Spiritual growth in yoga ashram. *Journal of Humanistic Psychology, 22,* 43–55.

Winchester-Nadeau, J. (1998). *Families making sense of death.* London: Sage.

Wright, S. (1996). *Adapting Milan style systemic therapy: From family therapy to research.* Unpublished manuscript.

Zinnbauer, B. J., & Pargament, K. I. (1996). *When worlds collide: On the integration of religion and spirituality, and psychotherapy.* Unpublished manuscript, Bowling Green State University, Bowling Green, OH.

11

Mass Violence and Secondary Trauma: Issues for the Clinician

Carol Tosone and Lisa Bialkin

In 1910 Joseph Conrad led an expedition deep into the "heart of darkness," a terrifying abyss he called the human soul, in which morality had no place. Indeed, since then many have written about the precariousness of the human condition and the perils involved in negotiating a safe course in a world fraught with dangers and unpredictability. Among them was Freud who, in his work *Civilization and its Discontents* (1930/1961), attempted to make psychoanalytic sense of the human psyche at a time when civilization found itself on the brink of exposure to unfathomable evil. Less progress has been made, however, in our understanding of how human beings confront the emotional turbulence that is part of our experience of living in the modern world—including reactions to mass violence.

Many survivors of trauma have had the experience of directly confronting terrors and atrocities, ranging from personal experiences of violence and assault such as sexual abuse, rape, and incest, to more collective assaults, such as war, persecution, torture, and terrorism. Viktor Frankl (1945) poignantly described his terror-filled experiences in a Nazi concentration camp and his need for meaning and purpose in order to withstand the inhumanity he endured.

The accounts of trauma victims are often too horrifying for most people to hear. The stories told by such survivors, whether shared consciously with others or released unconsciously in the terrifying nightmares and intrusive thoughts that often characterize their existence, give the rest of us who have been spared such encounters glimpses into that terror-filled netherworld from which, despite all our good intentions, we are only too eager to retreat. Most people "dread being drawn into the vortex of such darkness," wrote Danieli (1994, p. 543), who documented extensively the intergenerational transmission of victimization and the attitudes and difficulties of mental health professionals working with Holocaust survivors. Those who have been exposed to these kinds of horrors through the experience of others, whether they were drawn into that world because they are family, friends, or those whose profession calls on them to be involved with survivors, often do not emerge unscathed, experiencing secondary trauma.

The purpose of this chapter is to explore the effects of working with survivors of mass violence on social workers and other mental health professionals. It is through their work with trauma survivors that professionals themselves become secondarily exposed to trauma. Although less has been written about these kinds of secondary effects than about the accounts of persons primarily experiencing the trauma, interest in secondary victimization has been generated and dealt with in the literature. This phenomenon has been given various names and descriptions, which will be referred to collectively as *secondary trauma.*

Dynamics of Secondary Trauma

The symptoms resulting from exposure to trauma have been generally recognized as normal responses to abnormal conditions (Ursano, Fullerton, & McCaughey, 1994). These symptoms emerge as individuals and society do their best to integrate what was heretofore unfathomable into the fabric of their everyday lives. It has been well documented that persistent, normative, and primary exposure to severe trauma can result in acute psychological distress, including posttraumatic stress disorder (PTSD). In the most recent definition of PTSD as set forth by the American Psychiatric Association (2000), the understanding of the disorder has been broadened to include not only those persons who have been directly affected, but also those who are witnesses to or are confronted with an event that results in serious injury, physical threat, or death of others.

How an individual responds to trauma varies greatly and is "a complex interaction of the event itself and the individual's past, present, and expected future as well as biological givens and social context" (Ursano et al., 1994, p. 5). The role that memory plays in this process is also crucial (Van der Kolk, 1996). Ursano and colleagues (1994) have noted that "the meaning of a traumatic event changes over time with the individuals' ever changing psychosocial context" (p. 20).

Since the 1970s, much has been written about those who in some way are witnesses to the stories told by the survivors of trauma—persons who, while they might not have suffered the effects of the trauma directly, have become involved with and even "experienced" the effects of the trauma indirectly (McCann & Pearlman, 1989, 1995; Pearlman & Saakvitne, 1995). Such individuals, depending on their degree and amount of exposure to trauma, as well as on their own personal histories and characteristics, develop symptoms that can at times parallel those of the survivors themselves. These secondary trauma symptoms have been reported in the context of people living with a traumatized spouse or other family member, young children brought up by traumatized parents, and adult children of war veterans (Figley, 1995). Social workers and other health and mental health professionals repeatedly dealing with traumatized persons may also experience secondary trauma (McCann & Pearlman, 1989, 1995; Pearlman & Saakvitne, 1995).

Components of Secondary Trauma

The effects of dealing with traumatized clients on mental health professionals have been characterized in many different ways and have been given numerous meanings and names.

Among the terms that have been used to capture secondary reactions to trauma are: "burnout" (Pines & Maslach, 1978), "traumatic countertransference" (Herman, 1992), "compassion fatigue" (Figley, 1995), "secondary victimization" (Figley 1995), "secondary traumatic stress disorder" (Figley, 1999), and "vicarious traumatization" (McCann & Pearlman 1989, 1995; Pearlman & Saakvitne, 1995). While each of these concepts was originally developed in a specific context and with individual nuances, they have also been used interchangeably in connection with the phenomenon of secondary trauma—the reactions of clinicians to the traumatic events experienced by their clients. Some of the most commonly used terms are discussed below.

Burnout

The concept of *burnout* has been used not only in the context of trauma but in the therapeutic context in general (Gabriel, 1994). The "burned-out" clinician becomes emotionally or psychologically drained due to the toll taken by continuously empathizing and working with difficult clients. It occurs when the expectations and goals of the mental health professional are unrealistically high and do not adapt to the realities of the situation, either in terms of the clients' functioning or due to obstacles that exist in the clients' environment. An important factor contributing to burnout of clinicians is professional isolation and lack of professional support.

Clinicians experiencing burnout may show symptoms of depression, loss of interest and compassion, and discouragement. They may become cynical toward the ability of the society to meet the needs of their clients or cynical toward their clients, blaming them for creating their own difficulties and maintaining emotional distance from them (Farber & Heifetz, 1982). As a consequence of burnout, clinicians may even develop specific psychosomatic symptoms such as exhaustion, insomnia, and headaches, as well as increased interpersonal difficulties.

Countertransference

Although the definition and application of the term *countertransference* continues to evolve, in the context of working with trauma survivors, it can be said to include the emotional reactions of the clinician based on both the clinician's own life experiences and the many painful feelings, images, and thoughts that can be induced by working with survivors.

Different types of trauma-related countertransference have been listed in the literature. For example, Danieli (1980, 1988) identified the most prevalent countertransference reactions of clinicians working with Holocaust survivors, including bystander's guilt; overwhelming feelings of rage, dread, and horror; shame about the potential boundlessness of human evil; and the tendency to dwell exclusively on the traumatic event and to neglect the client as a whole.

In the context of work with Vietnam veterans, Lindy (1988) was one of the first authors to describe how the powerful and unusual imagery of war trauma may be more than clinicians can handle and how the clinicians' own character defenses may be inadequate to cope with these images. In some cases it may lead the clinician to the development of his or her own symptoms of PTSD. Lindy (1988) suggested several possible countertransference responses, including: (1) affect, such as rage, fear, guilt, shame, horror, voyeurism, excitement, disillusionment, and condemnation; (2) defenses, such as avoidance of and distancing from clients, disavowal of or clinging to the professional role, isolation, generalization, intellectualization, overprotection, and counterphobic engagement; and (3) symptoms, such as nightmares, intrusive images, reenactments, amnesia of the event, alienation, irritability, and psychophysiological reactions.

The importance of empathy in the therapeutic relationship with survivors of trauma has been noted by Lindy and Wilson (1994). Clinicians may have difficulties in sustaining an empathic position, leading to negative countertransference and the possible rupturing of the therapeutic relationship.

Vicarious Traumatization

The concept of *vicarious traumatization* has provided a theoretical framework for understanding the psychological impact of working with trauma survivors. Central to this concept is the idea that working with trauma victims is different from working with other client populations because of the continual exposure to clients' traumatic experiences, which may include shocking images of horror and suffering (McCann & Pearlman, 1989, 1995; Pearlman & Saakvitne, 1995).

The symptoms of vicarious traumatization can manifest themselves in emotional, cognitive, behavioral, or physical reactions. They can include a variety of posttraumatic symptoms similar to those of the victimized clients, including the experience of traumatic images via flashbacks, dreams, and intrusive thoughts, but without the original context of the client's trauma (Miles, Demi, & Mostyn-Aker, 1984; Pearlman & Saakvitne, 1995; Steed & Downing, 1998). The clinician's self-protective beliefs about safety, control, predictability, and attachment may be challenged when working with trauma survivors. Clinicians also may experience changes, such as feeling overwhelmed and without energy to care for themselves, increased cynicism, sadness, anger, grief, despair, and increased sensitivity to violence. They also may find themselves becoming more anxious and avoidant of potentially dangerous situations (Steed & Downing, 1998).

Vicarious traumatization also can affect the clinicians' basic sense of self. This may impact their frame of reference, such as identity, worldview, and belief system; their sense of their ability to work effectively professionally; their psychological functioning, such as esteem, control, intimacy, independence, and even memory; and their cognitive schemas, in particular their beliefs about safety, predictability, and trust (Astin, 1997). For example, a clinician who believed that the world is just and fair may be left without a meaningful way to understand or process the trauma resulting from mass violence.

Vicarious traumatization teaches us that clinicians can be just as vulnerable as their clients and that bad things can happen to people randomly. While this realization can make clinicians more aware of their own helplessness, particularly in cases of mass violence, it also helps to bring clinicians closer to the struggles of their clients (Astin, 1997). Thus it becomes crucial that clinicians remain vigilant about the possibility of being impacted by these processes and take appropriate steps to address them, as will be discussed below. Vicarious traumatization is illustrated in the case of Rachel.

> Rachel, whose maternal grandmother was a Holocaust survivor but never talked to her family about her experiences in the concentration camp, developed a private practice specializing in work with Holocaust survivors and their families. As her caseload increased, she found herself immersed in the stories of her clients, particularly female survivors who were children or adolescents at the time of their concentration camp incarceration. Many of these women reported symptoms of residual trauma as a result of their experiences. One such survivor, Judith, suffered frequent panic attacks in anticipation of showering and also exhibited symptoms of agoraphobia. She talked about her experiences in the concentration camp and her fear that if she took a shower she would not know whether there would be water or lethal gas coming from the showerhead.
>
> Although Rachel became accustomed to hearing the horrific and vivid recollections of Judith's captivity, one memory stood out that Rachel could not erase from her mind and that she revisited in flashbacks during the day and in her dreams at night. Each day the guards would separate those who would live from those who would die. Judith, her mother, and the mother's young sister stayed close together, each night planning how they might handle that eventuality. When the day came that the guards separated her mother from Judith and her aunt, the aunt pleaded with Judith to speak to the guard and to do whatever was necessary to bring the mother back. Judith, who was too terrified and feared for her own life, refused to do anything to save her mother. To this day, she remained haunted by feelings of guilt and shame and by the image of her mother's face as she was being pried from her aunt's arms.
>
> Rachel found herself particularly attuned to Judith's narrative, but remained unaware that it was impacting her own personal life. Rachel became more withdrawn and depressed without understanding why. She spent increasingly more time at home and became more fearful for her children's safety. She also became more socially anxious, and her level of anxiety was often out of proportion to the specific situation. For instance, several times she precipitously left movie lines while waiting with friends, citing an uncomfortable, claustrophobic feeling.
>
> Rachel's professional world contracted as well. Previously, she had been enthusiastically involved in a peer supervision group, but as the number of female survivors in her caseload increased, her interest in the group waned. She felt that her colleagues could not fully appreciate the meaning or intensity of her work, and she was deeply disappointed in their response to her presentation of Judith's case. When Rachel mentioned the intrusive image of Judith being separated from her mother in the concentration camp, her fellow clinicians suggested to Rachel that she return to therapy. Rachel felt that they were reducing her experience to one of pathology. It took considerable effort on the part of her colleagues to convince Rachel that her reactions were understandable, that they represented vicarious traumatization, and that it was important that Rachel focus on meeting her own needs.

Shared Trauma

Shared trauma, a relatively new concept in the United States, has been receiving increased attention in the literature following the attacks of September 11, 2001 (Altman & Davies,

2002; Saakvitne, 2002). Shared trauma refers to the clinician's and the client's experiencing the same trauma at the same time. Disasters such as explosions, war, terrorist attacks, as well as other kinds of mass violence, are examples of events and situations that can lead to traumas that are shared simultaneously by the survivors and their helpers. This concept was discussed briefly in the context of the bombing of the Alfred P. Murrah Federal Building in Oklahoma City in 1995: "The pressure of work is so constant and immediate that you forget you are part of this community and its bereavement as much as you are its therapist. A terrorist act simultaneously assaults physical lives and their cultural underpinning. More than simple displacement occurs, and despite discipline and training, you begin to experience the mania and exhaustion that accompany such an intense shared experience" (Krug, Nixon, & Vincent, 1996, p. 103). Other authors (Sprang, 1999; Tucker, Dickson, Pfefferbaum, McDonald, & Allen, 1997; Tucker, Pfefferbaum, Vincent, Boehler, & Nixon, 1998) have also addressed the contradictory and sometimes overwhelming feelings of clinicians experiencing mass violence while also working with victims of that violence.

The tragic events surrounding the September 11, 2001, attacks and the fear of the spread of anthrax that followed are examples of this kind of a collective shared trauma. Professionals in such situations function in a dual capacity, as both fellow victims and professional helpers, sometimes leading to a blurring of their perspectives (Golan, 1978). In instances of shared trauma, issues of countertransference and secondary trauma are exacerbated. The co-constructed reality of the therapeutic process results from the merging of the clinician's and the client's unconscious, preconscious, and conscious experiences, and the resulting shared experience of each clinician and client is unique to that particular dyad. This is particularly significant in light of the fact that the nature of the response to trauma profoundly affects each person's schemas, or fundamental views, about life. Consequently, it may be difficult for clinicians to remain neutral as they help clients deal with their responses to trauma.

An Example of Shared Trauma. Tosone et al. (in press) describe second-year MSW social work students processing these events in the aftermath of the September 11, 2001, tragedy in New York City. The outcome of the students' work illustrates some of the complexities involved for individuals trying to understand their own reactions, while at the same time attempting to provide help to clients suffering from some of the very same reactions to the trauma. The reactions of this student group encompassed a broad range of intense personal emotions, including, among others, denial, anger, shock, disbelief, bewilderment, fear, anxiety, hysteria, sadness, depression, hopelessness, and confusion. In addition, some students felt thankfulness, strength, hope, defiance, and love, as well as a renewed desire to find meaning in life.

The students also identified how their own responses to the traumatic event impacted their work with clients. Their reactions to clients ranged from increased desensitization and lack of empathy, difficulties in helping others when preoccupied with their own personal feelings, and increased feelings of insecurity, uselessness, and helplessness with respect to their clinical abilities. On the other hand, some students were able to find comfort and strength in the fact that they were experiencing many of the same emotions as their clients, and therefore they felt less alone. These students felt increased feelings of empathy and connection toward clients, greater need to feel involved and communicate with them, and a newfound sense of confidence as professionals.

This study demonstrated the crucial interplay between the social work students' personal reactions to trauma and their ability to treat clients who were experiencing many of the same reactions. If there was a theme to be drawn from the collective and individual experiences of these students, it was that the ability of clinicians to work with clients in the context of shared trauma depends as much on the abilities of the clinicians to process their own personal reactions to the events as on their dedication to the needs of their clients. More specifically, the way that clinicians are able to best respond to the needs of their clients when there is shared trauma is inextricably interwoven with how they personally have interpreted and responded to these events for themselves. This, in turn, is dependent on how the clinicians have internalized and responded to earlier events in their own lives.

Only by taking care of themselves can clinicians truly be in a position to help others. This issue of the clinician's self-care has been well documented in the secondary trauma literature (Catherall, 1999; Levine, 2001; Steed & Downing, 1998) and will be discussed below. The case of Robert illustrates shared trauma.

> Robert, a seasoned social worker of twenty years, was meeting with his client, Ed, in downtown Manhattan when the first hijacked plane hit one of the towers of the World Trade Center. Both Robert and Ed were distracted by the loud noise of the plane overhead and perturbed by the sound of the plane hitting the building. At the time they were unaware of what had occurred, attributing the loud noise of the plane to atmospheric conditions, and the actual impact to trucks hitting the ubiquitous New York City potholes. Only the subsequent sounds of sirens from police and emergency vehicles alerted them to the magnitude of the situation.
>
> Following the session, Robert and his client learned independently about the disaster, and each witnessed the burning towers and the resulting mayhem in the downtown streets. While each experienced his own personal trauma, Robert had the added responsibility of attending to the needs of his clients, most of whom lived downtown and were firsthand witnesses to the disaster. In the days following the disaster, Robert also found himself comforting family members, reassuring his mother of his safety, and volunteering in a community agency. He was immersed in all aspects of the September 11th experience, both professionally and personally. He was more vigilant about his safety and that of his family, had difficulty eating and sleeping, and had difficulty concentrating when meeting with clients.
>
> Robert found most client sessions difficult, especially when clients questioned the importance of the topics they had discussed prior to the disaster. Suddenly such topics as test anxiety, lack of available mates in New York City, and parental insensitivities in childhood seemed trivial concerns when one was facing daily bomb and anthrax threats. Robert's cognitive schema of the world as relatively safe had changed in an instant, as did that of his clients. He both looked forward to and dreaded sessions with Ed; they processed together what had occurred, but were also sensory reminders for one another of their shared trauma.

Clinician Self-Care

Much has been written about what clinicians can do to protect themselves against secondary and vicarious trauma, particularly the need to establish clear boundaries between their personal and professional activities (Miller, 1998; Newman & Gamble, 1995). Many authors have suggested that clinicians need to take the same advice they give their clients—to nurture themselves and maintain their health through adequate nutrition, rest, and exercise (Astin, 1997; Frazier & Schaul, 1995; McCann & Pearlman, 1989, 1995). They noted the need to participate in leisure activities, such as going to the movies and reading. The importance of developing a spiritual life has also been identified as important to self-care, and Levine (1996) has emphasized the value of keeping up with friends and developing new social support networks. Participating in personal therapy has also been highly recommended so that the clinician can stay aware of his or her own trauma history and vulnerabilities, shore up defenses, build self-awareness, process the material of trauma victims, and maintain professional boundaries (Charney & Pearlman, 1998).

It is noteworthy that while there are numerous measures to evaluate PTSD in clients, there are very few ways to evaluate secondary traumatic stress disorder in clinicians. Recently, a Secondary Trauma Questionnaire was developed by Motta, Kefer, Hertz, and Hafeez (1999) that can be used by all professionals.

In terms of the profession, it is important that agencies and organizations warn and protect their staff against the possibility of vicarious traumatization and that they offer appropriate support (Newman & Gamble, 1995). Clinicians need to limit the number of trauma cases in their caseload. Further, they should obtain clinical supervision and may benefit from participation in peer supervision and continuing education.

Self-care and self-awareness on the part of clinicians is not only self-protective but also may prevent the intrusion of the clinicians' vulnerabilities into their relationships with clients, thereby further traumatizing their clients (Friedman, 1996). Berzoff (1996) has stated that trauma "can actually become contagious," and "if the clinician shares the client's experiences of helplessness *too* much, she can become afraid of the client and turn away, again traumatizing the client" (p. 423). Therefore, clinicians need to develop sufficient insight into their own reactions to avoid the emotional abandonment of their clients. In addition, the clinician needs to be careful about self-disclosure that might further harm the client.

Rachel and Robert, the case illustrations described earlier in the chapter, needed to use a combination of these self-care strategies. Specifically, Rachel reduced the number of cases of Holocaust survivors in her caseload. She took the advice of members of her peer supervision group and returned to her own therapy, where she gained new insights about her reactions to Judith and other trauma clients and the intergenerational impact of her own grandmother's trauma; she also joined a peer group specifically for clinicians working with trauma survivors. Robert, the clinician exposed to the shared trauma of September 11th, spent more time with family and friends and also took time alone to ponder the meaning of these catastrophic world changes to his personal life. Both Robert and Rachel found discussions with colleagues who were similarly impacted by their work with trauma survivors to be invaluable in helping them to appreciate the challenges, rewards, and necessity of their work.

Conclusion

Social workers and other mental health professionals dealing with clients who have been impacted by mass violence may become profoundly affected by the experiences of their clients. As a result, they may experience secondary traumatization, whereby they have reactions that are similar to those of their clients. Such secondary trauma forces clinicians to deal with their own personal experiences, the shattering of assumptions (Janoff-Bulman, 1992) regarding their worldview, and the unpredictability of living in the modern world Both the clinician and the client must individually confront the radical assault on their own cognitive perceptions of the world, themselves, and others and work through the painful transformations that such a confrontation entails (McCann & Pearlman, 1995). In the case of vicarious traumatization, clinicians are forced to see the world through the eyes of their clients. This may lead to their unconscious identification with their clients' terror of annihilation, shattering their previous view of a safe world. In these situations, clinicians need to become aware of this overidentification with clients and take responsibility for their own self-care.

In the unique situations arising from collective traumatic events of mass violence that result in shared trauma, both the clinician and the client respond to the event at the same time and simultaneously experience the same processes of mourning and disruption of their existing schema. Clinicians, however, have the added responsibility of dealing with their own traumatic alterations while fulfilling their professional responsibilities to clients and helping clients work through their responses to trauma.

In cases of secondary traumatization, clinicians need to open themselves up to their own fears and terrors that may be lying just below the surface, helping to make their personal anxieties conscious. In reality, both the client and clinician are dealing with the painful process of looking into a "heart of darkness" (Conrad, 1910), with its losses, mourning, and need for reconstruction. In spite of the darkness, however, the clinician needs to maintain her or his professional role and be available to help the client through the complex healing process. Both the client and the clinician need to develop a worldview that accommodates the new reality, a process that while painful and frightening, contains within it the seeds for greater awareness, personal growth, and wisdom.

References

Altman, N., & Davies, J. M. (2002). Out of the blue: Reflections on a shared trauma. *Psychoanalytic Dialogues, 12(3),* 359–360.

American Psychiatric Association. (2000). *Diagnostic and statistical manual of mental disorders*—Text Revision (DSM-W-TR) (4th ed.). Washington, DC: Author.

Astin, M. C. (1997). Traumatic therapy: How helping rape victims affects me as clinician. *Women & Therapy, 20*(1), 101–109.

Berzoff, J. (1996). Anxiety and its manifestations. In J. Berzoff, L. Melano Flanagan, & P. Hertz (Eds.), *Inside out and outside in: Psychodynamic theory and practice in contemporary multi-cultural context* (pp. 397–427). Northvale, NJ: Jason Aronson.

Catherall, D. (1999). Coping with secondary traumatic stress: The importance of the clinician's professional peer group. In B. H. Stamm (Ed.), *Secondary traumatic stress: Self-care issues for clinicians, researchers and educators* (pp. 80–94). Baltimore, MD: Sidran Press.

Charney, A. E., & Pearlman, L. (1998). The ecstasy and the agony: The impact of disaster and trauma work on the self of the clinician. In P. M. Kleepsies (Ed.), *Emergencies in mental health: Evaluation and management* (pp. 418–435). New York: Guilford.

Conrad, J. (1910). The heart of darkness. In *Heart of darkness and the secret sharer* (pp. 65–158). New York: Harper and Brothers.

Danieli, Y. (1980). Countertransference in the treatment and study of Nazi Holocaust survivors and their children. *Victimology: An International Journal, 5* (2–4), 355–367.

Danieli, Y. (1988). Confronting the unimaginable: Psychoclinicians' reactions to victims of the Nazi Holocaust. In J. P. Wilson, Z. Harel, & B. Kahana (Eds.), *Human adaptation to extreme stress from the Holocaust to Vietnam.* New York: Plenum Press.

Danieli, Y. (1994). Countertransference and trauma: Self-healing and training issues. In M. B. Williams & J. F. Sommer (Eds.), *Handbook of post-traumatic therapy* (pp. 541–563). Westport, CT: Greenwood Press.

Farber, B. A., & Heifetz, L. J. (1982) The process and dimensions of burnout in psychotherapists. *Professional Psychology, 13,* 293–301.

Figley, C. R. (1995). Compassion fatigue as secondary traumatic stress disorder: An overview. In C. R. Figley (Ed.), *Compassion fatigue: Coping with secondary traumatic stress disorder in those who treat the traumatized.* New York: Brunner/Mazel.

Figley, C. R. (1999). Compassion fatigue: Toward a new understanding of the costs of caring. In B. H. Stamm (Ed.), *Secondary traumatic stress: Self-care issues for clinicians, researchers, and educators* (pp. 3–28). Baltimore, MD: Sidran Press.

Frankl, V. (1945). *Man's search for meaning.* New York: Washington Square Press.

Frazier, L., & Schaul, P. (1995) Vicarious trauma: The effects on female counselors of working with sexual violence survivors. *Psychology of Women Quarterly, 19,* 49–64.

Freud (1930/1961). Civilization and its discontents. *The standard edition of the complete psychological works of Sigmund Freud, 21,* 59–145. London: Hogarth Press.

Friedman, M. (1996, April). PTSD diagnosis and treatment for mental health clinicians. *Community Mental Health Journal, 32*(2), 173–189.

Gabriel, M. (1994). *AIDS trauma and support group therapy: Mutual aid, empowerment, connection.* New York: Free Press.

Golan, M. (1978). Natural and man-made disasters. In *Treatment in crisis situations* (pp. 125–148). New York: Free Press.

Herman, J. (1992). *Trauma and recovery.* New York: Basic Books.

Janoff-Bulman, R. (1992). *Shattered assumptions: Towards a new psychology of trauma.* New York: Free Press.

Krug R., Nixon, S. J., & Vincent, R. (1996). Invited editorial: Psychological response to the Oklahoma City bombing. *Journal of Clinical Psychology, 52*(1), 103–105.

Levine, J. (1996). Oklahoma City: The storytelling of a disaster. *Smith College Studies in Social Work, 67* (1), 21–38.

Levine, J. (2001). Working with victims of persecution: Lessons from Holocaust survivors. *Social Work, 46* (4), 350–360.

Lindy, J. D. (1988). *Vietnam: A casebook.* Philadelphia: Brunner/Mazel.

Lindy, J., & Wilson, J. (1994) Empathic strains and countertransference. In J. P. Wilson & J. D. Lindy (Eds.), *Countertransference in the Treatment of PTSD* (pp. 5–30). New York: Guilford.

McCann, I. L., & Pearlman, L. A. (1989). Vicarious traumatization: A framework for understanding the psychological effects of working with victims. *Journal of Traumatic Stress, 3,* 131–149.

McCann, I. L., & Pearlman, L. A. (1995). Vicarious traumatization: An empirical study of the effects of trauma work on trauma clinicians. *Professional Psychology: Research and Practice, 26* (6), 558–565.

Miles, M. S., Demi, A. S., & Mostyn-Aker, P. (1984). Rescue workers' reactions following the Hyatt Hotel disaster. *Death Education, 8,* 315–331.

Miller, L. (1998). Our own medicine: Traumatized psychotherapists and the stresses of doing therapy. *Psychotherapy, 35,* 137–146.

Motta, R. W., Kefer, J. M., Hertz, M. D., & Hafeez, S. (1999). Initial evaluation of the secondary trauma questionnaire. *Psychological Reports, 85,* 997–100

Newman, D., & Gamble, S. (1995). Issues in the professional development of psychotherapists: Countertransference and vicarious traumatization in the new trauma therapist. *Psychotherapy, 32,* 341–347.

Pearlman, L., & Saakvitne, K. (1995). Vicarious traumatization: How trauma therapy affects the clinician. In L. Pearlman & L Saakvitne (Eds.), *Trauma and the clinician: Countertransference and vicarious traumatization in psychotherapy with incest survivors.* New York: W. W. Norton.

Pines, A., & Maslach, C. (1978). Characteristics of staff burnout in a mental health setting. *Hospital Community Psychiatry, 29,* 233–237.

Saakvitne, K. (2002). Shared trauma: The therapist's increased vulnerability. *Psychoanalytic Dialogues, 12,* 443–450.

Sprang, G. (February, 1999). Post-disaster stress following the Oklahoma City bombing. *Journal of Interpersonal Violence, 14* (2), 169–184.

Steed, L., & Downing, R. (1998). A phenomenological study of vicarious traumatisation amongst psychologists and professional counselors working in the field of sexual abuse assault. *The Australasian Journal of Disaster and Trauma Studies, 2.* http://www.massey.ac.nz/~trauma/issues/1998-2/steed.htm. Accessed 7/14/02.

Tosone, C., Bialkin, L., Campbell, M., Charters, M., Gieri, K., Gross, S., Grounds, C., Johnson, K., Kitson, D., Lanzo, S., Lee, M., Martinez, M., Martinez, M. M., Millich, J., Riofrio, A., Rosenblatt, L., Sandler, J., Scali, M., Spiro, M., Stefan, A. (in press). Shared trauma: Group reflections on the September 11th disaster. *Psychoanalytic Social Work, 10* (1).

Tucker, P., Dickson, W., Pfefferbaum, B., McDonald, N., & Allen, G. (1997). Traumatic reactions as predictors of post-traumatic stress six months after the Oklahoma City bombing. *Psychiatric Services, 48*(9), 1191–1194.

Tucker, P., Pfefferbaum, B., Vincent, R., Boehler, S., & Nixon, S. J. (1998). Oklahoma City: Disaster challenges mental health and medical administrators. *Journal of Behavioral Health Services & Research, 25,* 93–99.

Ursano, R., Fullerton, C., & McCaughey, B., (1994). Trauma and disaster. In R. Ursano, C. Fullerton, & B. McCaughey (Eds.), *Individual and community response to trauma and disaster: The structure of human chaos* (pp. 3–27). Cambridge, UK: Cambridge Press.

Van der Kolk, B. (1996). Trauma and memory. In B. Van der Kolk, A. McFarlane, & L. Weisaeth (Eds.), *Traumatic stress: The effect of overwhelming experience on mind, body and society* (pp. 279–302). New York: Guilford.

Section V

Mass Violence, Social Welfare Policy, and Social Justice

12

Mass Violence and Social Welfare Policy

Norma Kolko Phillips

Social welfare policies impact on clients, social workers, and social service agencies and organizations, determining what services clients will receive, who receives the services, who delivers them, and often the very existence, as well as the functions, of social service agencies and organizations. While this occurs regardless of existing political and social circumstances, the impact of social welfare policies becomes more immediate and discernable during times of mass violence.

Social welfare policies in the United States have served several functions: to protect and improve the quality of life for particular groups, to create opportunities for economic and social mobility for some, to boost the national economy, to maintain or restore public confidence in the government, and to preserve the power structure. During and in the aftermath of mass violence, public perception of safety and claims of national security take precedence over all other objectives.

This chapter will look at the nature of social welfare policy change and will present a model of a policy change cycle. This pattern of policy change helps us to anticipate future changes and their consequences, particularly those growing out of an atmosphere of fear and mass violence. The cycle will be applied to situations of mass violence historically and in the present, and dilemmas growing out of conflicting interests that impact on policies will be identified. Implications of policy changes for the social work profession will be discussed.

The Nature of the Social Welfare Policy Change Process and the Policy Cycle

Social welfare policies may be seen as "principles that govern actions directed towards given ends" (Titmuss, 1974, p. 23); as the "ends" change, policies also change. Historically, social welfare policies have responded to crises in society, shifting as a specific crisis and public attention to it subsides. Consequently, as public attention to a particular social problem diminishes, policy commitments to programs may lose their zeal over time, leading to a lack of vigilance and underfunding of programs (Phillips & Straussner, 2002).

Using the model of a social welfare policy change cycle, policies can be viewed in four consecutive categories, based on function. These categories, elaborated below, are preventive, incentive, protective, and compensatory. The failure of one category to fulfill its function leads to the creation of the next category. As with any model, policies can overlap and at times meet the criteria for several categories simultaneously.

Preventive policies are usually developed when a social problem has been identified by professionals, the public, and/or the mass media. The issue is taken up by politicians who then advocate for legislation and funding of programs that are intended to curtail the impact of the problem. For example, in the area of elder abuse, additional policies and preventive programs are needed (St. James, 2001), and the problem of HIV/AIDS among older adults, though a sizable problem, has received little attention (William & Donnelly, 2002). On the other hand, in the case of child abuse, a problem that is recognized and that society has responded to, preventive services for families at risk for child abuse are funded, such as supportive services, parenting classes, and counseling programs (Gonzalez-Ramos, 1997). Similarly, in the case of substance abuse, prevention programs such as the DARE program have been implemented in schools (Nadel & Straussner, 1997). Preventive policies also impact programs on the community level; following an incident of police brutality, training courses for police officers may be introduced to help prevent similar incidents in the future (Gootman, 2002).

Incentive policies are intended to promote behaviors that comply with government policies. Incentives can take various forms. A common form is financial, which may be offered through tax relief. For example, tax relief for contributors to nonprofit organizations, referred to by Titmuss (1969) as fiscal welfare, serves as an incentive for philanthropists to donate money or services to nonprofit agencies and organizations that provide social services. On another level, when a government makes an offer of money to the family of a suicide bomber, that too, may serve as an incentive to carry out the act.

Incentives may not be financial but may be in-kind. For example, for years condoms have been distributed in schools in the interest of curtailing the spread of HIV/AIDS as well as for birth control. Another form of incentive is a voucher, such as is used by the federal Women's, Infants' and Children's (WIC) program. Food vouchers make it possible for parents of nutritionally at-risk children to get specific foods for their young children, with the goal of preventing developmental difficulties related to nutrition.

Some incentives are intangible and have symbolic rather than monetary value. Examples might include giving a sticker to a person who has donated blood, or, as occurred immediately after the September 11th attacks, to those donating money for families of the victims. Intangible incentives can also be based on recognition, such as an awards ceremony honoring volunteers in a nursing home or a printed program listing donors to a particular social service agency.

There are also policies that serve as *disincentives;* these carry negative consequences for behaviors that interfere with preventive policies. For example, students may not be permitted to attend school if they have not been vaccinated.

Protective policies may be directed toward people or property. They may serve the function of preservation of safety, as in the case of police protection, or protection from exploitation, as seen historically in the development of child labor or minimum wage laws. While policies in all four categories are value-laden and often result in conflicts of interest, protective policies, which are a result of the failure of preventive and incentive policies, have more serious legal consequences and tend to be more controversial. For example, what are the limits a society can go to in order to "protect" children from what may be seen as physical abuse or to require immunizations for children? What are the rights of parents to determine how they discipline their children?

Compensatory policies provide financial or other kinds of benefits to people for harm experienced as a result of a particular incident or condition arising from a problem in society. Once it has been determined that a person is innocent and has suffered as a result of failure of preventive, incentive, and protective measures, compensation may be provided to the survivor or to the family of the victim. For example, if a violent mentally ill person who has not been adequately served by preventive and protective programs attacks someone at random, the survivor or the victim's family may demand compensation. Determinations about compensation may be arrived at either through legislation or court decisions and are usually aimed at helping survivors or the families of victims make up for their losses. Such determinations also highlight the inadequacies of existing policies and programs and often lead to the strengthening of preventive policies, thereby serving a preventive function as well (Rohde, 2000).

Mass Violence and the Policy Cycle

In the case of mass violence, the perceived needs of particular groups or of the government in general take precedence over other concerns. The assessment of a situation as a national crisis is, of course, subjective, but nonetheless, the impact of the ensuing social welfare policies affect everyone. Policies can also be used to promote political goals; Titmuss (1974) has suggested that political propaganda "frequently masquerades under social policy labels" (p. 23).

The decision of a nation to engage in warfare—whether a traditional war, terrorism, or other forms—is based on particular ideological, economic, or political commitments. However, once involved in a national crisis, all policies shift so that the focus is on the crisis; this impacts not only public policies, but social welfare policies and services as well. Existing services suffer as funding is diverted toward defense and security efforts, compromising their scope and even the continuation of social service programs. For example, a year after the September 11, 2001, attacks, while the United States saw extensive military buildup, Donald Rumsfeld, Secretary of Defense, responded to efforts to pass legislation providing for additional benefits to disabled veterans: "We simply cannot continue to add ever-expansive obligations.... This would divert critical resources away from the war on terrorism, the transformation of our military capabilities and important personnel programs such as pay raises and facilities improvements" (Loeb, 2002).

Building on works of Max Weber and Herbert Spencer, Titmuss (1969) claimed that social welfare policy decisions during wartime are determined by who is directly involved in the war effort. In situations where war efforts are confined to the military, funding is directed toward those who are involved. However, if, as in the case of World War II in England, the general population is involved, then services must be offered to them, too. "The aims and content of social policy, both in peace and in war, are thus determined—at least to a substantial extent—by how far the cooperation of the masses is essential to the successful prosecution of war. If this cooperation is thought to be essential, then inequalities must be reduced and the pyramid of social stratification must be flattened" (p. 86).

Mass Violence and Preventive Policies

During times of mass violence, preventive policies may be instituted to curtail further damage to people and property and to prevent further civil disruption. The new circumstances that arise from the experience of mass violence require new solutions; consequently, preventive policies are natural outgrowths of war and social unrest.

Historical Perspective. Early efforts to involve the federal government in preventive legislation were seen during the Civil War. The U.S. Sanitary Commission and the Freedmen's Bureau were established to prevent illness and social disorganization by meeting the health, social, and educational needs of the military, the freed slaves, and war victims. While these efforts, which also involved the voluntary sector, were not permanent, they did introduce the role of the federal government in meeting health, education, and welfare needs of the population (Axinn & Levin, 1997).

Another critical example of preventive legislation growing out of social chaos in the United States occurred during the Great Depression, with the passage of the Social Security Act of 1935—the first permanent federal program to meet some of the pressing economic and health needs of the general population. Over the years, this piece of legislation also has been expanded incrementally. During the 1960s, once again in response to civil unrest, a new approach was taken as attempts were made to engage diverse groups in the goals of the society. To this end, new legislation was passed and numerous programs were created, such as Head Start, the Food Stamp Program, and the extension of the Social Security Act to include Medicaid and Medicare (Karger & Stoesz, 2002).

Unemployment insurance, one of the programs instituted as part of the Social Security Act of 1935, also serves as a marker for the rate of newly unemployed in the country. In times of economic crisis, including crises of mass violence such as the September 11th attacks, when businesses downsize and job scarcity develops, the length of time of eligibility to receive unemployment insurance may be increased. This serves both to sustain the long-term unemployed and their families and to prevent social and economic instability (Associated Press, 2002; Straussner & Phillips, 1999).

The Example of Prevention of Mass Violence in Schools and the Workplace. As a result of disastrous school shootings and the attacks of September 11th, we have seen intensified preventive policies in schools and the workplace. Efforts to gain more stringent gun control laws, which tend to increase following incidents such as sniper attacks and school shootings, are seen by some as a challenge to the right to own firearms. With gun control inadequate, and also serious questions raised as to its role in the prevention of school shootings (Klein & Chancer, 2000), school districts may introduce security measures such as metal detectors to screen all students and others entering the school building. Many school districts also turn to hiring guards to patrol schools, both to act as a deterrent to violence and to intervene in the event of a violent incident.

Efforts have also been made to prevent mass violence in the workplace. Since September 11th, we have seen new policies that require employees and visitors to show identification before entering a building. While this had been the practice in some government agencies and private organizations prior to September 11th, it has become more widespread.

Although there has been some objection to procedures to increase safety in the workplace, many of the policies and resulting procedures related to prevention of mass violence in schools are highly controversial. For example, some school districts have policies of suspending students if they bring toys that could be considered weapons to school, or if they write fictional stories that involve violence. Security policies are also controversial, such as requiring children to pass through metal detectors in order to enter the school building.

Mass Violence and Incentive Policies

While incentive policies generally provide inducements to comply with preventive policies, during times of mass violence, or in its aftermath, incentive policies are used as inducements to support government actions, such as furthering the goals of national security or of economic development.

Historical Perspective. Incentives have been used to induce people to join the military in this country since the Revolutionary War. They are still used today and include sign-on bonuses as well as many educational incentives. Presently, after completing 36 months of active duty, an individual can become eligible to receive up to $23,700, which is tax free, toward a college or technical school education. Additional programs are offered as inducements for college graduates to join the military, including programs that will repay their student loans (U.S. Marine Corps, 2001).

At critical times, the federal government offers incentives, such as educational grants to motivate individuals to enter educational programs for particular professions. For example, educational grants may be made available for students preparing to be nurses and for other medical personnel, which might be needed in the event of further wartime activities. During the period of social unrest in the 1960s, numerous federal scholarships were made available for social work students to work in the area of community mental health. Currently, the Social Workers Omnibus Act of 2003, which will be introduced in the 108th Congress by Congresswoman Stephanie Tubbs Jones, is another effort to provide government-funded financial incentives for people to enter the social work profession. This legislation would provide licensed social workers with student loan forgiveness and a housing program, similar to that offered by the Teacher/Police Next Door Program of the U.S. Department of Housing and Urban Development (Simmons & Kola, 2002).

The Example of Incentives in Higher Education. Incentives are used in the area of higher education to engage universities in research and training that meet the needs of government. Incentives may focus on the development of technology and products, as well as preparing personnel for specific jobs. This becomes more apparent in times of national crises. For example, after September 11th, the CIA approached many universities around the country in order to establish programs that would meet federal defense needs (Golden, 2002). Proposals have been made for the funding of additional projects, hiring economists and political scientists on university faculties to serve as consultants, and recruiting graduates. There is a particular interest in reaching graduates of Middle East Studies programs to fill staff openings at the CIA, which have increased by 85 percent (Golden, 2002).

Grant programs that serve as incentives to link defense needs of the government with universities are being established as the country moves further into a military posture. For example, in December 2002, the National Science Foundation announced grants totaling $1,000,000 for research related to "...preparedness, response and recovery regarding disasters and other extreme events" (NSF, 2002).

Serious ethical and educational questions are raised by federal policies that stipulate that international students who are not U.S. citizens must be excluded from participating in research funded by several federal agencies, such as the CIA. There is also the fear that CIA-funded projects will interfere with academic freedom, dictating course content and curriculum (Golden, 2002). One could wonder if and how any interference with academic freedom, which is so central to social work education, might affect education for the profession. Some educators, however, agree with the views of the president of Rochester Institute of Technology, who stated that, "We may have to suspend some freedoms for a little while.... I'm less afraid of losing freedoms due to loss of democracy than of losing freedoms because we're all dead due to terrorist attacks" (Golden, 2002, p. A8).

Mass Violence and Protective Policies

As indicated previously, the outbreak of mass violence signifies the failure of preventive and incentive policies. A declaration of war is, in itself, the ultimate protective policy, with its broadly stated objectives of freedom, or safety, or being a war that will end all wars. In such times, new and harsher protective policies, which are designed to support the new reality, affect social welfare services and the day-to-day life of people.

Historical Perspective. According to Marden, Meyer, and Engel (1992), throughout our history, even during peaceful times, policies have been constructed with national security as a priority. In 1798 the Alien and Sedition Acts were passed, "giving the president somewhat arbitrary authority to deport dangerous aliens and those suspected of treason" (p. 61). During periods of mass violence, policies have been used to suspend protection of individual freedom in favor of fulfilling national objectives. For example, in 1861 in order to accomplish the goals of the Civil War, Lincoln suspended the writ of habeas corpus, and used military force to overcome draft rioters in New York City. During the First World War, civil liberties were curtailed by the Espionage Act of 1917 and the Sedition Act of 1918 in order to suppress opposition to the war (Marden et al., 1992).

The United States has a history of policies targeting specific racial or cultural groups during times of national crisis in the effort to curtail the level of subversive activities. Immigration policies are utilized to control who can enter and who can remain in this country. For example, during World War II, the Alien Registration Act made it possible for the government to use surveillance methods and deport immigrants who were not citizens. The infamous detention of 77,000 Japanese and Japanese Americans in internment camps in the United States following the attack on Pearl Harbor was another effort to "protect" the country: "The FBI...rounded up 'enemy aliens'...on the slightest pretexts, such as having contributed money to Japan or owning a knife or flashlight" (Marden et al., 1992, p. 403). Similarly 600,0000 Italian residents of the United States were targeted as "enemy aliens" during the same period, travel restrictions and requirements were imposed on them, and they were required to carry identification cards (John D. Calandra Italian American Institute, 2002).

After each of the two World Wars, the country was consumed with the "Red Scare" of communism, and repressive public policies that limited civil liberties emerged, including the 1950 Internal Security Act, which required the registration of alien residents and expanded powers of deportation. These policies were in the name of protecting the country from subversives (Marden et al., 1992).

Protective policies during wartime have also been used in the interest of furthering freedoms; the Emancipation Proclamation would be the prototype for this. Freedoms were furthered during World War II with Franklin Roosevelt's seminal policy contained in his 1941 Executive Order establishing the Fair Employment Practices Committee. This gave protection to oppressed groups by prohibiting discrimination due to race, creed, color, or national origin in defense industries or government employment. This Order not only accomplished its immediate goal of increasing the labor force to fill positions in industry that had been vacated when people joined the war effort, but also opened opportunities for groups that had been discriminated against in hiring—women, blacks, Native Americans, Mexican Americans, and Puerto Ricans. It made it possible for a million African American men and women and 25,000 Native Americans to serve in the military during World War II, also becoming eligible for veterans' benefits, including housing, employment, and education programs. Axinn and Levin (1997) make the point that in addition to opportunities for economic advancement, Roosevelt's 1941 legislation offered increased opportunity for social equality, and it "laid the groundwork for the civil rights and feminist movements of the 1950s and 1960s" (p. 227).

Protective Policies and Civil Liberties. In October 2001, a month after the September 11th attacks, the USA PATRIOT Act ("Uniting and Strengthening America by Providing Appropriate Tools Required to Intercept and Obstruct Terrorism" Act) introduced new surveillance strategies and provided new guidelines for how the government handles confidential information about people. The USA PATRIOT Act made it possible for government agents to gain access to information about individuals, "including library records, books store receipts, subscription lists, credit and banking records, e-mails, phone conversations and student files" (Rosenfeld, 2002). Then, in November 2002, the Department of Homeland Security was established "to reorganize broad elements of a scattered federal government around a focused response to terrorism" (Firestone, 2002, p. A1). The new department, which was the largest reorganization in the federal government in over fifty years, absorbed twenty-two different functions, such as intelligence analysis, emergency management, immigration, and border protection; 170,000 employees situated around the world were brought into this one department (Firestone, 2002).

In spite of security threats to the United States following the 2001 terrorist attacks, there has been a great deal of controversy over the PATRIOT Act and the establishment of the Homeland Security Department. It has been suggested that "in the nation's history, the greatest battles over the reach of government power have occurred against the backdrop of wartime" (Liptak, Lewis, & Weiser, 2002). Civil libertarians have objected to these measures, both from the point of view of how much information about individuals would become available to the federal government and also how much information the federal government would withhold from the public. Regarding the PATRIOT Act, while U.S. Attorney General John Ashcroft claims that "the measures are needed to prevent terrorism and that criticism of them aids terrorists...Civil libertarians say the measures go too far and undermine constitutional principles" (Rosenfeld, 2002, p. A1). There was also a great deal of criticism of the Department of Homeland Security: "Privacy watchdogs are up in arms about a new 'office of information awareness' which, they say, could put all e-mails, credit-card transactions, drug prescriptions and every bit of electronic information you generate on one vast, Orwellian database" (United States: Washington's Mega-Merger, 2002, p. 52).

Also in the name of protection of public safety, some of the procedures that emerged after the September 11th attacks reflected a policy of racial profiling—a pattern that was seen earlier in our history. For example, in November 2002, "Thousands of Iraqi citizens and Iraqi-Americans with dual citizenship who are attending American universities or working at private corporations, and who might pose a risk in the event of a United States-led war against Iraq [are being arrested and detained] if they are believed to be planning domestic terrorist operation" (Johnston & Van Natta Jr., 2002, p. 1). In the same month, the U.S. Attorney General ordered "virtually all male noncitizens over the age of 16 who come from 18 countries, mostly Arab and Muslim, to be interviewed, photographed and fingerprinted by federal authorities. The program affects tens of thousands of immigrants from those countries, most of whom hold valid work and study visas" (Broder & Sachs, 2002, p. A20).

Mass Violence and Compensatory Policies

Those who are affected by mass trauma may benefit from compensatory policies, which have functions that are similar to those of social welfare policies—to protect and improve the quality of life, to create opportunities for economic and social mobility, to preserve the power structure, to boost the national economy, and to maintain or restore public confidence in the government. Compensation can take many forms. It could be credibly argued that the social legislation of the 1960s was a form of compensation for groups who experienced oppression in society. However, the policies related to benefits for war veterans is a clearer example of compensation.

Historical Perspective. Benefits providing compensation to people adversely affected by military service have been around as long as armies fought. Military pensions for impoverished veterans were first seen in the United States in 1818 for Revolutionary War veterans, and during the Civil War, a pension system was developed but was limited to Union servicemen who were disabled while on duty or the dependents of servicemen who were killed. A military hospital was started in 1865 for totally disabled Union servicemen; this legislation was later strengthened and led to a system of federally supported institutions for disabled veterans. In 1890, federal legislation provided for a pension system for war veterans, widows, and orphans based on need rather than disability. In the South, too, legislation was enacted to provide relief for needy servicemen and their families, first through voluntary agencies and then through government programs (Axinn & Levin, 1997; Trattner, 1999).

Policies regarding benefits to veterans have become particularly complex as veterans of different wars have not only been received differently by the public, but they also received different compensation. Veterans of World War II benefited from the GI Bill of Rights, which opened opportunities for them to obtain higher education and buy homes in the rapidly growing suburbs (Palen, 1995). Perhaps because the two World Wars had much public support and the wars were perceived as having been "won," while military actions that followed were less popular and were not so clearly "won," and perhaps because of the expansion of public sector services during the decade of the 1960s, some services to veterans have shifted from the Veterans' Administration to the broader public sector. For example, with the introduction of the Medicaid program, financially eligible veterans in need of medical care could turn to public programs other than Veterans' Administration hospitals.

Policy changes related to veterans benefits have occurred frequently and persist until today. For example, policies related to compensation for people in the military who might have been exposed to biological and chemical agents have been in flux. Today everyone who served in Vietnam is presumed to have been exposed to Agent Orange and certain illnesses are presumed to be a result of the exposure. Those who suffer from Hodgkin's disease, multiple myeloma, non-Hodgkin's lymphoma, prostate cancer, and respiratory cancers, such as lung, larynx, and trachea, are entitled to compensation. Similarly, special benefits are also available to children of Vietnam veterans who have spina bifida and other birth defects. In addition, veterans of the 1992 war in the Persian Gulf who are suffering from undiagnosed illnesses are now eligible for compensation in the form of monetary benefits (Vietnam Services, 2002; Vietnam Vets, 2002).

Homelessness is a particularly pervasive problem among Vietnam veterans. Although the Department of Veterans' Affairs claims that while the rate of occurrence of posttraumatic stress disorder among Vietnam veterans is high, epidemiologic studies have not found connections between service in Vietnam, exposure to combat, and homelessness (Department of Veterans Affairs, 2002). Yet in 2002, one-third of the adult homeless population in the country, or 250,000 people, were veterans. The number of homeless Vietnam veterans has surpassed the number of service personnel who died during that war. Desert Storm veterans are also becoming part of the homeless population (Department of Veterans Affairs, 2002). The Department of Veterans Affairs (2002) has found that the incidence of mental illness among homeless veterans is about 45 percent, similar to the general homeless male population. Also similar to the general homeless population is the incidence of substance abuse problems, which is slightly higher than 70 percent. While the Department of Veterans Affairs recognizes these problems and makes ambitious efforts to provide services, the problems persist (Department of Veterans Affairs, 2002).

Current Compensatory Policies: Benefits to Families of Victims and to Survivors of the 2001 World Trade Center Attacks. One might draw a comparison between the survivors of the September 11th attacks and war veterans, and between the families of the victims and families of those who perished in the military. As with war veterans, compensation was made available to the survivors and the families of victims. However, as this was not a traditional case of compensation to people in the armed forces, it took different forms. Controversies around who is eligible for compensation arose for the survivors and families of victims of the September 11th attacks, as they do for war veterans and families of war victims.

Compensation for families of victims of the September 11th attacks was offered immediately by several agencies. In addition to the millions of dollars raised by voluntary donations, most of which was administered by the American Red Cross, public funding was also made available.

A critical source of assistance to people who suffered economic hardship because of the disaster came from the Federal Emergency Management Agency (FEMA). Controversies arose around who would qualify for compensation because of FEMA's stringent eligibility requirements. Although the agency developed new guidelines in June 2002, so that anyone living or working in Manhattan who suffered financially was eligible for compensation (Chen, 2002), the agency continued to come under attack for its handling of the situation (Hernandez, 2002). Compensation from FEMA was directed not only to people affected by the disaster, but also to the cities that suffered damage. For example, in addition to money given to New York City to help pay for expenses resulting from the September 11th attacks, $80 million was also given to New York City schools to cover instruction time in schools that had been lost after the attacks (Kelley, 2002)

However, the major source of compensation for the families of victims came through the federal government's Victim Compensation Fund. Offers of compensation were made to victims' families in the average amount of $1.85 million per family, which would be tax-free. However, attached to this was the stipulation that once the money was accepted, the relatives surrender their right to sue the government or any corporation in the United States. For those who choose to sue, a loss in court would leave them with no money at all. In spite of the possibility of this consequence, a 30-year-old wife of a victim on one of the planes that crashed into the World Trade Center rejected a settlement by the government. She decided to sue both United Airlines and the airport security company that, she maintained, "should have prevented terrorists from hijacking Flight 175.... She wants the government and the airlines to admit that the hijackings didn't have to happen. She hopes, exposing flaws in aviation security, to make another terrorist attack less likely.... If the suit leads to protracted legal wrangling, she will spend the next few years revisiting the events that led to [her husband's] death" (Eig, 2002, p. 1).

This woman's efforts to expose negligence may not be without cost to her emotionally. Appearing in court during litigation can be an overwhelming experience, especially for individuals suffering with posttraumatic stress disorder. The need to relive the traumatic experience and hear it discussed again and again in court can even result in retraumatization (Pitman, Sparr, Saunders, & McFarlane, 1996). Consequently, while opportunities for compensation are presumably available to all families of those who were killed, some people, particularly those with symptoms of posttraumatic stress disorder, will be unable to pursue litigation and will choose to settle with the federal government's offer instead. Economics is another factor in determining who can sue; many families cannot risk the financial consequences of not winning in court.

Mass Violence and the Social Work Profession

Bremner (1956) made the observation that war can change a nation's assumptions as well as its priorities. Writing about the impact of the Civil War on the understanding of the causes of poverty, he stated, "To a certain extent the war made Americans as a whole more cognizant of the impersonal causes of destitution operating in society" (p. 44). This recognition of economic and social causes of poverty, on the eve of emancipation of slaves, phenomenal immigration, industrialization, and migration and urbanization, had a profound influence on the rugged course of social welfare policy and on the development of the profession of social work.

In spite of the new recognition of the causes of poverty, efforts to increase taxes during the war, both for payment of bounties as incentives to join the military and for assistance to families of servicemen, brought objections from property owners. In the effort to avoid higher taxes, property owners argued that publicly funded relief was both inefficient and invited dishonesty among public officials, and they advocated instead for voluntary giving. While this served to further delay federal government involvement with social welfare needs of people, the focus on voluntarism encouraged the participation of women as volunteers in the war effort. This new role for women contributed to the development of women's movements in the United States, to the eventual social, political, and economic transformation for women, and to the participation of women in developing the social work profession. "For countless American women war-relief work was an emancipating experience. After the war a number of them were unwilling to retire serenely to the management of households.... [These women were] the forerunners, and often in a literal sense the teachers" (Bremner, 1956, p. 45) of the social reformers of the Progressive Era.

War not only changes a nation's priorities, but also the priorities of professions. The impact of war on social welfare policy and the social work profession was seen during World War I, when new approaches were developed to both the funding and the function of social work services. Rather than relying on public funding for war relief, the concept of corporate responsibility for philanthropy emerged as business gifts to the war relief effort increased in order to meet the needs of private philanthropy. Agencies such as the Red Cross, YMCA, and the United War Work Campaign managed major national and local fundraising drives. Following the war, the war chests, consisting of these voluntary contributions, were converted to community chests, with chambers of commerce providing leadership in fundraising, thereby establishing the somewhat shaky but ongoing relationship between social work and corporate philanthropy (Abelson, 2000; Heald, 1970).

At the same time, spurred by the needs of traumatized World War I veterans for counseling, the social work profession turned away from its prewar social reform focus and instead moved in the direction of the newly found scientific base of psychoanalytic thinking of the 1920s. Bertha Reynolds (1963) commented on this trend: "We had acquired an outlook almost like that of private practice in psychiatry, even though we were doing our counseling in social agencies" (p. 147). Following the war, the Settlement House movement also shifted to a new concept of "professionalism," moving from its concern with social reform to a new methodological approach of helping through recreational and educational activities. The new professionalization was symbolized and promoted by the establishment of the American Association of Social Workers in 1921. Concern with issues of economic and social need were left behind, and during this time government and business surpassed the social work profession in searching for new ways of responding to problems of economic and social need (Phillips, 1982).

The social unrest of the Great Depression and the subsequent passage of the Social Security Act once again transformed the profession of social work, and what was to become the vast sector of publicly funded social services was created (Fisher, 1980; Phillips, 1985). Although the change did not come gracefully and has not proceeded smoothly, the profession eventually responded as it was called upon to provide the gamut of social services associated with financial need and financial assistance. The unrest that occurred during the 1960s reinforced, at least for that decade, the interest and commitment of social work to a concern with the impact of poverty on individuals and groups and to social reform (Phillips & Straussner, 2002).

Since the 1990s, with the events of terrorism and other incidents of mass violence—and most recently the terror attacks of September 11th—the social work profession has been called upon to respond and provide services to those who are severely affected by violence. This has required that the profession address a number of new issues, including developing appropriate clinical skills to help the traumatized (Robbins, 2002); finding ways to help emergency workers experiencing posttraumatic stress disorder (Harvey-Lintz & Tidwell, 1997); reassessing and readjusting agency functions, including long-term as well as emergency intervention (American Red Cross Announces Long-Term Program, 2002); dealing with issues of insurance reimbursement for services provided (National Association of Social Workers, 2002); responding to lowered public funding for existing services due to crisis spending (Altman & O'Connor, 2003); understanding the need for cooperation among public and voluntary agencies (SAMHSA, 2001); and developing funding streams for research related to clinical approaches and community initiatives to help people affected by mass violence (NIMH, 2002; Project Liberty, 2002).

At the same time, policies regarding privacy of information introduced in the USA PATRIOT Act and the Department of Homeland Security raise potentially difficult questions for the social work profession. One might wonder how this legislation will affect confidentiality in social work practice and the practice of other mental health professionals.

Librarians have already questioned how these policies affect their work, and how they can "protect patron privacy without breaking the law" (Minow, 2002, p. 52). Social workers may be faced with similar concerns.

Conclusion

We have seen that every aspect of social living is affected by mass violence, and that social welfare policies are needed to guide public response to them. Whether the issue is the curtailment of civil rights; mass violence in schools, the workplace, and community; poverty; housing; education; homelessness; medical care of veterans and their families; mental health care for surviving individuals, families, and communities; or the numerous other issues arising out of events of mass violence, government must make choices about what actions to take. Controversy is at the heart of each policy; how it is resolved represents not only the moment in history but also the residues of critical moments that have passed. For social workers, including those working with survivors at the center of the event and with those affected elsewhere, it is essential not only to stay informed about changing policies affecting clients and agencies, but also to take an active role in informing the public of the social service needs of individuals, families, and communities, and, as policy practitioners, to work closely with communities, community leaders, and politicians.

References

Abelson, R. (2002, March 29). Foundation giving is at $23 billion high. *New York Times.* Retrieved December 21, 2001, from www.nytimes.com.

Altman, L. K., & O'Connor. (2003, January 5). Health officials fear local impact of smallpox plan. *New York Times.* Retrieved January 7, 2003, from www.nytimes.com.

American Red Cross announces long-term program. (2002, August 21). PR Newswire. Retrieved October 24, 2002, from http://memex.lehman.cuny.edu:2072/universe/.

Associated Press. (2002, December 17). Loss of jobless benefits taints holidays. *New York Times.* Retrieved December 18, 2002, from www.nytimes.com.

Axinn, J., & Levin, H. (1997). *Social welfare: A history of the American response to need* (4th ed.). New York: Longman.

Bremner, R. H. (1956). *From the depths: The discovery of poverty in the United States.* New York: New York University Press.

Broder, J. M., & Sachs, S. (2002, December 17), Threats and responses: The tightening border; Facing registry deadline, Men from Muslim nations swamp immigration office. *New York Times,* p. A20.

Chen, D. (2002, June 29). After criticism, U.S. broadens 9/11 aid pool. *New York Times,* p. A1.

Department of Veterans Affairs. (2002, November 15). Homelessness among veterans: Overview of homelessness. Retrieved December 2, 2002, from www.va.gov/homeless.

Eig, J. (2002, September 11). Litigating grief: Affixing the blame for Sept. 11 loss: A widow's choice. *Wall Street Journal,* pp. A1, A10.

Firestone, D. (2002, November 20). Senate votes, 90–9, to set up Homeland Security Department geared to fight terrorism. *New York Times,* p. A1.

Fisher, J. (1980). *The response of social work to the Depression.* Cambridge, MA: Schenkman.

Golden, D. (2002, October 4). Gown and dagger: After Sept. 11, the CIA becomes a force on campus. *Wall Street Journal,* pp. A1, A8.

Gonzalez-Ramos, G. (1997). Children living in poverty. In N. K. Phillips & S. L. A. Straussner, (Eds.). *Children in the urban environment: Linking social policy and clinical practice* (pp. 27–42). Springfield, IL: Charles C. Thomas.

Gootman, E. (2002, September 23). Five altering years for a police department. *New York Times,* p. B6.

Harvey-Lintz, T., & Tidwell, R. (1997). Effects of the 1992 Los Angeles civil unrest: Post traumatic stress disorder symptomatology among law enforcement officers. *Social Science Journal, 34,* 171.

Heald, M. (1970). *The social responsibility of business: Company and community, 1900–1970.* Cleveland, OH: Case Western Reserve Press.

Hernandez, D. (2002, November 22). Neighborhood group sues FEMA. *New York Times,* p. B8.

John D. Calandra Italian American Institute. (2002). Exhibit: Prisoners in our own homes: The Italian American experience as America's enemy aliens. Retrieved December 26, 2002, from www.ItalianAmericanMuseum.org.

Johnston, D., & Van Natta Jr., D. (2002, November 17). Agencies monitor Iraqis in the U.S. for terror threat. *New York Times,* p. 1, 22.

Karger, H. J., & Stoesz, D. (2002). *American social welfare policy: A pluralist approach* (4th ed.). Boston: Allyn and Bacon.

Kelley, T. (2002, October 19). U.S. to give New York schools $80 million in Sept. 11 aid. *New York Times,* p. B5.

Klein, J., & Chancer, L. (2000). Masculinity matters: The role of gender in high-profile school violence cases. In S. Spina (Ed.), *Smoke and mirrors: The hidden context of violence in schools and society* (pp. 129–162). New York: Rowman & Littlefield.

Liptak, A., Lewis, N., & Weiser, B. (2002, August 4). After Sept.11, a legal battle on the limits of civil liberty. *New York Times,* p. 1.

Loeb, V. (2002, October 7). Bush threatens veto of Defense Bill; President wants costly new disabled military pension benefits eliminated. *Washington Post,* p. A2.

Marden, C. F., Meyer, G., & Engel, M. H. (1992). *Minorities in American society* (6th ed.). New York: HarperCollins.

Minow, M. (2002, October 1). The USA Patriot Act. *Library Journal,* 52.

Nadel, M., & Straussner, S. L. A. (1997). Children in substance-abusing families. In N. K. Phillips & S. L. A. Straussner (Eds.), *Children in the urban environment: Linking social policy and clinical practice* (pp. 154–174). Springfield, IL: Charles C. Thomas.

National Association of Social Workers. (2002, November 13). Update on mental health parity. Retrieved December 22, 2002, from www.socialworkers.org.

National Science Foundation (NSF). (2002). Multidisciplinary research into critical infrastructure and related systems-mitigation, preparedness, response and recovery regarding disasters and other extreme events. Retrieved December 23, 2002, from www.nsf.gov/cgi-bin/getpubs?nsf03578.

NIMH awards research grants to study Sept. 11 trauma. (2002. April 29, 2002). *Mental Health Weekly.* Retrieved November 2, 2002, from www.manisses.com.

Palen, J. J. (1995). *The suburbs.* New York: McGraw-Hill.

Phillips, N. K. (1982). *Social work, government, and social welfare: The Social Security Act.* Doctoral dissertation, Wurzweiler School of Social Work, Yeshiva University, New York City. Ann Arbor, MI: University Microfilms International.

Phillips, N. K. (1985). Ideology and opportunity in social work during the New Deal years. *Journal of Sociology and Social Welfare, 12,* 251–273.

Phillips, N. K., & Straussner, S. L. A. (2002). *Urban social work: An introduction to policy and practice in the cities.* Boston: Allyn and Bacon.

Pitman, R. K., Sparr, L. F., Saunders, L. S., & McFarlane, A. C. (1996). Legal issues in posttraumatic stress disorder. In B. A. van der Kolk, A. C. McFarlane & L. Weisaeth (Eds.), *Truamatic stress: The efforts of overwhelming experience on mind, body, and society* (pp. 378–397). New York: Guilford.

Project Liberty: Feel free to feel better. (2002). Retrieved December 14, 2002, from www.projectliberty.state.ny.us.

Reynolds, B. (1963). *An uncharted journey.* New York: Citadel.

Robbins, S. (2002). The rush to counsel: Lessons of caution in aftermath of disaster. *Families in Society: The Journal of Contemporary Services, 83,* 113.

Rohde, D. (2000, May 5). Subway killer apologizes at sentencing. *New York Times, p. B1.*

Rosenfeld, S. (2002, September 8). Looking back, looking ahead: A nation remembers; Patriot Act's scope, secrecy ensnare innocent, critics say. *San Francisco Chronicle,* p. A1.

Simmons, C., & Kola, L. A. (2002). Social Workers Omnibus Act 2003. E-Mail correspondence from L. Kola, Dean of Graduate Studies, Case Western Reserve University, Cleveland, Ohio.

St. James, P. (2001). Challenges in elder mistreatment programs and policy. *Journal of Gerontological Social Work, 36,* 127–140.

Straussner, S. L. A., & Phillips, N. K. (1999). The impact of job loss on professional and managerial employees and their families. *Families in Society, 80,* 642–648.

Substance Abuse and Mental Health Services Administration (SAMHSA). (2001, October 23). Report on federal disaster response: Helping the nation address the mental health and substance abuse effects of terrorist/bioterrorist events. Washington, DC: Author.

Titmuss, R. M. (1969). *Essays on the welfare state* (2nd ed.). Boston: Beacon.

Titmuss, R. M. (1974). *Social policy: An introduction.* New York: Random House/Pantheon.

Trattner, W. I. (1999). *From poor law to welfare state: A history of social welfare in America* (6th ed.). New York: Free Press.

United States: Washington's mega-merger; The new Department of Homeland Security. (2002, November 23). *The Economist,* 52.

U.S. Marine Corps. (2001, January). *Educational opportunities in the Marine Corps.* Pamphlet AXC45-4EXBAXX0100, Rev. 1/01.

Vietnam services—Veterans pensions and disability claims. Retrieved November 27, 2002, from www.senate. gov/~byrd/vets-svcs-pens-disclaims.htm.

Vietnam veterans benefit from Agent Orange rules, compensation and pension service. Retrieved November 23, 2002, from www.vba.va.gov/bln/21/Benefits/Herbicide/Aono1.htm.

Williams, E., & Donnelly, J. (2002). Older Americans and AIDS: Some guidelines for prevention. *Social Work, 47,* 105–111.

13

Social Justice in Times of Mass Violence

Richard Holody

Bertha Reynolds (1963) wrote that if social work were truly to be part of "the life of a period," it must participate in "the controversies by which a people determines its destiny" (p. 292). Today, then, to maintain social work's relevance in a world that includes mass violence and the conditions that give rise to such acts by individuals, groups, and nations, social work must reassess its values, define their relevance to changing conditions, and actively work to better the conditions of human life.

At first glance, the conjunction of "social justice" with "mass violence" seems absurd: The very notion of mass violence insults a value that is constructed on cooperation, equality, and respect. However, such a response, satisfying viscerally perhaps, leaves fruitful and relevant work undone; it also overlooks the contradictions of Western civilization. Looking only at the last hundred years, efforts reflecting a commitment to social justice resulted in the development of the League of Nations and the United Nations, the Geneva Conventions, the Universal Declaration of Human Rights, National Health Care in the United Kingdom, and the Civil Rights Acts in the United States. Yet in this same century the nations of the Western world also produced acts of carnage that force us to question our humanity (Glover, 2000): Verdun, Auschwitz, the fire bombings of Dresden and Tokyo, the massacre of Muslims at Srebrenica. From Scottsboro to Columbine and from Manson to McVeigh, the United States, the freest and wealthiest country in the world today, has been home to individual acts of appalling violence. If social justice is a guiding principle that defines professional purpose, then it must illuminate what social work's responses are to be in times when our society is shaken and threatened by mass violence, whether by individuals, groups, or nations. The terrorist attacks of September 11, 2001, intensify the need for social work to examine and reaffirm its commitment to social justice; so too do the subsequent war in Central Asia and the passage of the USA PATRIOT Act.

This chapter explores the nature of social justice both in general and within the more specific context of the profession of social work. It begins by analyzing the concept of social justice especially as argued by John Rawls, whose writings proceed in the tradition of the Western Enlightenment. Next, the significance of social justice within the profession is demonstrated with special attention to the link between Rawls's theory and the relevant section of the Code of Ethics of the National Association of Social Workers. There has been considerable effort in the popular and professional media to clarify our understanding of the perpetrators and circumstances of mass violence; this chapter validates this search and posits that a commitment to social justice supports the urgency of the task. The chapter concludes with a consideration of how social justice may guide the professional activities of social workers as we all, as individuals and citizens of the world, struggle with the threat and reality of mass violence.

Social Justice

In Aeschylus' (1999) *The Suppliants,* the Danaids, fifty women who have fled their land to avoid forced marriages with their cousins, seek asylum from Pelasgus, the leader of another city-state. Their situation is fraught with the potential for violence: If their request is denied, they will commit mass suicide; if accepted, Pelasgus risks war. At the play's conclusion, the Danaids will achieve vengeance with an act of retribution that bloodies the stage. Pelasgus is troubled by both their plight and the implications of what his response is to be.

> *Pelasgus: So how should I do my duty to you?*
> *Danaids: By not giving us back to Aegyptus' sons.*
> *Pelasgus: You drive a hard bargain; it will lead to war.*
> *Danaids: But remember, Justice protects her allies.*
> *Pelasgus: If she's on their side from the start.*
> *(Lines 315–319)*

Apart from demonstrating the enduring concern for social justice, this passage from one of the earliest extant plays in Western civilization illustrates the complexity of the notion of justice. It presumes that relationships exist between people beyond family and nation and that they entail responsibilities even if the specifics are uncertain. Social justice guides conduct and entails risk, and, as the last exchange argues, a commitment to justice begins not with today's problem but is ongoing and requires an ever-vigilant concern with societal conditions that give rise to unfairness, inequality, and oppression.

Introduction to Rawls

In 1971, John Rawls's *A Theory of Justice* was published; while its complexity and nuance are daunting, a brief explication of his theory is necessary because of the seminal nature of his work. Rawls's theory derives from the intellectual tradition of Western Enlightenment, which, as Kramnick (1995) summarizes, favored science over superstition, reason over religion, and individual liberty over restraint that was based on tradition. The Enlightenment was radical; it demanded that all assumptions, be they supportive of kings or clergy, be challenged. An intellectual movement of a burgeoning middle-class, it was fueled by and in turn fueled revolutions in England, France, and North America. "Central to the Enlightenment agenda was the assault on religious superstition.... Religion [would be] removed from public life and public authority [and] would be reserved" for private life (Kramnick, 1995, p. xii).

Rawls is a contract theorist whose work is in the Enlightenment tradition of Locke and Rousseau. He begins by imagining a social contract among people who, behind a "veil of ignorance" and "in an initial position of equality," form a society in which they would all want to live. Because they are unaware of the social meaning and consequences of their own characteristics (race, gender, etc.) yet are motivated by their individual need to advance, they will devise a society that rationally will benefit all, and consequently benefit each individual. This society will be characterized by reciprocity, equality, and cooperation and is one where justice is understood as fairness; it will be "neither a society of saints nor a society of the self-centered" (Rawls, 1996, p. 54). Thus, in Wakefield's (1988a) view, Rawls is attempting to make explicit justice "as we already intuitively understand it, or...[would] understand it if we took a rational and sustained interest in doing so" (p. 195). It is "not a world we think of much virtue until we find ourselves without it" (Rawls, 1996, p. 54).

Two Principles of Justice

Rawls seeks to reconcile freedom and equality and does so by positing two principles of justice that the original contractors would have concluded were rational. "First, each person is to have equal right to the most extensive scheme of equal basic liberties compatible with a similar scheme of liberties of others" (Rawls, 1999a, p. 53). Such freedom requires that each human have equal access to basic social goods. These goods or "values" include "liberty and opportunity, income and wealth, and the social bases of self-respect" (Rawls 1999b, p. 54). Were that not to be true, people would advance not because of inevitable innate differences such as physical strength or creativity, but rather because the social structure unfairly assisted them to the disadvantage of others: The original contractors would not agree to a system that might disadvantage themselves individually. Wakefield (1988a) illustrates the principle this way. Health is not a social good as each of us has different genetic endowment that will affect, for example, our eyesight or susceptibility to cancer. However, "the opportunity to be served by those who are expert in preventive or curative health is a social good and therefore must be fairly distributed" (p. 203). This principle underscores the importance of the imaginary "veil of ignorance": the original contractors would be acting against their own self-interest if they created a society wherein they would be penalized for personal characteristics over which they have no control, such as gender or race.

Because the original individual contractors would want to achieve whatever would be possible as a result of their own intelligence, prowess, or other personal quality, social and economic differences inevitably occur. Rawls's (1999a) second principle states that these "inequalities are to be arranged so that they are both (a) reasonably expected to be to everyone's advantage, and (b) attached to positions and offices open to all" (p. 53). Again, remembering that the original contractors are unaware if their talents or characteristics will bring them reward or disadvantage, inequality would be rational only if everyone benefited from that inequality and if everyone had the equal opportunity to achieve positions and offices of influence and power. Jim Crow voting laws, for example, violated this principle because only whites were allowed to hold office and when in office they perpetuated a society that worked to the advantage only of some members of the community. Yet, experimentation, creativity, and genius need to be rewarded because their fruits (e.g., harnessing electricity, developing computer chips, devising air travel) benefit all.

This necessarily brief review of Rawls's views requires two additional points relevant to the problem of mass violence in the contemporary context: a consideration of the "social bases of self-respect" and the problem of the "irrational" or "intolerant." The inclusion of "self-respect" as a basic social good may seem surprising, as most would understand it to be solely an internal, psychological construct. But for Rawls, self-respect is also social because it is a rational precondition for pursuit of one's own plan and it "normally depends on the respect of others" (Rawls, 1971, p. 178). His inclusion of the social bases of self-respect broadens substantially people's reciprocal obligations.

The Problem of the "Irrational"

Rationality must also confront the irrational. The Enlightenment intellectuals struggled with the notions of people who believed rather than sought truth through rational inquiry. Kant argued that because enlightenment would inevitably follow only from freedom, a theocratic state, because it allowed no freedom, would be "absolutely null and void, even if confirmed by the supreme power" (In Kramnick, 1995, p. 4). Separation of religion from a political state was necessary for Locke because the state was formed precisely "to secure every man's possession of the things of this life"; concern for things of the next life "is left entirely to every man's self" (In Kramnick, 1995, p. 90). What of secular threats to a rational state? James Madison acknowledged there would always be "factions" that would threaten the rights and interests of others. He opposed a pure democracy and instead argued that a republic, based on representative democracy, would control the effects of factions. He believed that apart from the impossibility of forcing each citizen to share the exact same beliefs, the causes of factionalism could be removed only by the "folly" of "destroying the liberty which is essential to its existence" (in Kramnick, 1995, p. 461).

Rawls agrees with his Enlightenment predecessors that "no particular interpretation of religious truth can be acknowledged as binding upon citizens generally" (Rawls, 1999a, p. 191) and that each religion would have equal opportunity to engage with the populace. The problem arises with sects, religious and secular, that are intolerant; in effect, with "unreasonable" people, those who do not accept the original contract. "Reasonable persons...desire for its own sake a social world in which they, as free and equal, can cooperate with others on terms all can accept.... By contrast, people are unreasonable...when they plan to engage in cooperative schemes but are unwilling to honor, or even to propose, except as a necessary public pretense, any general principles for specifying fair terms of cooperation" (Rawls, 1999a, p. 50).

He considers whether the freedom of the intolerant can be limited and finds that restriction of liberty can occur "only when the tolerant [i.e., those who are "reasonable" as defined above] sincerely and with reason believe that their own security and that of the institutions of liberty are in danger" (Rawls, 1999a, p. 193). Though war may be "irrational or wasteful," it may come when an impasse occurs between peoples who have "final ends that require them to oppose one another without compromise" (Rawls, 1999b, p. 123). Peace is secured "by preparing the way for peoples to develop characteristics that support a reasonably just ordered regime" (Rawls, 1999b, p. 123).

Social Justice and Social Work

The current National Association of Social Workers Code of Ethics (1996) lists social justice as one of six "core values" that are "ideals to which all social workers should aspire." The ethical principle under the value of "social justice" states that:

> Social workers challenge social injustice.
>
> Social workers pursue social change, particularly with and on behalf of vulnerable and oppressed individuals and groups of people. Social workers' social change efforts are focused primarily on issues of poverty, unemployment, discrimination, and other forms of social injustice. These activities seek to promote sensitivity to and knowledge about oppression, and cultural and ethnic diversity. Social workers strive to ensure equality of opportunity, access to needed information, services, resources, and meaningful participation in decision making for all people.

The concept of social justice is new to the NASW Code of Ethics. Neither the phrase "social justice" nor the word "justice" is mentioned in the first Code of Ethics (NASW, 1960), its amendment (NASW, 1967), or its first major revision (NASW, 1979). Only in 1993 does the phrase appear, though not until the next to last sentence of the Code: "The social worker should advocate changes in policy and legislation to improve social conditions and to promote social justice" (NASW, 1993, Section V, p. 6).

Clearly, social work has a history of challenging injustice and working for equality of opportunity and resources, a history that considerably predates its formal commitment to social justice in the Code of Ethics. Reamer (1998) notes that the settlement house movement's "attention to structural and environmental causes" of poverty and other social problems reflected a commitment to social justice and reform (p. 489). Jane Addams worked for expanded economic and political opportunity on the levels of the immediate community and city and fought as well on the national and international level for social change and peace, culminating in her shared Nobel Prize for Peace in 1931. The life and work of Bertha Reynolds concerned what she called the "titanic struggle for human welfare... [and] the battle for social justice" (Reynolds, 1963, p. 293). As a result of the civil rights, anti-war, feminist, and other social movements of the 1960s and 1970s, "[t]housands of new practitioners were attracted to the profession primarily because of social work's abiding concern about values" such as social justice (Reamer, 1998, p. 489). Currently, the Council on Social Work Education requires that content on social justice be integrated throughout the social work curriculum, both at the baccalaureate and master's levels, and that students be educated to promote social justice (CSWE, 2001).

Social Work and Rawls

More recently, social work scholars have explicated the connection between social work and Rawls's theory of social justice. Wakefield (1988a, 1988b) sought to establish what he called "minimal distributive justice" as the organizing value of the profession, appropriately so because only social work "of all the secular professions" has its purpose "to pursue specifically moral goals of fairness and justice" (p. 207). He argued that social justice applied to therapeutic or clinical social work, an idea supported and further developed by Swenson (1998). Figueira-McDonough (1993) uses Rawls to clarify the social worker's role as policy practitioner, acting "as the social conscience of liberal democracies" (p. 180). Scanlon and Longres (2001a, 2001b) begin their explorations of the meaning of social justice to the profession by summarizing Rawls's theory and his influence on other social work scholars.

The clearest indication of the influence of Rawls on the professional Code of Ethics is the wording of the professional value itself: "access," "needed" resources, "equality of opportunity," and "meaningful participation" are concepts that are developed and have particular resonance in his theory of justice. Ethical standards 6 (Social Workers' Responsibility to the Broader Society) and 6.04 (Social and Political Action) reinforce the notion that the pursuit of social justice, especially at the macro level, is a positive obligation for all social workers: It is something they "should" do.

Social Justice and Mass Violence

A striking phenomenon in the post–September 11th period is the persistent and ongoing search for answers to explain the terrorists' attack. These inquiries take many approaches: interviewing relatives of Palestinian "human bombs" in Israel (Hassan, 2001), explaining the various types of terrorist threats (Garwin, 2001), trying to understand their motives and diverse circumstances (Lelyveld, 2001), asking "what terrorists want" (Lemann, 2001), relating the history of Islam to its contemporary reality (Lewis, 2001), and understanding how the United States is viewed in the Muslim world (Judt, 2001). For most commentators this journey reflects a need to understand the motivations and conditions of existence of those who practice mass violence before devising appropriate strategies of response. The exploration is fraught with peril and so requires considerable self-reflection as well as the study of others. Part of us wants simply to condemn; part of us fears what we may find; throughout, we struggle with and even recoil from the results of our inquiry. Understanding mass violence—the events and their context—is both difficult and a prerequisite for practicing social justice; it is a form of starting where the client is.

The Search for Answers in Literature

This search for answers is not new and not limited to social scientists or political analysts. Consider the disparate thoughts of two internationally acclaimed novelists writing about mass violence at either end of the twentieth century, as well as those of a contemporary

American writer responding to September 11th. What they share with social workers is the struggle to understand humans: the need both to understand the conditions of violence and to be courageous and humble in empathizing with those whose behavior we must condemn. Joseph Conrad's *The Secret Agent* (1953) was inspired by contemporary accounts of a failed anarchist bombing.

> I remember, however, remarking on the criminal futility of the whole thing, doctrine, action, mentality; and on the contemptible aspect of the half-crazy pose as of a brazen cheat exploiting the poignant miseries and passionate credulities of a mankind always so tragically eager for self-destruction. That was what made for me its philosophical pretenses so unpardonable....; a blood-stained inanity of so fatuous a kind that it was impossible to fathom its origin by any reasonable or even unreasonable process of thought. For perverse reason has its own logical processes. (p. 9)

Yet when Conrad learned more details about that incident of "absurd cruelty," he became absorbed in writing what became a classic novel because he felt he had to—"It was a necessity" (Conrad, 1953, p. 11).

Where Conrad began with anger and incomprehension, Haruki Murakami would conclude with seeing commonalities between terrorists and himself (and his readers). In *Underground* (2000), Murakami reports his interviews with survivors of the 1995 sarin attack on the Tokyo subway, an event of chemical warfare that he describes as one "of the gravest tragedies in Japan's postwar history" (p. 237). He also interviewed members of the Aum religious cult that included the perpetrators.

> However we need to realize that most of the people who join cults are not abnormal; they're not disadvantaged; they're not eccentrics. They are the people who live average lives (and maybe from the outside, more than average lives), who live in my neighborhood. And in yours.
>
> Maybe they think about things a little too seriously. Perhaps there's some pain they're carrying around inside. They're not good at making their feelings known to others and are somewhat troubled. They can't find a suitable means to express themselves, and bounce back and forth between feelings of pride and inadequacy. That might very well be me. It might be you. (Murakami, 2000, p. 364)

The award-winning U.S. novelist Don DeLillo (2001) comments that after September 11th "the sense of disarticulation of the term 'Us and Them' has never been so striking, at either end."

> We are rich, privileged and strong, but they are willing to die. This is the edge they have, the fire of aggrieved belief. We live in a wide world, routinely filled with exchange of every sort.... The terrorist...builds a plot around his anger and our indifference.... We can tell ourselves that whatever we've done to inspire bitterness, distrust, and rancor, it was not so damnable as to bring this day down on our heads. But there is no logic in apocalypse.... [The terrorist] pledges his submission to God and meditates on the blood to come. (p. 34)

Social Justice as a Rational Activity

Not all observers see the need to explore the underlying conditions of mass violence or the psychology of the perpetrators of global terrorism. Friedman (2000) doubts there is anything the world can do but to isolate terrorists. "Feeling their [terrorists'] pain will not turn them around, and neither will social work" (p. 405). Even if Friedman is referring only to doing good works, not the activities of the profession, his impatience is shared by other commentators. For example, Rothstein (2001) argues that terror perpetrated by fundamentalist religious groups should be viewed as simply "a variety" of totalitarianism; "it [then] becomes clearer just how limited the injustice theory and the question of 'root causes' are" (p. A17).

Friedman and Rothstein may be correct in part: The war against terrorists necessarily may be a military, bloody, destructive war. But such analyses ignore three factors that we can learn from Rawls. First, the fight for social justice does not begin in response to acts of mass violence and does not need mass violence as a precondition of its value. It may well be true that a national and global fight for social justice, sincerely and sufficiently waged, may still result in persons or groups that will strike out at others in ways of horror and carnage; such a result does not mean that promoting social justice was futile. Social justice is a rational activity in itself and indeed, in Rawls's scheme, forms the very basis of society. Second, even when nations must use their might against terrorists, their goals and their means must be in the service of justice; otherwise, the tolerant will have joined the unreasonable, outside the original contract.

But the most fundamental answer to Friedman and Rothstein is this: Understanding the conditions that promote mass violence is itself an activity that promotes social justice. Rawls's theory may rest on an act of imagination, but it is through such activity that we humans seek to extend ourselves beyond our corporal nature and quotidian concerns and come closer to realizing that understanding the needs and prerequisites for life of "the other" is simultaneously a way of understanding ourselves. To recall the phrase of DeLillo, we need to reduce the disarticulation of "us" and "them." Social justice then defines our behavior with others and in doing so defines our selves.

Strategies for Promotion of Social Justice

What are the implications of this analysis for social work? How do social workers promote social justice in a world scarred by mass violence? How do we translate into reality our ethical obligation to address those conditions that contribute to mass violence—address them not just in individual practice and in the agency setting, but beyond the work environment and indeed beyond national boundaries? Social workers practice in many different fields, with different client systems, with different immediate and long-term objectives. The terrorists' attack of September 11th and subsequent events no doubt affect the morale and hope of social workers in the United States, who, like many in society, may fear "that the future is newly lost/ to an unfocused dread/ of what may never happen/ and nobody can stop" (Salter, 2002, p. 73). Still, we are an action-oriented profession united by our ethics and core values that infuse the mission of the profession (NASW, 1996), and social justice is a value that commands action. Rather than propose different strategies for different practitioners, this chapter proposes a social justice agenda that has five facets: immediate social needs, ongoing social needs, political work within our country, global work, and ongoing reconceptualization of the value of social justice. This agenda informs the behavior of social workers as individual practitioners as well as members of professional organizations.

Social work's agenda is immediate. People who are directly and indirectly affected by mass violence need help at the moment and afterwards; social justice demands that efforts be made to ensure that people receive immediate help and support. Such work includes crisis intervention; provision of food, clothing, shelter, and cash; counseling about short- and long-term planning; grief and bereavement counseling; and identification of and assistance with stress-related disorders. This restorative work is done not only with individuals and families but with communities as well: participating in the dialogue that identifies the community's needs, resources, and aspirations, social workers are uniquely equipped to process the rational and emotive components of this work.

The confusion and outrage that has surrounded charitable fundraising and dispersal of assistance following September 11th suggests that social work's professional role in society needs further explanation and augmentation. How can money be raised quickly? Who should be helped? What kind of help is needed? Who should provide the help? These are questions of social welfare policy that the profession has always struggled with. Social workers know that these questions pose fundamental value conflicts: private contributions versus government grants or equality of treatment versus equitable response, to select only the most obvious dilemmas. Much as the cleanup of the ruins of the World Trade Center needed to be done by expert personnel, the work of helping is also a professional activity that must be guided by professional values.

The crises that surround events of mass violence may result in additional harm to people and communities; irrational acts may beget irrational responses. Hatred, discrimination, and violence may occur against persons because of their membership in religious, ethnic, or national groups. Such excesses strike to the core of social justice because they exclude people from society's contract not because of what they did (e.g., criminal acts, which require that society protect itself) but of who they are. Onken, Franks, and Lewis (2001) describe a framework of understanding this process of moral exclusion. Derived from post-Holocaust work, the model is a way for individuals and groups to examine how their reasoning about people affects how they respond to the behavior of others. It seeks to turn the value of social justice into action. Social work's response to this danger cannot be limited to practice models; political advocacy is needed as well, to guard against unthinking and unqualified support of government actions (military or domestic) and to ensure that basic constitutional rights are secured and maintained for all.

Social work's agenda is ongoing. Because "the primary mission" of social work is enhancing "human well-being" and helping "meet the basic human needs of all people" (NASW, 1996), it can be argued that from the perspective of Rawls all professional activity promotes social justice. The profession historically has been concerned with poverty, discrimination, oppression, and with conditions of vulnerability. This focus is self-evidently related to Rawls's principles of freedom and equality. What his theory of justice compels, however, is that social workers work to eliminate poverty, end discrimination, fight oppression, and help the vulnerable not simply because it may prevent the conditions that give rise to mass violence but rather because social justice itself is necessary, ongoing, and good.

In this context, social justice requires that social work do more to institutionalize basic services and to expand the availability of preventive services in all fields of practice. This point is critical. Services that are provided in a residual model often are perceived as stigmatized and typically are available in a delivery system that is filled with gaps or duplication or are wasteful, time-consuming, and difficult to access either by geography or bureaucratic procedure. These barriers to professional helping mean that those who need help are less likely to receive it, thus injustice prevails. For example, the extraordinary and persistent disproportionately higher rate of incarceration of African American and Latino persons compared with people of European heritage reflects not only an unjust outcome but ongoing oppressive conditions that support white privilege (Pewewardy & Severson, in press). The need for preventive service programs as a matter of social justice is best illustrated by the field of child welfare. The interrelationship between poverty and child abuse and neglect is well known (Lindsey, 1994). Yet typically it is foster care, the most expensive service program that operates after a crisis has occurred, that garners a disproportionate share of public attention and financing away from community-based prevention programs. Instead of institutionalizing services, the tendency has been to institutionalize people. Yet, as Meyer (1976) wrote, it is far better that social work should provide its help "where people *are*" instead of "where people end up" (p. 75).

Social work's agenda is political. Social workers may feel the challenge of doing political work to be too far removed from their daily concerns with their clients. Domanski (1998) found that while almost all social workers say they are informed about political and policy issues, less than half do any active work in the electoral process apart from voting. Such limited political participation does not fulfill a commitment to social justice. Traditional client practice, whether it be with individuals or groups, seeks to improve the well-being only of the specific client in question; its "objective is not to ensure a more equitable distribution of opportunity," a principle of social justice (Figueira-McDonough, 1993, p. 180).

Over the last decade, considerable scholarly attention has been devoted to the development of the social work role of "policy practitioner." Traditionally, policy work had been viewed as being a specialization or field of practice and often limited to analysis of existing policy and its effects. The work of Jansson (1990), Wyers (1991), Figueira-McDonough (1993), and Haynes and Mickelson (2000), to name only a few authors, has significantly reexamined, redefined, and expanded the social worker's connection to policy, including explicit recognition of the need for political activity. Jansson and Scranton (2001) state that as policy practitioners, social workers need to make efforts to "change the cast of decision makers" and "influence how resources are allocated" (p. 2).

Political silence compromises social justice. Following World War I, there occurred in the United States the first "Red Scare," an extended period of baseless accusations of Bolshevism, unwarranted government imprisonment of immigrants, and an overall climate of fear and suspicion. Jane Addams (1960), criticizing those social workers who did *not* speak out in protest, said they "exhibited many symptoms of this panic and with a kind of protective instinct carefully avoided any identification with the phraseology of social reform" (p. 237). As Dworkin (2002) asserts, "patriotism now demands" that because constitutional and legal rights are most jeopardized in time of crisis, we must protect them "even as we fight the terrorists" (p. 49).

Some social workers have been elected to political office, and there is an interesting historical coincidence about the votes of two such officials. Jeannette Rankin was the first social worker elected to Congress. Her bid for reelection in 1919 failed because she had cast the only vote against U.S. entry into World War I. Twenty years later, elected again to the House of Representatives, Congresswoman Rankin cast the only vote against this country's declaration of war against Japan (Haynes & Mickelson, 2000). And in today's crisis, the only vote in the House that did not support a military response to September 11th was cast by a social worker, Barbara Lee of California. The gestures may seem quixotic, but they affirm that principle and value are not to be compromised in times of emergency or public clamor for action.

Social work's agenda is global. Globalization refers to the processes of economic integration across national borders. It includes limiting trade and transportation barriers between countries, increased reliance on new electronic technologies—especially the immediate transfer of information, and the ideology of free-market capitalism. Globalization is seen by many as the primary way poverty can best be fought in the world; many others see it as the primary cause of increasing the worldwide disparity of worth (Globalization and its critics, 2001). While the merits of each view are hotly debated, it is beyond contention that globalization has brought the world closer, interconnected and interdependent in ways unimaginable just years ago. Globalization made September 11th possible: It demonstrated the new power now possessed by individuals to "act on the world stage directly—unmediated by a state" (Friedman, 2000, p. 14) and allowed the world to view the fall of the World Trade Center towers as it was occurring.

The struggle for social justice is also global. As U.S.-based corporations develop profits from labor in other countries (resulting from freer and capitalist-friendly trade agreements), or when political and economic oppression deprive people of basic human rights, the conditions in those countries become a concern for social work. The agenda for possible action is extensive, and this chapter offers only four examples where social work advocacy, by individuals as well as by profession organizations, is needed.

- If the United States increased its international health aid by 0.1 percent of Gross Domestic Product for the next five years, at least 8 million lives per year now lost to poor health worldwide would be saved (Health of Nations, 2001).
- Nobel Prize-winning economist Amartya Sen (2001) provides an outline for international reform needed to reduce global inequity. He too includes the need for greatly expanded health care and educational opportunity, as well as a relaxation of restrictive trade practices and restrictive "patent laws which inhibit the use of life-saving drugs—vital for diseases like AIDS" (p. 50). But he is especially concerned with ongoing sales of arms from developed to undeveloped countries. In the last five years, the United States alone was responsible for 50 percent of the world's arms sales, two-thirds of it to developing countries. "The world powers bear an awesome responsibility for the subversion of democracy in Africa. Global arms exports continue that evil tradition" (Sen, 2001, p. 50).

- Social workers can also ally with organizations that have an explicit international agenda of social justice. For example, Amnesty International works to free political prisoners, aims to eliminate the death penalty worldwide, and supports such causes as HIJOS (Children for Identity and Justice Against Oblivion and Silence), a now worldwide group that began in Argentina to protest the unexplained disappearance of tens of thousands of people in the 1970s (Lajoie, 2001).
- One can hardly imagine a need more concretely illustrative of social justice than access to clean water. Yet today one-sixth of the world's population lack such access, and millions die worldwide yearly because their water was dirty and disease-ridden. The World Bank and the International Monetary Fund now favor the privatization of water in developing nations despite considerable evidence that transforming clean water from a public utility to a private commodity does not improve people's access to this fundamental need (Finnegan, 2002).

There are, of course, other issues of global importance. Common to the above concerns are the reality of the gross disproportion of wealth and power between developed and developing nations, as well as a need for a frank exploration of the role of the U.S. government and American-based corporations in the affairs of other countries. Social workers participate in this reality on a daily basis and so must participate in dialogue and activities that shape the global issues that affect our lives and the lives of the people in the communities we serve.

Social work's agenda is philosophical. As this chapter has discussed, the conception of social justice that is reflected in the NASW Code of Ethics reflects Rawls's theory of justice, which in turn is embedded in a tradition of thinking known as the Western Enlightenment. Rawls's theory, and indeed the Enlightenment, are not without their critics. Even before September 11th some writers wrote of an ongoing fundamental clash of Western and Islamic civilizations (Huntington, 1996; Sullivan, 2001). Giddens (2000) presents a more nuanced view. While accepting that fundamentalist beliefs and actions are problematic for what he calls cosmopolitanism, nevertheless he argues that

> [w]e shouldn't accept the Enlightenment idea that the world should rid itself of tradition altogether. Traditions are needed and will always persist, because they give continuity and form to life.... Fundamentalism isn't just the antithesis of globalizing modernity, but poses questions to it. The most basic one is this: Can we live in a world where nothing is sacred?... I don't think we can. Cosmopolitans, of whom I count myself one, have to make plain that tolerance and dialogue can themselves be guided by values of a universal kind. None of us would have anything to live for if we didn't have something worth dying for. (pp. 62–63, 68)

But are there values of a universal kind? Postmodern theorists argue no, that our "truths" are constructs reflecting the time, space, and position in which we find ourselves. More specifically, the leading postmodernist writer Stanley Fish (2002) clarifies that relativism means that our truths are unprovable to others: Whatever else can be said about terrorists, they do view truth differently. This is so whether the terrorist is McVeigh or bin Laden.

While there may be no hope of convincing the perpetrators of mass violence that their beliefs are false, there is hope that we can examine our own truths. Here lies an area where social work can make an apt contribution. Because we have committed ourselves to recognizing and working with the strengths of diverse cultures, social workers can understand the importance of tradition—the continuity of cultural norms—in the lives of people. Where others may see blind superstition, social workers make an ethical commitment to study and be sensitive to differences. This orientation to diversity in its fullest implications is derived from the ethical value of "Dignity and Worth of the Person" (NASW, 1996); it serves not only as a guide to social work practice but can shape philosophical inquiries by social work scholars into what one writer described as "a struggle (*jihad*) against the flaws within one's own traditions" (Asani, 2002, p. 60).

There is another product of Western Enlightenment thought that has profound political implications: the conception of civil rights as opposed to human rights. Civil rights define the relationship between people within a nation-state and between those people and their government. They are inherent in individuals (who are "by nature all free, equal, and independent," Locke, in Kramnick, 1995, p. 401) and are protected by the nation-state to which "we the people" consented. The Western Enlightenment, civil rights, and nation-states are thus intertwined and developed in a particular historical era.

Human rights, however, are based not on contract within nation-states but on a recognition of the human condition beyond borders. Globalization and the changing nature of states challenge the rights of people in new and overwhelming ways. Human rights activists now face

> a world where many of the most urgent human rights challenges come not from strong states, but from collapsing or rogue states. The main problem is often not the civil and political repression of individuals, but the genocide, ethnic cleansing, and massacre of entire communities. The challenge is not just civil war and human violence, moreover, but the catastrophic impact of HIV on governance and development in sub-Saharan Africa. (Ignatieff, 2002, p. 20)

Whereas civil rights are protected by constitutional and political strategies within a nation, human rights need to be protected through supra-sovereignty arrangements—less by imposition of might, but more through agreements that recognize that the condition of human existence is a matter of international concern. In effect, human rights extend the contract model of the Enlightenment from contracts between individuals to contracts between nations. This understanding of human rights seeks to counteract the worst tendencies of global capitalism, which, Barber (2001) argues, may be productive economically but "it fails miserably at distribution and hence at safety and justice" (Barber 2001, p. xxxi). Social justice, then, must be developed further to meet the reality of the global era and be protected internationally as well as within nations.

Social workers have chosen to be guided by social justice as a value that structures its behavior; consequently, we must participate in the ongoing work of understanding that social justice means in this global era. The brief comments about diversity and human rights are meant only to illustrate where fruitful work can be done in reconceptualizing social justice. What is critical is that we recognize the historical character of social justice and Western Enlightenment and be willing to risk exploring the assumptions that support this value and worldview.

Conclusion

This chapter has sought to explore the implications of mass violence in the context of social work's commitment to social justice. It explored the historical context of the value of social justice so that its worth and relevance can be maintained in today's world. As formulated by Rawls, social justice derives from Western Enlightenment and therein lies both its vigor and its limitations for social workers. The rationale for social justice, its foundation in common human needs and contracting among people, speaks with special resonance for social workers. It is the function of social work to respond to the crises that result when such needs are not met and when the structure of society is based not on assent but through domination and oppression.

However, in this postmodern global world, our understanding of social justice seems fragile when the words and actions of terrorists indicate that they stand outside our historical tradition and covenant. It is understandable that sudden and overwhelming incidents of mass violence challenge our personal and professional selves, including our moral commitments. They cause all of us to question and doubt, to be angry, to demand solutions to the despair that is felt so immediately; these responses, more than the actual violence, are the greatest threats to a commitment to social justice for they are within ourselves and thus within our control. Marx wrote that humans are agents, who "make history, though not in the circumstances of their own choosing" (In Giddens, 1984, p. xxi). Social workers did not choose to live in this world of suicide bombings any more than they chose to live in the nineteenth century world of social and economic disparity arising from industrialization and the rise of cities. The challenge to fight against injustice exists no less today than when our profession began.

It may well be that acts of terror will continue, performed by actors of various political and religious and even unknown motivations, fueled by grievances real and imaginary. It may further be true that faced with mortal threats from those who refuse any possibility of compromise, armed defense, including preemptory measures, must be taken, even though death and destruction will result. Neither statement diminishes the need to reaffirm social justice as a guiding value for the social work profession. To paraphrase Pelasgus, our only hope for justice to prevail is to be guided by justice in all of our actions.

References

Aeschylus. (1999). The suppliants. In D. R. Slavitt & P. Bowie (Eds.), *Aeschylus 2.* Philadelphia: University of Pennsylvania Press.

Addams, J. (1960). *A centennial reader.* New York: Macmillan.

Asani, A. S. (2002). Pluralism, intolerance, and the Qu'ran. *The American Scholar, 71,* 52–60.

Barber, B. R. (1995, 2001). *Jihad vs. McWorld.* New York: Ballantine Books.

Conrad, J. (1953). *The secret agent.* Garden City, NY: Anchor.

Council on Social Work Education (CWSE). (2001). Educational policy and accreditation standards. Alexandria, VA: Author.

DeLillo, D. (2001, December). In the ruins of the future. *Harper's Magazine,* 33–40.

Domanski, M. D. (1998). Prototypes of social work political participation: An empirical model. *Social Work, 43,* 156–167.

Dworkin, R. (2002, February 28). The threat to patriotism. *The New York Review of Books,* 44–49.

Figueira-McDonough, J. (1993). Policy practice: The neglected side of social work intervention. *Social Work, 38,* 179–188.

Finnegan, W. (2002, April 8). Leasing the rain. *The New Yorker,* 43–53.

Fish, S. (2002, July). Postmodern warfare. *Harper's Magazine,* 33–40.

Friedman, T. L. (2000). *The Lexus and the olive tree* (expanded edition). New York: Anchor.

Garwin, R. L. (2001, November 1). The many threats of terror. *The New York Review of Books,* 16–19.

Giddens, A. (1984). *The constitution of society.* Berkeley, CA: University of California Press.

Giddens, A. (2000). *Runaway world* New York: Routledge.

Globalization and its critics. (2001, September 29). *The Economist* (Special Survey), 1–32.

Glover, J. (2000). *Humanity.* New Haven, CT: Yale University Press.

Hassan, N. (2001, November 19). An arsenal of believers. *The New Yorker,* 36–41.

Haynes, K. S., & Mickelson, J. S. (2000). *Affecting change: Social workers in the politicalarena* Boston: Allyn and Bacon.

Health of nations. (2001, December 21). *The Economist,* 83–84.

Huntington, S. P. (1996). *The clash of civilizations.* New York: Simon & Shuster.

Ignatieff, M. (2002, June 13). The rights stuff. *The New York Review of Books,* 18–20.

Jansson, B. (1990). *Social welfare policy: From theory to practice.* Belmont, CA: Wadsworth.

Jansson, B., & Scranton, A. (2001, June). *Teaching social welfare practice.* Paper presented at The Policy Conference, Charleston, S. C.

Judt, T. (2001, November 15). America and the war. *The New York Review of Books, 4–6.*

Kramnick, I. (Ed.). (1995). *The portable enlightenment reader.* New York: Penguin.

Lajoie, R. (2001, Winter). Against oblivion. *Amnesty NOW,* 4–7.

Lelyveld, J. (2001, October 28). All suicide bombers are not alike. *The New York Times Magazine,* 49–53, 62, 78–79.

Lemann, N. (2001, October 19). What terrorists want. *The New Yorker,* 36–41.

Lewis, B. (2001, November 19). The revolt of Islam. *The New Yorker,* 50–63.

Lindsey, D. (1994). *The welfare of children.* New York: Oxford University Press.

Meyer, C. (1976). *Social work practice* (2nd ed.). New York: The Free Press.

Murakami, H. (2001). *Underground.* New York: Vintage.

National Association of Social Workers (NASW). (1960) *NASW Code of Ethics.* New York: Author.

National Association of Social Workers (NASW). (1967). *NASW Code of Ethics.* Silver Springs, MD: Author.

National Association of Social Workers (NASW). (1979). *NASW Code of Ethics.* Silver Springs, MD: Author.

National Association of Social Workers (NASW). (1993) *NASW Code of Ethics* Washington, DC: Author.

National Association of Social Workers (NASW). (1996) *NASW Code of Ethics* Washington, DC: Author.

Onken, S. J., Franks, C. L., & Lewis, S. J. (2001, November). Acting bravely in intolerant times. *Currents* (New York City Chapter, NASW), 5, 8.

Pewewardy, N., & Severson, M. (In press). A threat to liberty. *Journal of Progressive Human Services.*

Rawls, J. (1971). *A theory of justice.* Cambridge, MA: Harvard University Press.

Rawls, J. (1996). *Political liberalism.* New York: Columbia University Press.

Rawls, J. (1999a). *A theory of justice.* (rev. ed.) Cambridge, MA: Belknap Press of Harvard University Press.

Rawls, J. (1999b). *The law of peoples.* Cambridge, MA: Harvard University Press.

Reamer, F. G. (1998). The evolution of social work ethics. *Social Work, 43,* 488–500.

Reynolds, B. (1963). *An uncharted journey.* Silver Springs, MD: NASW Press.

Rothstein, E. (2001, November 17). Exploring the flaws in the notion of the "root causes" of terror. *The New York Times,* p. A 17.

Salter, M. J. (2002). After September. *The American Scholar, 71,* 71–73.

Scanlon, E., & Longres, J. (2001a). Social work and social justice: A reply to Leroy Pelton. *Journal of Social Work Education, 37,* 441–444.

Scanlon, E., & Longres, J. (2001b). Social justice and the research curriculum. *Journal of Social Work Education, 37,* 447–463.

Sen, A. (2001). Addressing global poverty. *The Economist.* Special Issue: The World in 2002, 50.

Sullivan, A. (2001, October 7). This *is* a religious war. *The New York Times Magazine.* pp. 44–47, 52–53.

Swenson, C. R. (1998). Clinical social work's contribution to a social justice perspective. *Social Work, 43,* 527–537.

Wakefield, J. C. (1988a). Psychotherapy, distributive justice, and social work: Part 1. *Social Service Review, 62,* 187–210

Wakefield, J. C. (1988b). Psychotherapy, distributive justice, and social work: Part 2. *Social Service Review, 62,* 353–382

Wyers, N. (1991). Policy-practice in social work: Models and issues. *Journal of Social Work Education, 27,* 241–250.

Index